William Skeen

Adam's Peak

Legendary, traditional, and historic notices of the Samanala and Sri-Pada: with a

descriptive account of the pilgrims' route from Colombo to the Sacred Foot-Print

William Skeen

Adam's Peak
*Legendary, traditional, and historic notices of the Samanala and Sri-Pada: with a descriptive
account of the pilgrims' route from Colombo to the Sacred Foot-Print*

ISBN/EAN: 9783337292065

Printed in Europe, USA, Canada, Australia, Japan

Cover: Foto ©ninafisch / pixelio.de

More available books at **www.hansebooks.com**

Adam's Peak.

Dedicated

BY SPECIAL PERMISSION

TO

HIS ROYAL HIGHNESS ALFRED ERNEST ALBERT,

DUKE OF EDINBURGH,

EARL OF KENT, AND EARL OF ULSTER,

DUKE OF SAXONY, AND PRINCE OF SAXE COBURG GOTHA,

K. G., K. T., G. C. M. G., G. C. S. I.

THE FIRST PRINCE OF THE BLOOD ROYAL OF ENGLAND
WHO HAS VISITED THE ISLAND OF CEYLON.

BY

HIS ROYAL HIGHNESS'S

MOST OBEDIENT AND VERY HUMBLE SERVANT,

THE AUTHOR.

CONTENTS.

ERRATA.

Owing to an unfortunate mistake, the accompanying Map, engraved and printed in London, is not so accurate in its delineation of the country and route from Palábaddala to Diyabetma as it should have been.

North of Palábaddala, trending to the east, rises the mountain Kunudiya-parvaté, the western face of which is a tremendous precipice. South of and forming an angle with this mountain runs a range consisting of the mountains Kondagala, Nílihela, and Kękillagala. The route from Palábaddala is first between Kondagala and Nílihela, then up and over the latter, on to a range that culminates at Diyabetma, the watershed of the district; the streams to the east of Diyabetma, between it and Dharma-rája-gala, Sítá-gangula-hena, and Hęramițipáoa, flowing in a northerly direction. The source of the Kalu-gaṇga is west of Diyabetma, whence it runs south, finding its way down among the mountains and passing north of Palábaddala, between it and the lower southern slopes of Kunudiya-parvaté.

The following sketch will shew the position of the mountains.

P. Palábaddala.	4. Diyabetma.	8. Hęramițipáoa.
1. Kunudiya-parvaté.	5. Idikațupána.	9. Adam's Peak.
2. Kondagala.	6. Dharma-rája-gala.	10. Bęna Samanala
3. Nílihela.	7. Gangula-hena.	

The ranges of mountains where Kondagalla and Níhilagalla are marked on the map, are wrongly placed, and the valley between Kondagala and Diabetna should be high mountainous ridges.

The following errors and corrections are also here noticed :—

page 15, line sixth from bottom, for " west" read " east."

"   65,   line eighth from top, for " south westerly" read " south-easterly."

"   88,   line thirteenth from bottom, for " C." read " G."

"   104, and 107, for "Captain" Forbes, read " Major."

"   117, the inscription on the stone is in memory of Eknęligoda Disáwa, the son of the builder of the vihára.

"   184, after " rice conjee" in first line, add "—rice."

"   218, line fifth from bottom, for " least," read " last."

The names of persons and places are so variously spelt by different writers, that it has not been possible to preserve uniformity of orthography throughout the work. In the Index, however, all names have been carefully revised, and are correct as they appear there.

PREFACE.

THERE is perhaps no mountain in the world of which so wide-spread a knowledge exists, as Adam's Peak. Almost every traveller to, or writer on, India and the East, has alluded to, noticed, or more or less described it. But, considering the sanctity in which it is held by Buddhists, Hindus, and Mohammadans; the numerous legends and traditions connected with it; and the immense number of pilgrims who annually visit the alleged Foot-print upon its summit; it is surprising how little has been recorded by any one author, and what wide and glaring discrepancies appear in the different accounts respecting it which have from time to time been given to the world.

An excursion to the summit of the Peak, in the early part of 1869, having led to considerable research upon the subject, as well as to two subsequent excursions, the results of the observations and inquiries made on each journey, and in the intervals between, are set forth in the following pages.

My principal endeavour has been, to bring into one common focus all attainable information; and to describe more fully than has hitherto been done, the Pilgrims' route from Colombo to the Srí-Páda, or Holy Foot-print, that crowns the summit of the Samanala.

In the prosecution of this task I have received from many quarters much valuable assistance. And for aid most freely rendered my thanks are specially due to the Hon'ble H. T. IRVING, the Colonial Secretary; to Messrs. RUSSELL, SAUNDERS, MACREADY, and STEELE, of the Civil Service; to Captain FYERS, the Surveyor General, and officers of his Department; to Mr. THWAITES, the Director of the Royal Botanic Gardens, Pérádeniya; to the learned Advocates of the Supreme Court, Messrs. LORENZ, FERDINANDS, ALWIS, and BRITO; to the Reverends BAILEY, ONDAATJE, and NICHOLAS; to HIKKADUWA SUMANGALA NA'YAKA UNNA'NSE', High-priest of the Peak, and SUBHUTI TERUNNA'NSE' of Waskaduwa vihára; to Mudaliyar LOUIS DE SOYZA, the Chief Translator to Government, and L. WIJAYASINHA, Mudaliyar of the Ratnapura Kachcheri; to EKNELIGODA Ratémahatmayá of the Kuruwite Kóralé; as well as to the learned pandit C. ALWIS, and others, whose names are mentioned in the body of the book.

As a contribution to the literature of the Island, I trust that the work now published may be deemed worthy of a place alongside those of others whose pens in times past have illustrated the history and antiquities of Ceylon. Much as they did, they yet left much to be done; and fields rich in historic and legendary lore still await investigation at the hands of diligent explorers. To those whose tastes incline them to such pursuits, investigations of the nature indicated are most attractive. Hardly less interesting is the work of detailing the results of such investigations. What may be interesting to an individual may not, however, interest the public at large; although to excite that interest should be the aim of every writer. Indulging in the hope that I may to some extent succeed in that aim, I will only add, that I have been scrupulously regardful of accuracy in every statement of a matter of fact; that the opinions I have advanced have been adopted only after much consideration and care; and that no pains have been spared to do justice to the subject upon which I have written.

W. S.

Colombo,
April 22nd, 1870.

Adam's Peak.

Turn eastward now thine eyes, and in the sun-light bold
The Samanala peak, that sacred rock, behold,
Where with his goddess train, great SUMANA ador'd
Th' illustrious lotus Foot-print of BUDDH', Omniscient Lord;
Bow'd reverently before, and offerings made the sign
Of Parasat' and Mandar, flowers of hues divine.

SELLA LIHINI SANDESE.

CHAPTER I.

INTRODUCTORY REMARKS.—ON THE ORIGIN OF BUDDHIST, HINDU, AND MOHAMMADAN PILGRIMAGES TO ADAM'S PEAK.

ADAM'S PEAK,—known amongst the Siṇhalese as the Samanta-kúṭa, or peak of the Samanala mountain; by Hindus* as the Sivan-oli-padam, and by Mohammadans as the Baba-Aadamalei,—is one of the most noted mountains in the world, celebrated alike for its singularly prominent

---

* Or, more correctly, Sivaites; Sivá being esteemed the supreme divinity in the Hindu Mythology. The worshippers of Sivá are divided into the following sects:—Vairavas, Vámas, Kúlámuk'bas, Mahávratas, Púsupatas, and Saivas. The Saivas are the predominant sect among the Tamils of Ceylon.

and striking appearance, and for the interesting religious associations connected with it. On its summit is a shrine which covers the renowned Foot-print, claimed by the respective votaries of India's old beliefs, as that of Sivá, or of Gautama Buddha; but by the followers of the Prophet of Mecca, as that of the first created man,—the great progenitor of the human race.* To that alleged foot-print, held sacred and reverenced by far the largest portion of mankind, annual pilgrimages are made, alike by Hindus, Buddhists and Moslems; and from times remote to the present day it has been visited by devotees, the representatives of those forms of faith, from every region where they maintain their sway.

As to the cause why and the time when this particular mountain peak first became an object of worship, and its summit a favorite spot for pilgrims to resort to, the following remarks which recently appeared in the published sketch of a journey thither,† may not be considered irrelevant. The writer says:—

"Without attempting to discuss the history, or the mythological legends connected with this place, I cannot help speculating regarding the origin of its sanctity in the first place. Here is a place which the Buddhist considered to be sanctified by the impress of Buddha's foot, which the Hindu reverences as being marked by the foot of Sivá, which the

---

* For further information as to the supposed origin of the Foot-print see Appendix A.

† In the "Ceylon Observer," October 2nd, 1869,

Mohammadan considers a holy place as bearing the foot-print of Adam, and which the Christians, or rather some of them, delight to believe is stamped with the foot of St. Thomas. Now I ask, whence this *consensus?* How came all of these to regard this place as holy, and to associate their traditions and legends with it? How is this to be accounted for? I at once dismiss from the inquiry this wretched imitation of a foot-print, since the very question is, how did the necessity arise to induce these various faiths to look on this shapeless mark as the representation of a foot at all? Standing there, surrounded by that matchless prospect, there on that proud pinnacle and above that enchanting view, one may well refuse to accept that rock-mark as the answer to his question. I want a higher, nobler answer, and is it not afforded? Let each decide for himself, but I like to believe that these legends are all after-thoughts; that the place was already sacred to the primal religion of humanity—the worship of nature,—as the enduring, all originating, all absorbing universal whole:—that to this faith, man's first, and perhaps his last, this spot was already consecrated as its most fitting temple. In a question of this kind I care little for historic evidences or their absence. There are many things of which history knows nothing, many more of which it has not chosen to tell."

Whether the "primal religion of humanity—the worship of nature," was man's first and will perhaps be his last faith, may be doubted, nay denied, while at the same time the fact is admitted, that the worship of false gods upon the high places

of the earth is a practice that has prevailed from times of a
very remote antiquity. And although history may not know,
or may have failed to furnish, an answer to the questions
when and how Buddhists, Hindus, and Moslems, came to
attribute the special sanctity they do to this hollow in the
rock, which all alike bow down before, and to which with
one consent they render reverential homage, the subject is
of too much interest to be dismissed without an attempt at
investigation in these pages.

Referring to the Rámáyana,* the oldest known work which
gives undoubted historic notices of Ceylon, it does not appear
in the descriptions that are there given of events which
happened 3000 or 4000 years ago, that any particular
sanctity was at that ancient date accorded to the mountain;
or that the worship of any special deity was connected with

---

* "The Adventures of Ráma," by the poet Valmíki, is an Indian epic
poem of great antiquity, and unsurpassed interest and beauty. It refers
to events considered by some chronologers to have happened upwards of
4000 years ago. In a note to Professor M. William's Indian Epic Poetry,
p. 68, the following passage occurs. "How many centuries have passed
·since the two brothers (Ráma and Lakshmana) began their memorable
journey, and yet every step of it is known, and traversed annually by
thousands of pilgrims! Strong indeed are the ties of religion, when entwined
with the legends of a country! Those who have followed the path of
Ráma from the Gogra to Ceylon stand out as marked men among their
countrymen. It is this that gives the Rámayana a strange interest; the
story still lives; whereas no one now, in any part of the world, puts faith
in the legends of Homer."

it; but there can be no question that at a period not long subsequent, the district of which it forms the most conspi-cuous feature, was identified, under the name of Saman, with Lakshmana, the brother of the principal hero of the poem, by whose aid and with that of Vibhíshana, Ráwana, the king of the island was overthrown. Both Lakshmana and Vibíshana* were deified, and became the tutelary divinities of portions of the island; but the worship of the former, as an incarnation of Vishnu, the deliverer and restorer, now alone maintains its hold upon the native mind, especially in connection with the great Saman déwále near Ratnapura, and the Samanala mountain, of which he is still believed by both Buddhists and Hindus to be the potent guardian god. During Buddha's lifetime, and for ages previous, this mountain was the central seat of Samanite worship in Ceylon, and the Buddhist legends impute to Saman's special entreaty the fact that Buddha stamped his foot-print upon the summit of its peak. This was of course an afterthought on the part of some one in the Buddhist hierarchy, in order

---

* Vibhíshana is stated in the Rájawaliya to have succeeded to the throne of Lanka on the death of his brother, which event occurred 1844 years before Buddha, or B. c. 2387; and to have fixed his Capital at Kęlaniya, his sovereignty extending over a large extent of country long since submerged by the ocean. To Lakshmana was assigned the sovereignty of the Western and Southern parts of the island, the laws of which he much improved. The groves of scarlet rhododendron trees which clothe the eastern slopes of the Samanala from base to summit are dedicated to him.

to add weight to the claim upon the belief of the worshippers
of Saman that Buddha was the Lord supreme, whom even
Gods adored, just as the early Buddhist missionaries taught
the serpent worshippers, that the king of the Nágas (cobras)
recognised and protected Gautama when he attained the
Buddhahood—a legend thus commemorated by Srí Ráhula
of Toṭágamuwẹ in his poem "Sẹla Lihini Sandése,"*
written A. D. 1444.

> Thence to the Serpent chamber, where good it is and meet
> The image there beheld, thy worship to repeat;
> For there to eye depicted is seen how by the lake—
> The lake of Muchalinda,—when fierce on Buddha brake
> In his sixth week the rains, from ten directions falling,
> The Nága-king himself through all that storm appalling
> Housed him in circling coils, and o'er the Omniscient's head
> His hood expanding wide a roof-like shelter spread.

The earliest approach to an authentic record of the mountain having been dedicated to Buddha, as well as to Saman, or
Sumana, is that contained in the 32nd chapter of the Mahawanso.† It is there recorded that the king Duṭṭhagámini,
being at the point of death at Anurádhapura, [B. C. 140,]

---

* "The Sella's Message." The Text, and a literal Translation, with
Notes and a Glossary for the use of Students, was published in 1867, by
W. C. Macready, Esq., of the Ceylon Civil Service.

† The *Mahawanso*, which literally means "*Genealogy of the Great*,"
is considered by competent scholars, "an authentic and unrivalled record"
of the national history of Ceylon. It is written in Páli verse, and was
compiled from annals in the vernacular languages existing in Anurádha-

wished for the presence of the thero Théraputtábhayo, one of his old military chiefs who had entered the priesthood, and that the said thero, "who was resident at the Panjali mountain at the source of the river Karindo, cognizant of his meditation, attended by a retinue of 500 sanctified disciples and by their supernatural power travelling through the air,* descended, and arranged themselves round the monarch." The king lamenting his approaching end, was consoled by the thero. Recounting all his pious deeds, the dying king at last said, that of them all two only " administered comfort to his mind." The thero, referring to one of these—a donation of a mess of kangu seed to five eminent theros in a time of great famine— said "the chief thero, Máliyadéwo, one of the five priests who had accepted the kangu mess, dividing the same among 500 of the fraternity resident at the mountain Sumano,

---

pura. The record of events up to A. D. 301, was written by Mahánámo, uncle of the reigning king Dhátu Sena, between the years 459 and 477. The subsequent portions were composed from time to time, by order of the kings, from the national records. The first thirty-eight chapters were translated into English, and printed by the Hon'ble George Turnour in the year 1837.

* The distance in a direct line from Anurádhapura cannot be less than 110 miles; the Panjali mountain being one of a range about 40 miles west of Adam's Peak. The river Karindo is that now known as the Kirindi oya. More than twenty-eight centuries ago the wisest of kings declared that there was nothing new under the sun. May not Gautama Buddha and his principal followers have been acquainted with what in modern days is termed Mesmerism, and a state of clairvoyance be understood to mean their supernatural power of travelling through the air?

himself also partook of it." This passage certainly intimates
that the mountain Sumano (the same as the Samanala) was
believed to be a place of residence for priests at that time;
but it does not settle the point as to whether the mountain
peak was then a place of pilgrimage, and the alleged foot-print
an object of worship.

A tradition of a later period, current in the locality, with
much of probability in its favor, attributes to king Walagambáhu the discovery of the Srí-páda* on the mountain top.
This king ascended the throne B. C. 104, and after a reign of
five months was driven from it by Malabar invaders. For 14
years and 7 months following, he wandered a fugitive amongst
the hills and fastnesses of the mountain districts, dwelling in
caves and supporting himself by means of the chase. During
this period, while living on the Samanala mountain at Bha-
gawálcna (Buddha's cave), he saw a deer in the distance
which he resolved to kill; to his surprise however, he could
not approach near enough to secure it, the deer keeping just
beyond his reach, slackening or increasing its pace or stopping
altogether, in exact accord with its pursuer's movements. In
this way the king was led to the top of the mountain, and
when there the deer suddenly vanished. On reaching the
spot Walagambáhu discovered the Srí-páda; and it was
then revealed to him that in this manner the god Sękrayá,
to whom Buddha had entrusted the care of Ceylon and
Buddhism, had chosen to make known to him the spot on

---

* ල්‍රාපද "Srí-páda"—Sacred Foot-print.

which he had left the impress of his sacred foot. After his restoration the king caused the rock that bore the foot-mark to be surrounded with large iron spikes, which formed the first foundation for the terraced platform from the centre of which the Samanta-kúṭa now seems to spring. Thus far the local tradition. History then records that the king, having recovered his throne, B. C. 88, "brought together 500 of the principal and most learned priests at a cave at Mátalé called Alulena, and, for the first time, had the tenets of Buddhism reduced to writing; which occurred in the 217th year, 10th month, and 10th day after they were promulgated orally by Mahindo."[*] It is curious that a somewhat similar story of the deer is also made use of to introduce Mahindo the princely Buddhist propagandist, to the notice of king Déwánanpiyatissa, B. C. 307,[†] in whose reign and through whom the Buddhist religion was first established as the national faith of Ceylon.

---

[*] Turnour's Epitome of the History of Ceylon, p. 280, vol. ii. of Forbes's Eleven Years in Ceylon.

[†] "The king Déwánanpiyatissa departed for an elk hunt, taking with him a retinue; and in the course of the pursuit of the game on foot he came to the Missa mountain. A certain devo assuming the form of an elk stationed himself there, grazing; the sovereign descried him, and saying, it is not fair to shoot him standing, sounded his bowstring, on which the elk fled to the mountain. The king gave chase to the flying animal, and on reaching the spot where the priests were, the thero Mahindo came within sight of the monarch, but the metamorphosed deer vanished."— *Mahawunsó*, c. xiv.

Divested of the romance with which the local tradition
is clothed, there is no reason to doubt that it contains certain
germs of truth; for what more likely than that the king who
thus caused the whole of Buddha's tenets to be reduced to
writing, and whose subsequent reign was zealously devoted
to the restoration of Buddhism, the building of immense
dágobas, and the founding of rock temples throughout his
dominions, should resolve upon connecting so remarkable a
mountain,—already sacred to the renowned god Saman, and
the place which holy theros selected as their abode,—by
indissoluble ties to the religion to which he was himself so
enthusiastic an adherent. A vivid imagination pondering
upon the discovery of the hollow, or the interpretation given
to a dream, would be all-sufficient in an age of superstition
to account for a supernatural revelation; and aided by the
efforts of a powerful and restored priesthood, the account
of such a revelation industriously circulated amongst the
people, and followed by the more elaborate legends which
the priests concocted in their pansalas, would speedily es-
tablish the fame of the Samanta-kúta, and draw pilgrims to
the Srí-páda from every quarter of India and the East where
Buddhism had established itself.

So far therefore as the Buddhists of Ceylon are concerned,
it would seem that the belief in the existence of the foot-
print is not of an older date than a century and a half before
the Christian era, if even it is as old, for although the
legendary visits of Buddha to the island—(in the third of
which occurred the stamping upon the top of the Samanala

peak the impress of his left foot)—are duly recorded in the Mahawansó, it must be remembered that the early chapters of that work were not written until the latter half of the fifth century; more than a thousand years later than the date when the impression is said to have been made; and it is moreover noteworthy, that "except in the *historical* works of Ceylon, there is no account of this supposed impression of Buddha's foot in any of the earliest records of Buddhism:"*— a faith which was not accepted as national until nearly two and a half centuries subsequent to the death of its author; and the doctrines of which were not reduced to writing until

* J. D'Alwis's Attanagaluvansa, note 15, p. 9.—The evident object of the historians, (themselves Buddhist priests,) was to connect in a miraculous manner the invasion of Wijaya, the first king of Ceylon, with the propagation of the Buddhist faith; and for that purpose the seventh chapter of the Mahawansó opens with a revelation or command of Buddha to that effect—Wijaya's invasion, according to the record of the historian, taking place on the day of Buddha's death. But the logic of facts, as established by chronology, fixes the invasion at a period 60 years subsequent. As to Buddha's visits to Ceylon, the following is the deliverance of the late Rev. Spence Hardy, an authority on Buddhism of the highest rank. He says, in a paper published in the Journal of the Ceylon Branch of the Royal Asiatic Society for 1846, "I have little doubt that it will one day be proved, even from the most sacred books of the Buddhists themselves, that the accounts we have of his visits to Ceylon are a pure fiction. In all the Siṇhalese books that I have read, the narration appears out of the regular order of events, like an after-thought, and it is entirely at variance with the traditions of Nepal and Thibet."

a further period of 218 years had passed from the time of their oral propagation by Mahindo.

The statement concerning Máliyadéwo* and 500 of the fraternity of priests living on Sumano, quoted at page 15, will hardly be accepted as other than apocryphal by those who consider that the special object of the dying scene of the aged monarch, as depicted by the historian, was to elevate the order of the priesthood, and to shew that the smallest alms to them outweighed in merit the greatest of all other kingly deeds. That the mountain was a place of abode at a later epoch is evident from the fact, that Mihindo III. [A. D. 997—1013] repaired the edifices which in a previous reign had been destroyed by the Solíuns; and he is praised as a patron of the religious institutions of the country. It is not however clear whether these edifices were actually on the peak or only at the base of the mountain, nor is the foot-print at all mentioned in the record of their repair.

The first notice of the Srí-páda, after the legend of its formation in the opening pages of the Mahawansó, is contained

* Maliyadéwo thero was a kinsman of king Walagambáhu, and is stated in the Mahawansó to have been the last of Buddha's inspired disciples. It is significantly recorded, that on the reduction to writing of the doctrines of Buddha in the reign of Walagambáhu, the age of inspiration passed away. The inspiration then was connected with the capacity for acquiring and orally delivering the traditions and doctrines of Buddhism; and one may readily conceive how constantly additions and marvellous legends and tales of miracles would be made to these from age to age; the tendency to which would at once be checked, if not entirely stopped, by an authorised promulgation of the written word.

in the 64th chapter of the work, which treats of the accession
of Prákramabáhu the First, A. D. 1153; and the first royal
pilgrimage to Samanala is recorded in the Rájawaliya.* This
was performed on foot by the just named king, a zealous
Buddhist revivalist, who on reaching the mountain peak
worshipped the priest of the foot-print, and caused a shrine to
be built on the rock for Saman Déwiyo,—an act, considering
the hold that the Samanite worship had on the minds of the
natives of the mountain districts, and the recent subjugation
of the central and southern provinces to his rule, as much of
policy as piety on the part of the monarch. His example was
followed by Kirti Nissanga [A. D. 1192—1201], and this
king's is the first that is mentioned in the Mahawansó as
that of a pilgrimage to the foot-print itself. A period of
from 1200 to 1300 years is thus passed over without reference
in any way to the spot either in regard to its sanctity as a
place of pilgrimage or an object of worship to the followers of
Gautama; † and it is difficult to account for this silence in
a history where the praise of Buddha is a dominant strain

* The Rájawaliya was compiled by different persons, at various periods,
and has both furnished the materials to, and borrowed from the Mahawansó; but it is not considered so authentic a work.

† In the Rája-Taringini, the historical chronicle of Kashmir, it is stated
that the king Meghavahana, who according to the chronology of Troyer,
reigned A. D. 24, made an expedition to Ceylon for the purpose of extending Buddhism, and visited Adam's Peak, where he had an interview with
the native sovereign. Other authorities (Thomas, J. A. S., vol. xiii.), fix
the date of Meghavahana's reign at A. D. 144, which would make his expedition take place during the reign of Bátiyatissa II. [A. D. 137—161],

from the opening of the first to the close of the last chapter.
Two causes may however be assigned, with some shew of
reason, for this want of information:—(1) the destruction of
Siŋhalese records at various times by Malabar invaders and
apostate Buddhist kings;* and (2) the fact that the capital of
the island was, up to A. D. 1319, in the Northern kingdom,
the Pihiṭi Raṭa (called also the Rája Raṭa or country of
the kings); the Mountain zone forming the central kingdom
or Máyú Raṭa; and the Southern portion of the Island the
Ruhuna Raṭa. Up to about A. D. 1050 the Máyú and
Ruhuna Raṭas were under the dominion of independent
princes or petty kings, and were only at intervals subjected
to the sway of the northern potentate. Among those kings
who were acknowledged sole sovereigns of the island was
Duṭṭhagámeni. To the mountain fastnesses of the Máyá
Raṭa kings and priests naturally fled for refuge when the

---

who like himself was a zealous Buddhist. But no mention of such a visit
at either date is to be found in the Mahawansó, the Rája Ratnakari, or
the Rájawaliya.

* Of Malabar invasions 17 are recorded between B. C. 204 and A. D.
1391. The invaders were in almost every instance animated by the same
spirit of deadly hostility to Buddhism which led to the ultimate extirpa-
tion of that faith in Central India towards the end of the seventh century.
Of apostate or impious sovereigns, the principal were Chora Nága, D. C.
63; Kanijánitissa, A. D. 33; Maha Sen, A. D. 275; Mágha, A. D. 1219; and
Rája Singha I., A. D. 1581. This last king gave over the custody of the
Samanala to a body of Aandiyas, or Hindu Fakeers; who are described
by S. C. Chitty, as a sort of begging friars belonging to the Saiva sect.

Malabar invaders drove them from their throne and temples at Anurádhapura or Polonnaruwa; although at times they established themselves in the Southern division; ultimately indeed [A. D. 1059] the Máyá was annexed to the Ruhuna Raṭa, and the Island partitioned into two provinces, the Northern being occupied by the Solíans, and the Southern being retained by the native princes. Throughout the Southern kingdom the Samanala was ever present to view, while in the Northern the high Nuwara Eliya range would exclude it from sight.

Closed in on all sides by chains of mountains whose sides and valleys were overgrown with dense and all but impenetrable jungle, visits or pilgrimages to the Samanta-kúṭa must necessarily have been few and far between, and were probably only attempted at times when the influence and power of a paramount sovereign could make itself felt through every portion of his dominions. Such being the case, the widespread knowledge in the north of the existence, and the visibility in the west and south of the isolated cloud-capped peak that reared itself so loftily above all surrounding heights, would well keep alive in the minds of Buddhists the tradition, and foster the belief, that the founder of their faith had there indelibly impressed the foot-mark that was alleged to have sealed the isle of Lanka as his own; a tradition that was ultimately destined to become an article of faith whereever Buddhism was professed. A belief in the existence of such a foot-print was held, we know, amongst the Chinese, as early as the third century of the Christian era, since there

are records in their literature of pilgrimages to India at that
date. All the pilgrims were struck by the altitude of the
hills of Ceylon, and above all by the lofty crest of Adam's
Peak, which served as the land-mark for ships approaching
the island. They speak reverentially of the sacred foot-mark
impressed by *the first created man*, who in their mythology,
bears the name of Pawn-koo; and the gems which were found
upon the mountain, they believed to be his "crystallized
tears, which accounts for their singular lustre and marvellous
tints." The Chinese books repeat the popular belief, that
the hollow of the sacred footstep · contains water, "which
does not dry up all the year round," and that invalids re-
cover health by drinking from the well at the foot of the
mountain, into which "the sea-water enters free from salt." *
At a later period, the belief of the Chinese as to the origin of
the foot-print seems to have undergone a change, for Fa Hian,

---

* Sir J. E. Tennent's Ceylon, vol. i. p. 586-7. This early belief of the
Chinese that the mark on the top of Adam's Peak, was an impression of
the foot of the first created man, is so very remarkable, that one is inclined
to suspect there must be some error on the part of the translators of the
books in which it is recorded, unless indeed it be the record of some ancient tradition which was afterwards grafted on to Buddhism. Ibn Batutu,
in his account of the foot-mark, visited by him about A. D. 1340, says " The
Chinese came here at some former time, and cut out from this stone the
place of the great toe, together with the stone about it, and placed it in
a temple in the city of Zaitun: and pilgrimages are made to it from the
most distant parts of China." The rock does not however bear any evidences of such an outrage ; and the story probably owes its origin to the

the Chinese pilgrim, who in the course of his travels visited
Ceylon, A. D. 413, says in the 38th chapter of his interesting
narrative, "By the strength of his divine foot, hè [Foe, i. e.
Buddha] left the print of one of his feet to tho north of the
royal city, and the print of the other on the summit of a
mountain." This visit took place in the reign of Maha
Náma, and the royal city alluded to was Anurádhapura,
where Fa Hian took up his abode. He did not however
visit the Srí-páda, and only thus incidentally alludes to it;
so that it does not appear to have then been a place of pilgrimage; nor does he mention that any of the priesthood
resided on the mountain, a fact which he would scarcely
have failed to note, had such really been the case.

From the time of Kirti Nissanga, pilgrimages to the foot-
print seem to have become a settled practice. The Rája
Ratnakari,* an authority only second to that of the Mahawansó, states, that Wijayabáhu, who established himself
[A. D. 1240—1267] in the Máyá Rata, and fixed his

craft of some of the Chinese mercenaries employed in the army of Prákrama III. A. D. 1266. One can imagine the inward chuckle with which,
after his return to "the flowery land," one of these mercenaries practised
the "old soldier" over his countrymen, in palming off a lump of stone with
a chiseled toe-mark, as a relic from the original impression of the foot-
print of Foe from the top of the sacred mountain of "Sze-tseu-kwo."

* The exact date of the composition of the Rája Ratnakari is not
known; but it would seem to have been written in, or immediately after,
the reign of Wikremabáhu of Kandy, whose life and acts occupy a
considerable space at the end of the work, and whose career the author,
Abhayarája of Walgampáye wihare, eulogises in glowing terms.

capital at Dambadeniya in the Seven Kóralés, repaired the
route to the peak, viâ Gampola, and with much pomp,
visited and worshipped the Srí-páda.   His successor Pandita
Prákramabáhu, improved the communications, and formed
a road from the Samanala to Bentota in the Southern
Province, bridging the ravines and rivers in the way, and
among others, throwing a bridge of timber 193 ft. 6 in. long
across the Kaluganga.   Two hundred and seventy years,
later, Wikremabáhu, whose capital was at Kanda Nuwara,
the modern Kandy, "caused bridges to be laid over the rivers,
repaired the road, and caused 780 steps to be cut in the
rock, in order that travellers might the more easily ascend;
and also caused resthouses to be made for the convenience of
travellers on the road.   And after expending a large sum of
money, he caused a great flambeau to be made which was
capable of containing 100 pots of oil, and this he lighted as
a beacon on the top of the peak, in order to make his works
visible to the world ; and thus this king accumulated an
infinite amount of merit." *   This route, there is reason to
believe, is the same that is now followed in ascending to the
peak, viâ Ratnapura.   The practice of lighting up the summit
of the mountain at sunset, during the pilgrim season, is continued to the present day, and the effect produced by the
multitude of flaming lamps in front of Saman's shrine, and
the Rayhili-gey, or temple of the foot-print, as seen either
from Díyabetme or Heramittipane is exceedingly fine.

---

* Upham's Rája-Ratnakari, p. 131-2.

The belief amongst the Hindus in regard to the origin and sanctity of the hollow on the summit of Adam's Peak varies. It is by no means universal; and among those who hold it the Vishnaivites maintain it is the foot-print of Vishnu, while the Siváites insist upon it that the impression was made by Sivá, the chief of the supreme triad of Hindu divinities, after whom it bears the name of Siván-oli-pádam. They base their belief on the legend, that Sivá in one of his manifestations retired to this mountain for the performance of certain devotional austerities, and that on their conclusion, in commemoration of his abode there, he left the impress of his foot upon the mountain-top. This legend does not appear in any of the eighteen Puranas; but is gathered from hints contained in several; and it was probably concocted at some bye-gone period more from political than any other motives. That there were occasions when such motives would be likely to sway the minds of both kings and priests, will be evident to all who have studied the history of the Tamils in Ceylon.

The religion of the aborigines of the island was Nága or Serpent worship, subsequently superseded by or incorporated with the worship of Lakshmana and Ráma after their deification as incarnations of Vishnu. The head quarters of this combination of religions were, Ratnapura, in Sabaragamuwa, and Dewi Newara or Dondra, the extreme southern point of Lanka, and boundary of Ráma's conquests in that direction. This was before the Buddhist historic period. After the Wijayan invasion, successive monarchs built and

endowed Hindu temples, introducing therein the worship of
Brahma, Vishnu, and Sivá, with that of other inferior deities.
This worship the people clave to, while still professing to be
Buddhists; and as it was tolerated by the Buddhist priests,
it gradually led to the anomalous sight now almost every
where to be seen, of Hindu déwáles in close proximity to
Buddhist viháras, and a people addicted alike to the adoration
of Buddha and the worship of Serpents and Demons.

Traditions of a remote age assert that a colony of
Malabars founded the city of Trincomalee 1589 years B. C.,
and the earliest authentic notices of the place record the
existence there of a very ancient and sacred Sivaite temple.
Other traditions traceable to a period long anterior to historic
times, make mention of a Tamil kingdom in the North-west
of the island, ruled over by an Amazon princess named
Alliarasamy, whose capital was Kudremale, where granite
ruins and rock inscriptions bear evidence to the truth of
the tradition; while a Tamil drama, founded on the story of
the queen, declares the people to have been Sivaites in their
religious faith.*   But

> "Hardly the place of such antiquity
>   Or note of these great monarchies we find ;
> Only a fading verbal memory
>   And empty name in writ is left behind."
>   PHINEAS FLETCHER.

---

* The places considered specially holy by the educated Tamils and
Hindus of Ceylon, in consequence of the presence of Sivá, are Trincomalee on the east, and Mardodde on the north-west coast.

Respecting the original peopling of the northern peninsula, the following account is given by Tamil writers.* A century and a half before the Christian era there lived in the Chola or Soli country, a certain minstrel named Yálpána Náyanár, otherwise Virarágaven. Being blind he depended for his subsistence entirely on the earnings of his wife. One day, however, she having delayed serving him with his meals at the accustomed hour, he quarrelled with her, and quitted the house, saying, that he was going to Ceylon; upon which she sneeringly observed,—"Ah! you are going to Ceylon to get a tusked elephant and a fertile field." On reaching Ceylon he made his way to Anurádhapura, where he obtained an audience of the king, and sang the monarch's praises to the accompaniment of his lute, in so agreeable a manner, that the well-pleased potentate did in fact present him with a tusked elephant, and moreover bestowed upon him in perpetuity the land on the northern extremity of the island; thus realizing the words with which his wife had ironically taunted him. The land was then covered with jungle and wholly uninhabited, but Yálpána induced a colony of Tamils from Southern India to settle upon and cultivate it; and in the course of years it became a populous, fertile and wealthy

---

* Extracted from the *Tamil Plutarch*, by the late Simon Casie Chitty, the talented District Judge of Puttalam, and author of the Ceylon Gazetteer. Several valuable papers were also contributed by him to the Journal of the Ceylon Branch of the Royal Asiatic Society, and other local Magazines and Journals, principally upon Tamil literature, and the history and customs of the Tamils, Moors and Mookwas of Ceylon.

district, which he named after himself *Yálpána nadu*, or the
minstrel's country—a name the origin of which is still preserved in the modern Jaffna and Jaffnapatam. He did not
however assume a personal sovereignty, but invited over a
prince of the Solian race, and crowned him king under the title
of Singariya Chakravarti, in the Kali year 3000, or B. C. 101.[*]

The preceding tale is by no means an improbable one, for
the early kings of Ceylon were of Indian origin, and always
more or less connected with that continent by matrimonial
alliances; and an Indian minstrel in the olden days would
count it no uncommon reward to receive gifts such as those
awarded to Yálpána by the king. The colonists he imported
were worshippers of Sivá, and that worship was known elsewhere in Ceylon as early as B. C. 426.

It is recorded in the Mahawansó that in the reign of
Pandukábhaya [B. C. 437—367] that monarch, who seems
to have been most tolerant in all matters of religion, built
places of worship in his capital, Anurádhapura, for all deno-
minations. The historian writes, chap. x. " He the king
who knew how to accord his protection with discrimination,"
established the yakkos in the royal palace itself and annually
provided demon-offerings. "He provided a nigródha tree

---

[*] The descendants of this king continued to reign in Jaffna, under the
title of ' Ariya Chakravarti,' until near the close of the sixteenth century.
They were frequently at war with the Sinhalese; and although at times
conquered and deposed, recovered and maintained their power until
finally subjugated by the Portuguese.

for the (dévatá) Wessawano, and a temple for the Wiyádho-
dévo." "He also constructed a dwelling for the various
classes of devotees." "The king built a temple for the
Nighantho Kumbhundo, which was called by his name. . To
the westward of that temple...... he provided a residence for
500 persons of various foreign religious faiths. Above the
dwelling of Jótiyo [a Brahman—his chief engineer] and
below the Gamini tank, he built a residence for the Paribájika
devotees. In the same quarter, but on separate sites, he
constructed a residence for the Ajiwako, a hall for the
worshippers of Brahma, (another for those) of Sivá, as
well as a hospital."

These Brahmans seem to have continued to reside peace-
ably in Ceylon, until B. C. 246, when two Malabar adventurers, military chiefs in the pay of the monarch Suratissa,
murdered the king and usurped the throne. Elála, of Solí
(Tanjore) on the Coromandel coast soon after their dethrone-
ment by Aséla, invaded the island, and defeating that king
possessed himself of the entire country, with the exception
of Ruhuna. He retained his power till B. C. 164, when in
his turn he was overthrown and slain in battle by Dutthága-
míne; and his followers driven out of the island. An army
of Malabars again invaded Ceylon in the reign of Walagambáhu, and held possession until B. C. 88. They seem to
have remained quiet after their expulsion by Walagambáhu
until A. D. 106, when the prince of the Solíans once more
ravaged the country with an army, and after plundering and
devastating it returned to his own land with immense booty

and 12,000 captives. Six years later, this invasion was·
avenged by Gajabáhu, the captives recovered, and a similar
number of Solíans led prisoners to Ceylon. Respecting these
transactions however, the Malabar and Siphalese annalists
give dissimilar accounts, the former asserting that the Solíans
voluntarily migrated to Ceylon at the request of Gajabáhu,
who made them large grants of land for the support of a
temple to Sivá, by way of expiation for a sin of intention,
he having at one time purposed to pull the said temple down.
It is at any rate certain that at the time alluded to a Solían
colony was established in Trincomalee, and that the colonists
were Sivaites. Another Malabar invasion took place A. D.
433, and the invaders again held possession of the land for
six-and-twenty years. Anarchy and internal discord more
or less prevailed from this time to the seventh century, in
which the Malabars every now and again took part. In A. D.
838 these inveterate invaders once more overran the country.
Driven back after awhile, they remained quiet until A. D. 954,
when war broke out afresh. A short peace ensued, and
again the Solíans ravaged the country; and the number of
Malabars increased so much in successive reigns that A. D.
1023, they menaced the throne, and an army of Solíans coming
to their aid, the king Mihindu IV. was captured, and with
his queen died a prisoner in the country of his foes. The
Solíans after this held the northern and mountain districts for
upwards of fifty years, when they were reduced by Wejaya-
báhu, who died A. D. 1126; and during this period the
Dhamilos [Tamils] succeeded in driving almost all the

Buddhist priests out of the island. Seventy years of peace followed, when a fresh period of internal discord tempted the Solíans to a fresh invasion, and the whole island became the prey of confusion, irreligion and anarchy, in which state it continued a third of a century. In other words, Hinduism prevailed, and Buddhism was all but extirpated under the strong hand of Mágha Rájá, the Malabar king.* He reigned for twenty-one years, when A. D. 1240 Wijaya succeeded in expelling the Malabars from the Máyá and Ruhuna divisions of the island; but they were too numerous and too firmly rooted in the Pihiṭi or northern kingdom to be driven thence; and their descendants remain there to the present day.†

The readiness with which the Siphalese associated the worship of Hindu divinities with that of their national faith is easily to be accounted for. Buddha, while neither

---

* The term "Malabar" is the common but improper name applied by Europeans to the Tamils of Ceylon, whether they come from Malabar proper, in the southwest of the Dekkan, from Tanjore, or from parts as far north as Cuttack and Orissa. The word never occurs in Siphalese writings. The term used in the Mahawansó and other Páli works is සමිළ Dhamilá, and in Siphalese works දෙමළු Demalu, corresponding to the Sanskrit word Draviḍa, Tamils. The king Mágha Rájá, was a native of Kálinga or Telegu, in the Northern Circars.

† The District of Nuwarakaláviya, however, which formed a large portion of the Kingdom of Pihiṭi, and in which was included Anurádhapura, the ancient capital, is still, as it always has been, occupied by the Siphalese, but with a large admixture of the Tamil race.

denying nor disputing the claims of these divinities to god-
ship, asserted his own immeasurable superiority over each
and all in every godlike attribute they were supposed to be
invested with: his followers therefore could worship whom
they pleased, so long as they acknowledged and took
refuge in him as the All-Supreme. But this assumption
of superiority was intolerable to those who rejected his
doctrines, and in their eyes his system was abominably obnoxious—in short, it was a most pestilent heresy. It
nevertheless made its way, for its originator was a king's
son, and kings and princes were its nursing fathers; and ere
long it became the dominant religion in the land of its
birth. In process of time, however, there came a reaction.
Brahmanism again prevailed, and proselytes were made with
facility; for when argument failed to convince, the sword
was brought to bear, and in the hands of its warlike wielders,
it wrought such effectual conversions, that ultimately Buddhism was either expelled from or extirpated throughout the
whole of Central India.

But, while the Hindus rejected Buddhism as heretical,
and extirpated it wherever they could, they have all along
manifested as ready a tendency as the most tolerant of
Buddhists to add to the number of their gods, though their
name already be legion. The ancient Tamil Poet Pudat-
tazhvár, a native of Mávilipuram near Sadras, has thus been
deified by the Vaishnavas, worshippers of Vishnu; in like
manner the two poetesses Uppei and Uruvei, who lived in
the ninth century of the Christian era, have been numbered

with the goddesses, and obtained elevated niches 'in the Hindu Pantheon; while in more recent times the founder of a temple at Nellore, in the north of the island, has become the divinity worshipped within it walls.

Such a tendency, it is but reasonable to suppose, would develope itself in connection with the Samanala peak, when the country in which it is situated became subjected to Hindu rule. The conquerors found the mountain dedicated to Saman, and its summit reverenced by Buddhists. Sivaite fakeers or ascetics discovered upon it medicinal trees and plants well known to them on the Himalayan ranges, the peaks of which are supposed to be Sivá's favorite abodes. They sought upon its slopes and surrounding valleys,—as their successors still continue the search for,—the plant "Sansévi," the tree of life and immortality, whereof whoso eateth he shall live for ever. Amongst them the mountain came to be called "Swargarrhanam," the ascent to heaven; and as all those whom Sivá destines to celestial bliss are said to receive upon their heads the impress of his sacred foot, by an easy process of transition the belief would become prevalent among the uneducated mass of his worshippers, that the foot-print upon the mountain top, alleged by the Sinhalese to be that of Buddha, was none other than Sivá's own. When once such a belief obtained a hold upon the Hindu mind, the legend to account for it would speedily be framed.

As already stated, however, many of the most orthodox of the Hindus repudiate the legend and decline to accept the rock-mark as a tangible memento of the presence of Sivá on the spot. In the Tiruvathavar Purana, generally supposed to have been written about the eighth century A. D.,* there is a chapter entitled "the vanquishing of the Buddhists in disputation," in which an account is given of a certain ascetic visiting Ceylon, (then called "the spotless kingdom of Ilá"),† and vexing the righteous souls of the "beautiful-shouldered" king, and the Buddhist hierarch, by proclaiming Sivá's superiority to Buddha. The king and the thero decided to go over to India and hold a public disputation upon the subject; but were there defeated and converted by the convincing arguments of the Sage Vathavuren. As this account appears in one of the works the Hindus esteem divinely inspired, and there is in it no mention whatever of the sacred foot-print or the Siván-oli-padam, it may be concluded that so late as the eighth century, both legend and belief were non-existent, so far at least as the Hindus are concerned.

The oldest probable period from which to date the legend, is that immediately following the invasion of the Solíans, A. D. 1023. The Siphalese king was then captured, and for fifty years after, the Hindu race held possession of the Máyá, or mountain, as well as the northern province of the

---

* A translation of this chapter, by S. C. Chitty, Esq., was published in the Journal of the Ceylon Branch of the Royal Asiatic Society for 1846.

† At that date, and previously, the old form of Siphalese, known as the "Elu," would doubtless be the language commonly spoken by educated natives.

island. Two years after this Solían invasion, A. D. 1025, a large body of Sivaites who fled in terror from Somnaut in India, where Mahmoud of Ghuznee had overthrown their temple, found a refuge in Ceylon; and this access of numbers no doubt largely contributed to strengthen the power of the Hindus in the land. The circumstances of the country however, in both the next and the succeeding century, were equally as bad, from a Buddhist point of view; and quite sufficient to account for the origination and confirmation of any belief that connected the Samanala peak with the worship of Sivá. There is no doubt about the fact, that the Sivún-oli-padam was resorted to by Hindu pilgrims in the early part of the fourteenth century, and as the pilgrimage was then an established custom, it may have been in vogue for a century or two earlier, for all that is known to the contrary. That observing old traveller Ibn Batutu,[*] after his arrival at Puttalam, on the North-west coast, thus describes his reception by " Ayarí Shakartí," the principal chief or sub-king of the district. " He said, Do not be shy; ask for what you wish. I answered, My only desire in coming to the island was to visit the blessed foot of our forefather Adam; whom these people call Bábá, while they style Eve 'Mámá. This, replied he, is easy enough. We will send some one with you who will conduct you thither.......He then gave me a palanquin which his servants carried upon their shoulders.

* The chapter of Ibn Batutu's travels relating to Ceylon, and containing the account of his ascent to the top of Adam's Peak will be found in Appendix B.

He also sent with me four Jogees, who were in the habit of visiting the foot-mark every year; with these went four Brahmans, and ten of the king's companions, with fifteen men carrying provisions."

From the fourteenth century to the present the custom has been kept up amongst the Hindu worshippers of Sivá. Hindus of other branches of Brahmanical faith seem to have frequented the mountain peak at the same period, but they either did not know or entirely ignored the legend that connected it with Sivá. They, in fact, held to the more ancient worship of Saman, a worship by no means repugnant to the feelings of the Siphalese. This is ascertained from the following dialogue between two Brahmans contained in the Siphalese poem entitled "Perakumbásirita," the life of Perakumbá, or Prákramabáhu VI., supposed by some to have been written by Srí Ráhula of Toṭagamuwa, a loyal panegyrist of that monarch, at whose Court at Jayawardhana, the modern Cotta, he resided;*——

කියන චලිය එහු ෙකාඨි ඔ, ඳ, සවනළ ෙගාඨිෂා
kiyaga magiya enu koyi siṭu, Dada, Samanula gosiná

එපුර අමුතු කිෙවක, බමුන, සුමන සුරිඳු විසිනා
epura amutu kimeka Bamuna Sumana, surindu wisiná

---

* For the extract in the text I am indebted to the Rev. C. Alwis, whose intimate acquaintance with the classic literature of his native land, and extensive knowledge of its legendary lore are surpassed by but few of his contemporaries. He has most obligingly assisted me in my researches, and furnished me with much valuable and interesting matter connected with the subject of this work. The extract was accompanied by the

කිය කල දෙදහස් පන් සිය රජෙක් එතෙයි දියනා
giya kala dedahas pan siya rajek eteyi Diyáná
කියලිය තන්වෙස් ඒනම් පෙරකුම් රජ මෙදිනූ
kiyaliya tanwęsi énam Pęrakum raja medinú.

O tell me, traveller, from whence you wend your way?
From Samanala, Brahman, have I arrived this day.—
What news from God Sumana, who holds thereo'er chief away?
When thousands twain, and hundreds five, of years have passed away,
The world to rule, a king shall come, so folk who dwell there say.—
King Pęrakum, then citizen, that is, whom all obey.

At a later date the Sivaites became the actual custodians of
the mountain, Rája Siṇha the Apostate from Buddhism
having delivered it over to a body of Aandiyás, Fakeers of the
Saiva sect, after putting to death the orthodox Bhikkhus,[*]
and burning all the sacred and historical books that he could
find of the faith which he had abandoned. These Aandiyás
retained possession of the mountain for a period of 160 years,
when the pious king Kirti Srí, restored it to the Buddhists,
bestowing the custody of the peak, with the royal village
Kuttápitiya, upon the priest Węliwita;[†] at the same time

following literal translation. "Tell (me) O traveller! where do you come
from?—O Brahman (I am returning) from having gone to Samanala.—
What news is there in that country, O Brahman! from the chief god
Sumana?—When two thousand five hundred years shall have elapsed,
they say that there would come a king, the chief of the world.—Then it
can be said, O citizen! that it is the king Pęrakum of this day."

[*] Bhikkhu, a person who lives on fragments; a Buddhist priest.

[†] A translation of the sannas or royal grant, is given in Appendix C.

conferring upon him, for his eminent services in restoring the religion· of Buddha, and procuring from Siam the Upasampadá ordination, the title of Sangha Rájah, or king of priests. The Aandiyás tried to regain possession, and in an appeal to the king for that purpose, made him a present of a splendid pair of elephant's tusks. The king accepted the present, but did not grant the petition; remarking, that the mountain belonged to Buddha and was not his to dispose of; at the same time he sent the tusks as an offering to the Srí-páda. The high-priests of the temple retained possession of these tusks until the British troops first entered the country, when they were removed to Kandy, and from thence to the Gadaládeni vihára in Udunuwara, where, in 1827, it was said they were still to be seen.

There is nothing recorded in the life of Mohammad, nor is there anything in the Kurán to shew that that enthusiastic Arabian iconoclast, the founder of the faith of Islam, was a believer in the tradition that connected Adam, the divinely created progenitor of the human race, and "greatest of all the patriarchs and prophets," with the holy mount of Serandib; yet the tradition was current amongst the Copts in the fourth and fifth centuries; and in a paper by Mr. Duncan, in the Asiatic Researches, containing historical remarks on the coast of Malabar, mention is made of a native chronicle, in which it is stated that a king of that country who was contemporary with Mohammad, was converted to Islam by a party of

dervishes on their pilgrimage to Adam's Peak.* But, as
the standard of the Crescent rose, and the prowess of its
turbaned followers, with almost incredible celerity, spread
far and wide the doctrines of him who called himself the
Apostle of God, and, after Adam, "the last and greatest
of the prophets," so, with like speed, did the wondrous tales
of the old Arab voyagers and traders of Ceylon† spread

---

* Asiatic Researches, vol. v. p. 9. This conversion "was effected by
a company of dervishes from Arabia who touched at Crungloor, or
Cranganore (then the seat of Government in Malabar) on their voyage
to visit the Footstep of Adam, on that mountain in Ceylon which mariners
distinguish by the name of Adam's Peak." In a note, Mr. Duncan adds:
" This Footstep of Adam is, under the name of Sre-pud or the 'holy foot,'
equally reverenced and resorted to by the Hindus."

† Arab traders were known in Ceylon centuries before Mohammad
was born, " and such was their passion for enterprise, that at one and the
same moment they were pursuing commerce in the Indian ocean, and
manning the galleys of Marc Antony in the fatal sea-fight at Actium.
The author of the *Periplus* found them in Ceylon after the first Christian
century, Cosmos Indico-pleustes in the sixth; and they had become so
numerous in China in the eighth, as to cause a tumult in Canton. From
the tenth till the fifteenth century, the Arabs, as merchants, were the un-
disputed masters of the East; they formed commercial establishments in
every country that had productions to export, and their vessels sailed
between every sea-port from Sofala to Bab-el-Mandeb, and from Aden
to Sumatra. The 'Moors' who at the present day inhabit the coasts of
Ceylon, are the descendants of these active adventurers; they are not
purely Arabs in blood, but descendants from Arabian ancestors by
intermarriage with the native races who embraced the religion of the
prophet."—Sir J. E. Tennent's Ceylon, vol. i. p. 607.

amongst their countrymen and co-religionists reports of the
beauty, the fertility, and the riches of India's utmost isle.
Not least in interest amongst the marvels told would be those
respecting the mysterious relic on the summit of Al-rohoun,[*]
the mighty mount they saw above the horizon for days before
they moored their ships beneath the shadow of the palms that
marged the coast. From what was recorded of Adam in
the Kurán, and the Coptic traditions, with which the Arab
traders would be well acquainted, connecting his name
with the mountain and the foot-print, the whole combined
failed not to invest the island with all the charms of an
earthly elysium, and fixed in the minds of Moslems the idea
that the mountain of Serandib, "than which the whole
world does not contain a mountain of greater height,"[†]
sprang from the site of Eden's garden, and was most probably that sacred spot,

<blockquote>" The Mount of Paradise, in clouds reposed,"</blockquote>

whence Adam was permitted to take his last long lingering
look at the abodes of bliss from which he was for ever
expelled, for

---

* So called from the Ruhuna division of the Island, in which Galle is
situated, and from which Adam's Peak is seen.

† The description given by TABARI, "the Livy of the Arabians,"
born A. D. 838, whose writings contain, it is believed, the earliest allusions
to Ceylon to be found in any of the Arabian or Persian authors.

"that mysterious crime,
Whose dire contagion through elapsing time
Diffused the curse of death beyond control;" *

or the pinnacle upon which he alighted, when, according to
other traditions, he was ·cast out from the Paradise of the
seventh heaven, and there "remained standing on one foot,
until years of penitence and suffering had expiated his
offence, and formed the footstep" that now marks the place
upon which he stood.†

The traditions vary in their details; but all true Islamites
hold to the belief that Ceylon was rendered for ever famous
by the presence upon it, and the residence therein, of the
Father of Mankind.‡   Sale, in the note already quoted from,

---

* James Montgomery's "World before the Flood."

"It is from the summit of this mountain, a tradition reports, that
Adam took his last view of Paradise, before he quitted it never to return.
The spot at which his foot stood at the moment, is still supposed to be
found in an impression on the summit of the mountain, resembling the
print of a man's foot, but more than double the ordinary size. After
taking this farewell view, the father of mankind is said to have gone
over to the continent of India; which was at that time joined to the
island; but no sooner had he passed Adam's Bridge than the sea closed
behind him, and cut off all hopes of return."—Percival's Account of
Ceylon, p. 206-7.

† Note to chap. ii. of Sale's Al-koran.

‡ "There is another tradition related in the Caherman-nameh, namely,
that Adam was banished to Serandib after his expulsion from Paradise,
and that Caherman-Catel, wishing to bequeath to posterity a monument
to record the birth of his son Sam-Neriman, caused a town to be built

mentions the further belief of the followers of the Prophet
of Mecca, that Eve, who had fallen from Paradise near Jed-
dah, or Mecca, in Arabia, was, after a separation of two
hundred years, reunited to Adam, who was conducted to her
by the angel Gabriel, and that they afterwards both retired
to Ceylon, where they continued to propagate their species.
Percival, in his notice of the mountain named after him to
whom

> " the evening breeze
> Had borne the voice of God among the trees;
>   .   .   .   .   .   whose morning eye
> Outshone the star that told the sun was nigh,"
> J. Montgomery.

states that one of the chains near the top is said to have
been made by Adam himself! but he gives no authority for
the statement. Sir W. Ousely, in his Travels, quoting from
the Berhan Kattea, a manuscript Persian dictionary, writes
" Serandib (or Serandil) is the name of a celebrated mountain,
whereon the venerable Adam, (to whom be the blessing of
God!) descended from Paradise and resided....it is likewise
reported, that here is interred the father of mankind."
Ashref, a Persian poet of the fifteenth century, holding this
belief, describes in the " Zaffer Nainah Skendari," a voyage

---

in the great plain at the foot of the mountain where Adam was interred,
and that he called the same Khorrem, place of joys and pleasures, such
as the Greeks and Latins believed the Elysian fields to have been."—
Bibliotheque Orientale of D'Herbelot, vol. iii. p. 308.

made to Ceylon by Alexander the Great, where, after landing and indulging himself and companions in feasts and
revels, he next explores the wonders of the island, and "with
the philosopher Bolinas [celebrated for the composition of
magical talismans] devises means whereby they may ascend
the mountain of Serandib, fixing thereto chains with rings,
and nails or rivets, made of iron and brass, the remains of
which exist even at this day; so that travellers, by the assistance of these chains, are enabled to climb the mountain and
obtain glory by finding the sepulchre of Adam, on whom be
the blessing of God!"* Unfortunately for Ashref's credibility,
his statements are not supported by any reliable authority,
and history is utterly silent in regard to this alleged voyage
of Alexander and his companions.† His own countrymen too,
are at issue with him as to the place of sepulture of the
father of mankind, for Hamdallah Kazwini, the Persian
geographer, says that Adam left Ceylon for the continent of
India, and "crossed the sea on foot, though ships now sail
over the place of his passage, during the space of two or
three days' voyage."‡

---

* Sir W. OUSELY's Travels, vol. i. p. 58.

† This belief amongst Easterns of the visit of Alexander the Great to
Ceylon existed long before the time of Ashref. Ibn Batúta, a century
earlier, mentions "the ridge of Alexander," at the entrance to the
mountain Serandib, "in which is a cave and a well of water," and a
minaret there "named after Alexander."

‡ Sir W. OUSELY's Travels, vol. i. p. 37.

The earliest account of the Mussulman tradition that
connects the story of Adam with the Peak is that contained
in the narrative of Soleyman, an Arab merchant who visited
Ceylon in the beginning of the ninth century. His attention
was particularly directed to the mountain called by his
countrymen "Al-rohoun," "to the top of which" he says,
"it is thought Adam ascended, and there left the print of
his foot, in a rock which is seventy cubits in length; and
they say, that Adam at the same time stood with his other
foot in the sea. About this mountain are mines of rubies,
of opals, and amethysts."* Ibn Wahab, another trader who
visited Ceylon about the same period, speaks of its pearls
and precious stones; and the narratives of both travellers
are related in a work entitled " Voyages of the two Mohammadans," written between the years A. D. 851—911, and
first printed in France in 1718.†

Sindbad the Sailor in his charming tales, written probably
about the same period as those of the two Mohammadans,
says in the account of his sixth voyage "The capital of
Serabdib stands at the end of a fine valley, in the middle of
the island, encompassed by high mountains. They are seen

---

* History of Ceylon, by PHILALETHES, 1817, p. 7. The opals referred
to by Soleyman must have been either cat's-eyes or moonstones; the
real opal not being found in Ceylon.

† By RENAUDOT; it was reprinted at Paris by REINAUD in 1845.
An English translation was included in both HARRIS's and PINKERTON's
collections of early travels.

three days' sail off at sea. Rubies and several sorts of
minerals abound. All kinds of rare plants and trees grow
there, especially cedars and cocoa-nut. There is also a
pearl-fishery in the mouth of its principal river; and in some
of its valleys are found diamonds.* I made, by way of
devotion, a pilgrimage to the place where Adam was confined
after his banishment from Paradise, and had the curiosity
to go to the top of the mountain." † The Arabian author
Edrisi, in his Geography compiled at the desire of the
Sicilian king, Roger the Norman, A. D. 1154, repeats details
of the height of the holy mountain of Ceylon, its gems
and odoriferous woods; and in the next century Kazwini
of Bagdad, the Pliny of the East, gives particulars of
Ceylon as then known to the travellers and voyagers of
his day.

Ibn Batúta, a Moor of Tangiers, the record of whose
thirty years' pilgrimage [A. D. 1324—1354] entitles him to
rank amongst the most remarkable travellers of any age or
country, whilst journeying through Persia, visited at Shíráz
"the tomb of the Imám El Kotb El Walí Abú Abd Allah

---

* Diamonds are not found in Ceylon, but white sapphires may have
been passed off for such gems. A species of zircon is found in Matura,
which goes by the name of the Matura diamond; these stones are
exceedingly hard, and some of them possess great lustre: but they are
seldom found of any size, and are of little commercial value.

† Arabian Nights' Entertainments, by TOWNSEND; Chandos Classics
Edit., p. 428.

Ibn Khafif, who is the great exemplar of all the region of
Fárs." Of him he says "This Abú Abd Allah is the person,
who made known the way from India to the mountain of
Serandib, and who wandered about the mountains in the
Island of Ceylon. Of his miracles, his entering Ceylon, and
wandering over its mountains in company with about thirty
fakeers is one: for when these persons were all suffering
from extreme hunger, and had consulted the Sheikh on
the necessity of slaughtering and eating an elephant, he
positively refused and forbade the act. They, nevertheless,
impelled as they were by hunger, transgressed his commands,
and killed a small elephant, which they ate. The Sheikh,
however, refused to partake. When they had all gone to
sleep, the elephants came in a body, and smelling one of
them, put him to death. They then came to the Sheikh,
and smelled him, but did him no injury. One of them,
however, wrapt his trunk about him, and lifting him on his
back, carried him off to some houses. When the people saw
him, they were much astonished. The elephant then put
him down and walked off. The infidels were much delighted
with the Sheikh, treated him very kindly, and took him to
their king. The king gave credit to his story, and treated
him with the greatest kindness and respect. When I entered
Ceylon I found them still infidels, although they had given
great credit to the Sheikh. They also very much honour
the Mohammadan fakeers, taking them to their houses and
feeding them, contrary to the practice of the infidels of
India; for they neither eat with a Mohammadan, nor suffer

him to come near them."[*] Sir James Emerson Tennent
observes upon this account:—"As this saint died in the year
of the *Hejira* 331, his story serves to fix the origin of the
Mohammadan pilgrimages to Adam's Peak in the early part
of the tenth century."[†]

Ibn Batúta's visit to Ceylon was the result of stress of
weather, he being at the time on a voyage from one of the
Maldive islands,—where his long residence and popularity
had excited the hatred of the Vizier,—to the "Manbar
Districts" on the coast of Coromandel. His narrative will
be found in the Appendix, accompanied with notes identi-
fying many of the places mentioned in his route from
Puttalam to Gampola, thence to Adam's Peak, to Dondra-
head, Galle, Colombo, and back to Puttalam.

---

[*] The Travels of Ibn Batúta, translated from the Arabic by the
Rev. S Lee, Professor of Arabic in the University of Cambridge, 1829,
p. 42–43 Robert Knox, writing three hundred and forty years later,
fully corroborates the statement of Ibn Batúta.

[†] Sir J. E. Tennent's Ceylon, vol. i. p. 579.

·· NOTE.

It is stated in page 19, on the authority of a note in
Mr. James D'Alwis's "Attanagalu-vansa," that except in
the historical works of Ceylon, there is no account of this
supposed impression of Buddha's foot in any of the earliest
records of Budhism." Since the printing of the sheet containing that page, I have been favoured with the following
communication from Mudaliyar Louis De Zoysa, the learned
Chief Translator to the Ceylon Government, whose merits
as a Puli and Sanscrit scholar are patent to all who have
occasion to consult him, but whose reluctance to publish the
fruits of his studious labours has hitherto prevented him
from taking that place amongst generally known Orientalists
to which his abilities entitle him.

"I have much pleasure in sending you an extract and its
translation from Buddhaghósa's Atthakathá on the Winayapitaka, entitled 'Samanta Pásádiká,' respecting the impression of Buddha's foot on the mountain of Samantakúta.
Buddhaghósa is the great commentator on the canonical
Scriptures of Buddhism. Atthakathá is a Comment, or
Glossary. Winayapitaka is that division of the sacred text
which treats of the Laws of the Buddhist Priesthood.

"Tíuikhópana Bhagavató padachétiyáni. Laŋkádípé ékaŋ.
Jambudípé Yónakaratthé dwéti. Tattha bódhitó atthamé wassé
Kalyániyaŋ Maniakkhi nágarújéna nimantitó Bhagavá paŋchahi

bhikkbusatéhi parivutó Laŋkádípamágamɪɴɴ Kalyáni chétíyaṭṭháné katé ratana-maṇdapé nisiɴnó bhattakichchaŋ katwá Samɴntakúṭe padaŋ dassotwá agamási."—SAMANTA PA'SA'DIKA'.

" There are three foot-impressions of the Deity of felicity: one in the Island of Lanká, and two in the Yónaka* country in Jambudípo. In the eighth year after his attainment of Buddhahood, the Deity of felicity, at the invitation of the Nága king Maniakkhi, arrived at Lanká attended by five hundred priests, and having taken his seat in the ratana-maṇdapa (gem-decorated-hall) on the site of the Dágoba at .. Kẹlani, and having partaken of his repast there, left the impression of his foot on the Samantakúṭa mountain and departed."

The above extract, however, only proves that the notice of the foot-print occurs for the first time in any other than an historical work, in the Aṭṭhakathá or commentary composed by Buddhaghósa, which, although esteemed by many as of equal authority with the Tripiṭaka, was nevertheless only written at about the same period as the corresponding statement in the Mahawansó, or but a short while before. For Buddhaghósa arrived in Ceylon from Maghada, near Patna, the original seat of Buddhism, during the reign of Mahanámó, A. D. 410—432; and he and the thero Mahanáma were both resident at the same time at Anarádhapura, where the latter completed the early chapters of the Mahawansó in the reign of his nephew Dhátu-Sena [A. D. 459—478]. The statements in the commentary and in the history are identical, and both

---

* Bactriana, or Affghanistan.

had, without doubt, a common origin.* The express object
of·Buddhaghósa's visit to Ceylon, was to translate from
Siṇhalese into Pali the Aṭṭhakathás on, as well as the text
of the Piṭakas, but during his residence in the island, he
himself composed additional comments, regarding which one
of the most learned priests of the·present day remarked,
"that any one who read them through would be able to
fulfil the office of Saṅgha Rájú, or supreme ruler of the
priesthood." † But at the same time, "they abound much
more with details of miraculous interposition than the
Piṭakas they profess to explain,"‡ and as there is absolutely
nothing in the text of the Winiyapiṭaka respecting the alleged
foot-mark, to give occasion to the extract quoted from the
comment, it seems evident that Buddhaghósa embodied in
his commentary, as in a kind of common-place book, everything that in any way tended to the glorification of Buddha,
however remotely connected it might be with the special
subject he had on hand.

---

* The *Dipawansa*, or history of the Island, written in Pali, perhaps a
century and a half earlier than the *Mahawansó*, is the oldest known book
in which the legend is stated. Both Buddhaghósa and Mahanáma seem
to have been indebted to its pages for what they have written on this
particular subject.

† HARDY's Manual of Buddhism, p. 512.

‡ HARDY's Eastern Monachism, p. 171.

Adam's Peak.

~~~~~~~~~

" All the giant mountains sleep
High in heaven their monarch stands,
Bright and beauteous from afar
Shining into distant lands
Like a new-created star."

J. MONTGOMERY.

——

CHAPTER II.

NOTICES OF THE PEAK AND FOOT-PRINT BY EARLY CHRISTIAN WRITERS.—ACCOUNTS BY MARCO POLO, SIR JOHN MAUNDEVILLE, CAPTAIN RIBEYRO, ROBERT KNOX, AND THE DUTCH HISTORIAN VALENTYN.

THE Gnostics, in framing their theological system, made Adam rank as the third emanation of the Deity; and in a manuscript of the fourth century, containing the Coptic version of the discourse on " Faithful Wisdom," attributed to Valentinus, the great heresiarch of that early corruption of Christianity, there occurs the oldest recorded mention of the sacred foot-print of " the primal man." The veneration they cultivated for *Ieû*, (the mystic name they gave to Adam) the protoplast of the human race, seems, after their dispersion under persecution, to have been communicated

by them to the Arabs, and it was probably under this
influence that Mohammad recognized him in the Kurán, as
the "greatest of all patriarchs and prophets," and the "first
of God's vicegerents upon earth."[*] It does not appear,
however, that pilgrimages were at any time made by Christians, as acts of devotion, to the sacred foot-print.

The Portuguese authorities, when they became interested
in the affairs of Ceylon, were not at all inclined to believe
in the impression, as being that of the foot-print of Adam;
some attributing it to St. Thomas, and others to the Eunuch
of Candace, Queen of Ethiopia.   Percival, in his account of
the island, apparently adopting this view, states, page 208,
that "the Roman Catholics have taken advantage of the
current superstitions to forward the propagation of their own
tenets; and a chapel which they have erected on the mountain, is yearly frequented by vast numbers of black Christians of the Portuguese and Malabar races." But in this
respect he seems to have fallen into an error; there are no
traces of such a chapel on the mountain at the present day,
nor does it appear, upon inquiry, that there had been any
such in former times. Probably, when writing his work, he
had present to his recollection traditions of the old Roman
Catholic church, which in the times of the Portuguese stood
on the spot now occupied as the great Saman Déwale, about
a couple of miles from Ratnapura, in which city there is

---

* Sir J. E. TENNENT's Ceylon, vol. ii. p. 135.

still a body of Roman Catholics, and a small chapel where they assemble for worship.

Early Christian travellers have not failed to make mention of the Peak in the narratives they have left of their voyages and travels to the far East. Chief amongst these stands Marco Polo, the celebrated Venetian whose travels through the dominions of the Emperor Kublaï Khan and adjacent countries, A. D. 1271—1295, led Sansivino, the historian of the city of Venice, to call him "the first before Columbus who discovered new countries." He thus refers (book III. ch. xxiii.) to the traditions that connect the mountain of Zeilan with both Adam and Buddha.

" I am unwilling to pass over certain particulars which I omitted when before speaking of the island of Zeilan, (ch. xix.) and which I learned when I visited that country in my homeward voyage. In this island there is a very high mountain, so rocky and precipitous that the ascent to the top is impracticable, as it is said, excepting by the assistance of iron chains employed for that purpose. By means of these some persons attain the summit, where the tomb of Adam, our first parent, is reported to be found. Such is the account given by the Saracens. But the idolaters assert that it contains the body of Sogomon-barchan,* the founder of their religious system, and whom they revere as a holy personage.

---

* Evidently a corruption of the terms Sákya-muni, chief sage of the Sákya race ; and Bhagawat, supreme spirit ; commonly used by Buddhists to designate Gautama Buddha.

Missing Page

Missing Page

king two large back-teeth, together with some of the hair,
and a handsome vessel of porphyry.   When the Grand Khan
received intelligence of the approach of the messengers, on
their return with such valuable curiosities, he ordered all
the people of Kanbalu (Pekin) to march out of the city to
meet them, and they were conducted to his presence with
great pomp and solemnity."

The first of the writers on Ceylon in the fourteenth century
was the Minorite Friar Odoric of Postenau in Fruili.* "In
it he saw the mountain on which Adam for the space of 500
years mourned the death of Abel, and on which his tears
and these of Eve formed, as men believe, a fountain;" but
this Odoric discovered to be a delusion, as he saw the spring
gushing from the earth, and its waters "flowing over jewels,
but abounding with leeches and bloodsuckers." In 1349
Giovanni de Marignola, a Florentine and Legate of Clement
VI., landed in Ceylon, at a time when the legitimate king
was driven away; his attention was chiefly directed to " the
mountain opposite Paradise."

Sir John Maundeville, a native of St. Albans, who died
at Liege in the year 1371, in his Voyages and Travels,†
says of Ceylon, " And there ben also many wylde Bestes, and
namelyche of Olifauntes.   In that yle is a gret Mountayne;

---

* He set out on his travels from the Black Sea, in 1318, traversed the
Asian Continent to China, and returned to Italy after a journey of
twelve years.—Sir J. E. Tennent's Ceylon, vol. i. p. 612.
† Chapter xviii. p. 238.   Edit. 1727.

and in mydd place of the Mount, is a gret lake in a full fair
Pleyne, and there is gret plentee of Watre. And thei of
the Contree seyn, that Adam and Eve wepten upon that
Mount an 100 Zeer, whan thei weren dryven out of Paradys,
And that Watre, thei seyn, is of here Teres: for so much
Watre thei wepten, that made the forseyde Lake. And in
the botme of that Lake, men fynden many precious Stones
and grete Perles. In that Lake growen many Reedes and
grete Cannes: and there with inne ben many Cocodrilles and
Serpentes and grete watre Leches."

Nicolo di Conti, a Venetian of noble family, and merchant
at Damascus, visited Ceylon in the early portion of the
fifteenth century. His adventures were related to Poggio
Bracciolini, apostolic Secretary to Pope Eugenius IV., by
whom they have been-preserved in a dissertation on " The
Vicissitudes of Fortune."* The notices of this work by
Sir Emerson Tennent make no mention of either the Peak
or the Foot-print; but Diego de Couto,† a painstaking
Portuguese writer, referring to Di Conti, says his description
of both are full of errors. De Couto rejects the idea that
the print of the foot was made by Adam, but insists very

---

* DI CONTI's account was printed at Basil, in 1538. The work was
translated into English for, and published by the Hakluyt Society, in 1857.

† DE COUTO was the continuator of a work written by ODOARDO
BARBOSA, a Portuguese captain who sailed in the Indian seas in the early
part of the sixteenth century. This work was a summary of all that was
then known concerning the countries of the East.

strongly on the claim made on behalf of St. Thomas, who also, he says, deeply impressed the marks of his knees upon a stone in a quarry at Colombo.

In 1506, Ludovico Barthema, or Varthema, a Bolognese, found it difficult to land in Ceylon "owing to the four kings, of the island being busily engaged in civil war," but he learned that "permission to search for jewels at the foot of Adam's Peak might be obtained by the payment of five ducats, and restoring as a royalty all gems over ten carats." The pearls of Manár and the gems of Adam's Peak were considered, in the early part of the 16th century, the principal riches of Ceylon.*

Captain Ribeyro, who gallantly fought on the losing side, and who records the downfall in Ceylon of the power of the race,† which more than two centuries ago had for the previous hundred and forty years

> " 'Neath flag of Portugal found place
> Till from each stronghold both were hurl'd
> And Holland standard proud unfurl'd,"

and the whole of the maritime provinces of the island passed

---

* Sir J. E. Tennent's Ceylon, vol. i. p. 135.

† History of Ceylon, presented by Captain John Ribeyro to the King of Portugal in 1685. Translated from the Portuguese by the Abbe Le Grand. Re-translated from the French, by George Lee, Postmaster General of Ceylon, 1847.

into the possession of the Dutch,* gives the following account of Adam's Peak:

"We have already said that Adam's-peak separates the kingdoms of Uwa, Kandy, and the Two Corles, from each other. This mountain passes for one of the wonders of the world. It is twenty leagues from the sea, and seamen see it twenty leagues from the land; it is two miles high, and before reaching its summit, we arrive at a very agreeable and extensive plain,† where that rest can be had of which the person who ascends is so much in need, as the mountain has then become very steep and rugged. This plain is intersected by many streams which fall from the mountain, and is entirely covered with trees; there are even very pleasant vallies in it.

"The heathens resort to this Peak on a pilgrimage, and never miss bathing in one of the rivulets, and washing their

---

* The Portuguese effected their first settlement in Ceylon at Colombo, A. D. 1518. The Dutch erected their first fort at Kattiar, near Trincomalee, in 1609; obtained a permanent footing (by treaty with the Portuguese) in 1646, and by 1658 made themselves masters of the entire sea-borde of the Island.

† Mr. LEE gives as a note here "Diabetme." But the plain of Diabetma is on a mountain top, and does not answer the description given by Ribeyro. The plain of Gilímalé, 9 miles from Ratnapura, is "intersected by many streams," is "covered with trees," and has moreover "pleasant vallies in it." Palábaddala however, is most probably the place meant, that being an elevated plateau, by and through which run streams and water-courses. It is the second halting station on the route, 15 miles from Ratnapura.

linen, their clothes, and all they have on them in it. They are persuaded that the place is holy, and they think that by these ablutions their sins are washed away.*

"After these superstitious observances, they clamber to the top of the mountain by chains which are attached to it, and without which it would not be possible to mount, so steep is the ascent from the plain to the top, and there still remains to be achieved a distance of quarter of a league. A person leaving the foot of the mountain very early in the morning will hardly reach its summit till two in the afternoon.†

"On the top of the Peak there is a large open square, 200 paces in diameter, and in the middle there is a very deep

---

* In chapter viii. of his history, Captain Ribeyro says, that the Queen Donna Catharina, widow of king Wimala Dharma [A. D. 1592—1627], married Senáratana, the brother of her deceased husband, who at the time of the king's death, was a priest "living in penitence on Adam's Peak." The native historians relate, that on the marriage of Senáratana, he was raised to the throne, and reigned for a period of seven years. He was succeeded by his son Rája Siṇha II., during whose reign of fifty years the Portuguese were expelled from Ceylon, being first driven by the king from all their possessions excepting their fortified towns on the sea-coast, after which, with the aid of the Dutch, he succeeded in finally expelling them from these; he then, by treaty with his allies, transferred to them the whole of the coast, with the exception of Batticaloa and Puttaḷam. It was while at Batticaloa, that Robert Knox and his companions were captured by order of Rája Siṇha II.

† This is about the time required, taking Palábaddala as the starting point.

lake of the finest water possible. Thence issue those streams
of which we have just spoken, and which collecting their
waters at the foot of the mountain form the three largest
rivers of the island.*

"Near the lake there is a flat stone bearing the impression
of a man's foot, two palms long and eight inches broad; this
impression is so well engraved that it could not be more
perfect if it were done on wax. All the heathens profess
great veneration for this relic, and assemble at the Peak
from all places to see it and render it their homage, and to
fulfil vows which they make regarding it. On the left of
the stone are some huts of earth and wood where the pilgrims
dwell: and on its right is a pagoda or temple, with the
house of the priest, who resides there to receive offerings
and to relate to the pilgrims the miracles which have been
wrought on the spot, and the favours and blessings which
have attended those who have come thither on pilgrimage;
and he never fails to impress on the minds of his hearers the
antiquity and holiness of that stone, which they wish the
heathens to believe is the imprint of the foot of our first
father.†

---

* The statement respecting the lake and the streams is erroneous.
There is however a small well near the top of the Peak.

† Ribeyro seems not to have known that the Sinhalese attributed the
foot-print to Buddha. He probably obtained his information from a
Mohammadan source. His account of the size of the foot-print differs
considerably from the reality. Its present length and breadth is about
four times larger than the dimensions stated in the text.

"Some trees have been planted round the stone to render the spot more venerable in appearance; and in order that the heathens may have no doubt as to the holiness of the place, the priest declares to them that two smaller mountains at the side of the Peak have stooped and bowed down before the sanctity of this mountain.* No man of common sense would believe this, any more than that the impression was made by a human foot, as the man who made it must have been of the most gigantic size; it is evident that it is the work of some heathenish hypocrite, a recluse on this spot, who sought to create a reputation for himself.

"One of the rivers falling from Adam's Peak runs towards the north, crosses the Four Corles, passes through Sittawacca and Malwana, and falls into the sea near Colombo, at a place called Mutwal; another flows towards the south, and waters the Two Corles, Saffragam, the Pasdun and Raygam Corles, and falls into the sea near Caltura; but the largest and most considerable of the three rivers is that which passes near Kandy, and after crossing the kingdoms of Trincomalee and Batticaloa, discharges itself into the bay dos Arcos, near the port of Cottiar. None of these rivers have any peculiar names, but take the appellations of the places they

---

* Sir J. E. TENNENT says, (vol. ii. p. 138,) "De Couto, in confirmation of the pious conjecture that the footstep on the summit was that of St. Thomas, asserts that all the trees of the Peak, and for half a league on all sides around it, bend their crowns in the direction of the relic; a homage which could only be offered to the footstep of an Apostle."

pass in their course, receiving as they flow onwards many smaller streams which entirely intersect the island."*

The assertion of the priests referred to by Ribeyro in the penultimate paragraph, is but the expression of a belief to which all true Buddhists tenaciously adhere. They appeal to the evidence of their senses; and plainly, the top of one the summits of the Bęna Samanala, the mountain which nearly faces Adam's Peak in a south-westerly direction, overhangs its base with a very apparent bend; while the tall rhododendron trees which flourish on the eastern side of the Peak, appear to lean over in the direction of the footprint, as their branches rise above the wall of the platform which surrounds the rock that bears it. There, they say, you have, on either hand, a miraculous proof of the divine supremacy of Buddha, and the sanctity of the seal of his power which he has impressed upon the mountain top. Five centuries and a half ago this belief, then as firmly held as now, was again and again referred to in the Samanta-kúṭa-wannaná, a poem descriptive of the Peak, and the origin of the Foot-print; and from which De Couto and others seem to have derived much of their information.

---

* This statement is not wholly correct. The first of the rivers named is the Kęlani-ganga, the second the Kalu-ganga. Both of these have their origin in the western slopes of the Samanala range of mountains, but not from Adam's Peak direct. The third is the Mahawęlli-ganga, the source of which is in Pędurutalágala, the highest mountain in Ceylon. One of its tributaries however flows from the eastern slopes of the Samanala range.

The following stanza is a fair sample of the poem:—

> වාලා වතංස සමකා ගිරයො සමන්තා
> Malú 'watansa samakú gírayo samantá
> හුත්වා නමන්ති අපි හන්ති සචේතනාව
> Hutwá namanti api hanti sachétanáwa
> සබ්බේපි තත්ථ තරවො චලන්තාදයොච
> Sabbépi tattha tarawo chalntádayocha
> නච්චන්ති දිබ්බ නටකා විය ඔනතග්ගා.*
> Nachchanti dibba natuká wiya onatnggá.*

Like canopies and garlands fair became the rocks around;
And graceful as the dancers, in heavenly mansions found,
The trees and floral creepers that clothe the mountains round,
Their heads, like sentient beings, bent lowly to the ground.

Robert Knox, in that most interesting account he has given of Ceylon in the narrative of his twenty years' captivity in the interior, during the reign of Rája Siṇha II., makes

---

* The author of Samantakúṭa-wannaná is generally believed to have been one WE'DE'HA, the chief priest of a temple called Patiraja Piriwena, who also wrote the Pali work Padya-madhu, and to whom is generally attributed the authorship of the Sidat Sangaráwa, the oldest known Grammar of the Siṇhalese language. He lived in the reign of king Pandita-Parakkramabáhu IV. A. D. 1320—1347. The Samantakúṭa-wannaná is a poem containing upwards of 500 stanzas, and describes, in flowing Pali verse, the legends which narrate the circumstances that led to the impression of Buddha's foot-print upon the summit of the Samantakúṭa. *Vide* Introduction to the Sidat Sangaráwa, by JAMES D'ALWIS. pp. clxxxii, clxxxiii, and cclxxxi. Colombo, 1852.

frequent mention of Adam's Peak.* He says, "The land is full of hills, but exceedingly well watered, there being many pure and clear rivers running through them...The main river of all is called Mavelagonga; which proceeds out of the mountain, called Adam's Peak (of which more hereafter); it runs through the whole land northward, and falls into the sea at Trenkimalay......On the south side of Conde Uda is a hill, supposed to be the highest on this Island, called, in the Chingulay language, Hamalell;† but by the Portuguese and the European nations, Adam's Peak. It is sharp, like a sugar loaf, and on the top a flat stone with the print of a foot like a man's on it, but far bigger, being about two feet long. The people of this land count it meritorious to go

---

* "An Historical relation of the Island of Ceylon in the East Indies; together with an account of the detaining in Captivity the Author, and divers other Englishmen now living there; and of the Author's miraculous escape. By ROBERT KNOX, a captive there near twenty years. [1659—1679]. Edit. 1817." This work was first printed in 1681. Captain Ribeyro's History was not presented to the king of Portugal until 1685; and remained unpublished till 1701; but as he lived in Ceylon, and took part in the occurrences he describes, previous to Knox's captivity, his account of the Peak is given first in order of time in the text.

† "The learned BRYANT, in his Analysis of Ancient Mythology, lays great weight upon this name; he says 'The Pike of Adam is properly the summit sacred to Ad Ham, the king or deity Ham, the Amon of Egypt. This is plain, to a demonstration, from another name given to it by the native Singalese, who live near the mountain, and call it Hamal-el: this, without any change, is Ham-eel-El, (Ham, the Sun,) and relates to the ancient religion of the Island. In short, every thing in

and worship this impression; and generally, about their new
year, which is in March, they, men, women and children,
go up this vast and high mountain to worship: the manner
of which I shall write hereafter, when I come to describe
their religion.   Out of this mountain arise many fine rivers,
which run through the land, some to the westward,* some
to the southward,† and the main river, viz. Mavelagonga
before mentioned to the northward."

"There is another great god, whom they call Buddou,
unto whom the salvation of souls belongs.   Him they believe
once to have come upon the earth; and, when he was here,
that he did usually sit under a large shady tree, called
Bogahah, which trees ever since are accounted holy, and
under which, with great solemnities, they do, to this day,
celebrate the ceremonies of his worship.   He departed from
the earth from the top of the highest mountain on the Island,
called Pico Adam;‡ where there is an impression like a foot,
which they say is his, as hath been mentioned before."

---

these countries savours of Chaldaic and Egyptian institution.'"—DAVY's
Account of the Interior of Ceylon, p. 348.   But Dr. Davy shews that
Bryant's explanation is entirely erroneous; that the sound of S and H
being indiscriminately used by the Siyhalese, the mountain is called by
them either Hamanala or Samanala, i. e. the rock of Saman; and that
in Pali its name is Somanó-kúṭa, and in Sanskrit Samanta-kúṭa-parwata,
the meaning, in each of the three languages, being exactly the same.

* Forming the Kẹlani-ganga.   † Forming the Kalu-ganga.

‡ Knox here followed the current native tradition.   Buddha's death
took place near the city Kusinára, in the year 543 B. C.   The exact site

"His great festival is in the month of March, at their New Year's tide. The places where he is commemorated are two, not temples—but the one a mountain, and the other a tree;* either to the one or the other they at this time go with their wives and children, for dignity and merit—one being esteemed equal with the other.

"The mountain is at the south end of the country, called Hammalella; but, by Christian people, Adam's Peak, the highest in the whole island; where, as has been said before, is the print of the Buddou's foot, which he left on the top of that mountain in a rock, from whence he ascended to heaven; upon this footstep they give worship, light up lamps, and offer sacrifices, laying them upon it as upon an altar.† The benefit of the sacrifices that are offered here do belong unto the Moors pilgrims, who come over from the other coast to beg, this having been given them heretofore

of this city has not yet been fixed. Different authorities suppose it to have been in the Province of Assam, the kingdom of Nepal, or at Hurdwar near Delhi. ||

* The Bo-tree at Anurádhapura, the oldest historical tree in the world, planted B. c. 288.

† "A beautiful pagoda formerly stood upon the top of this hill, respecting which many traditions are circulated, and many stories told. They say that it was the abode of Bhood, who was a disciple of the apostle Thomas. They add, that he stood with one foot upon this hill, and another upon a hill upon the coast of Madura, when such a flood of water burst forth, as to separate the island of Ceylon from the main land."—Philalethes, p. 210.

by a former king; so that, at that season, there are great
numbers of them always waiting there to receive their
accustomed fees."*

· The Rev. Philip Baldæus, "Minister of the word of God
in Ceylon," in his "True and exact Description of Malabar,
Coromandal, and also of the Island of Ceylon, &c.," printed
at Amsterdam in 1672, added but little to the stock of
information already known respecting the sacred foot-print.
In March, 1654, he states, that some Dutchmen, who had
gone purposely to examine it, were shewn by the Buddhist
priests a representation of it in gold, and of similar di·
mensions, on which different images were engraven, which
had before been exhibited upon the impression of the foot
in the rock. But, said they, when these images had been
pourtrayed in gold, they vanished from the stone.†

---

* KNOX has here, as in some other places, described the Hindus as
Moors. He refers in this instance to the Aandiyás, who from about 1590
to 1750, were the custodians of the Peak (see *ante*, page 39). In their
dress these fakeers somewhat resembled the Mohammadans, but smeared
their foreheads with ashes. Elsewhere, Knox particularly distinguishes
the Moors "who are Mohammadans by religion."

† This, according to a Buddhist tradition, implicitly believed by many
of the people, was not the first time impressions vanished from the surface
of that sacred rock. Each of the three Buddhas who preceded Gautama
Buddha left the impression of his foot-print on the spot; and each time
an impression was made, the former one sank through the rock to the
bottom of the mountain, where it still remains, and would be clearly
visible, if only the mountain could be turned upside down to exhibit it.

The historian Valentyn, in his great work on the Dutch East Indian possessions,[*] complains much of the want of information he found to exist among his countrymen, respecting the interior of Ceylon; what they had being chiefly derived from the statements of fugitives and spies. Of Adam's Peak, he says:—"This mountain is the Peak on the top of which Buddha, so say the Siŋhalese (or Adam, as others amongst them say,) left the great and famous footprint impressed on a certain stone, when he ascended to heaven. It is to this footstep that so many thousand pilgrims come from all lands to offer sacrifices." Elsewhere he furnishes a notable instance of the inaccuracy of his own information, by minutely describing the temples and images

---

[*] The following is the title of Valentyn's work:—"Keurlyke beschryving van Choromandel, Pegu, Arrakan, Bengale, Mocha, van 't Nederlandsch comptoir in Persien; en eenige fraaje zaaken van Persepolis overblyfzelen. Een nette beschryving van Malaka, 't Nederlands comptoir op 't Eiland Sumatra, mitsgaders een wydluftige landbeschryving van 't Eiland Ceylon, en een net verhaal van des zelfs keizeren, en zaaken, van ouds hier voergevollen; also ook van 't Nederlands comptoir op de kust van Malabar, en van onzen handel in Japan, en eindelyk een beschryving van Kaap der Goede Hoope, en 't Eiland Mauritius, met de zaaken tot alle de voornoemde ryken en landen behoorende. Met veele Prentverbeeldingen en landkaarten opgebeldert. Door FRANCOIS VALENTYN, Onlangs Bedienaar des Goddelyken woords in Amboina, Banda enz. Te Amsterdam, by Gerard Onder de Linden, 1726." This work is in five very large volumes in folio, and contains many hundred copper plates. One of these, a whole page plate, represents "Adam's Berg." The mountain is depicted as exceedingly high and steep, and is surmounted by two peaks like ragged

of Mulkirigala,—a precipitous rock near Mátara, called by
the Dutch Adam's Berg,—as if they existed on the mountain
of the Srí-páda. Philalethes, accepting this statement as
correct, endorses it in his history;* and Upham and others,
following him, perpetuate the error; although Cordiner,†
who is constantly quoted by Philalethes, and who does not

---

truncated cones, on the top of one of which the foot print is plainly
shewn. Groves of cocoa-nut and forest trees are scattered here and there;
and three rivers wind their way to the base of the mountain. One of
these, at the foot of the picture, is meant for the Sítagangulla. A company
of pilgrims are bathing in the stream a short distance from a waterfall;
and another company just come up, are preparing to do so. The pilgrims'
path is broad, and does not present any apparent difficulty, beyond its
steepness. Tremendous precipices however flank it on either side of the
mountain. About sixty pilgrims are seen on their way to the foot-print,
varying in the perspective from three quarters of an inch in size at the
bottom, to a mere speck at top. The whole forms a very curious
picture, and is as unlike the reality as one can conceive an artist would
make it, who, never having seen the Peak, was asked to design a representation of it from such confused and conflicting accounts as are given by
the historian.

    * " The History of Ceylon from the earliest period to the year MDCCCXV;
with characteristic details of the Religion, Laws and Manners of the
People, and a Collection of their Moral Maxims, and Ancient Proverbs.
By PHILALETHES, A, M., Oxon, 1817."

    † " A Description of Ceylon, containing an account of the Country,
Inhabitants, and Natural Productions, with Narratives of a Tour round
the Island in 1800, the Campaign of Candy in 1803, and a Journey to
Ramisseram in 1804. By the Rev. JAMES CORDINER, A. M., 2 vols.
1807."

seem to have been acquainted with Valentyn's work, in that part of his tour round the island which contains the route from Mátara to Tangalle, describes the same place, which was still called by Dutch residents Adam's Brecht or Berg.*

To compensate for his own lack of information in regard to particulars concerning Adam's Peak, Valentyn quotes, with approval, the following from De Couto:—

"On that mountain in Ceylon called Adam's Peak is an impression of the foot, in regard to which authors hold different opinions; some, as for instance, M. P. Venetus, [Marco Polo,] Nicolaus Conti, and other Venetians, having published very many errors concerning it.

"But we have the true story, as gathered from the old Siphalese and their books, and it runs thus:—

"This peak, called after Adam, is a mountain in the midst

---

* S. C. Chitty in the *Ceylon Gazetteer*, epitomizes from Cordiner the following account of this singular rock:—"*Adam's Berg*, a hill of considerable size, situated at the distance of 6 miles north-east of Kabawatte, in the district of Matura. It is known amongst the Singhalese by the name of Mulgirigal, and is mentioned in their history as early as the time of king Saidaitissa, who reigned at Anooraadhapoora from the year 140 to 122 B. C. The hill is about 300 feet in height, and is ascended by a winding flight of stairs, formed of five hundred and forty-five steps of hewn stones. On the summit, which is circular and level, stands a Dágoba, and about half way below it are two gloomy Wihares excavated out of the rock, close together, and in each of which there is (besides several figures of natural size standing in a row) a colossal image of Budha, in a recumbent posture, forty-five feet in length, and of a proportionable breadth, formed of stone."

of certain lands called Dinavaca, and it is so high that one, as he approaches this Island, can see it for more than twelve miles. It properly begins near Guilemale and Dinavaca, lying in a westerly direction from them. Guilemale lies twenty-four hours' journey from Colombo.

"The Siṇhalese name it Hammanelle Siripade, that is, the mountain of the foot-impression. It begins from below, gradually ascending, and divides itself on the summit into twelve tops,* on one of which is the foot impression. On either side of it, there are rivulets flowing from fountains above and branching off into streams. At the foot of the mountain is a river which flows nearly all around it.

"In this river, called Sitégangele,† the pilgrims, who come to the foot-impression to make offerings, wash themselves, and this washing is their baptism, they believing that by it they are cleansed.

"On the summit of one of these peaks is a plain,‡ and in the midst of the plain, is a tank of water, called Wellamallacandoere,§ surrounded on the top with large stones;

---

* De Couto is here confounding the mountain range with the mountain of the foot impression. There is but one summit, and one top on the Hammanelle, and that is the Peak itself.

† This river does not flow from Adam's Peak, but has its source in the Béna-Samanala mountain, and flows through the ravine which separates that mountain from Gangullahena, a mountain west of Adam's Peak.

‡ This answers to the plain on the top of Diabetma.

§ This tank lies in a ravine on the southern side of Heramiṭipána. About two miles further south is the village Welligalle. The stream

in the midst thereof is the shape of a great footstep which
they call Siripade, the foot much larger than a usual foot, and
of such a form that it appears to be impressed in the stone,
the same as if a seal was impressed in white wax.*

"Multitudes of pilgrims, as well Moors as Heathens,
flocking together here even from Persia and China, come to
this river for the purpose of cleansing themselves, and
putting on new and fine clothing. After cleansing themselves, they ascend a very high mountain. At a little
distance before reaching the top, they come to some steps,
on which are erected as it were two stone columns; over
these another stone is laid, to which is suspended a large
bell, made of the finest Chinese metal; to this hangs a great
clapper, bored through; through this hole passes a rope
made of leather, which each one must pull, the sound of the
bell indicating whether he who pulls it is clean or not;
for if he is still unclean, they believe that the bell will give
no sound, in which case he must return to the river and
cleanse himself with greater ceremony. The Devils seduce
them thus, although there is no one to whom the bell gives
no sound.

---

which supplies this village with water, is believed to take its rise at
Wellemalakandura; "kandura" signifying spring or head source of water.

* There is no foot-print here. DE COUTO is confused by his twelve
tops to the summit of his Hammancllc. Heramiṭipána, the pilgrim
station which gives its name to the place, is on the summit of a ridge
which is divided from the Samanala by a narrow valley; and the foot-
print referred to is that on the top of Samanala—the Srí-páda itself.

"As many as four or five hundred go thither together in
pilgrimage, and having arrived on the top, they can do no
more than kiss the stone with great reverence, and return;
they are not permitted to ascend by the pool or tank of
water, which pool is called in the Siṇhalese, 'Darroe-
pockoene'* that is, the tank of children. If women are
barren, they drink of this water; but they may not themselves
fetch it, it is brought to them by jogis. To ascend by this
pool or tank would be an unpardonable sin.

"The Moors also make offerings here, saying that it is the
footstep of Adam; that he ascended to heaven from thence,
and that he left his last foot-print in that stone.† This story
emanates from an old Eastern tradition, that Adam, when he
was driven out of Paradise was sent to an Island in India
called Serandive (that is, the Island of Ceylon).

"Marc P. Venetus says, that the Moors believe that
Adam was buried here. He says further, from the account
of these heathens, that the son of a King Sogomon Barcaon,
despising earthly dignities, resorted to this mountain for the
purpose of leading a holy life; that from thence he went
up to heaven; and that his father commanded that pagodas

---

* 'Daru' children; 'pokuna,' pond. This well is about 25 or 30 feet
from the top of the Peak, on its northwest side. It is reached by a steep
path from the northern angle of the platform which surrounds the Srí-
páda.

† "The fakirs of the Mohammadan religion take impressions of the
footstep on a piece of white cloth that has been previously covered with
pulverised sandur."—Hardy's Manual of Buddhism, p. 212.

should be built and images made in his memory, from which sprang the idolatry of India. But the Siphalese, having been asked about this, laugh at it; and their old writings, and principally their ballads, wherein are preserved their antiquities, and which they sing daily, (in order not to forget them,) tell quite a different tale.

"They say that there was a king who reigned over the whole East, who had been married many years and had no children; that in his old age, he obtained a son from God, who was the most beautiful creature that could be.

"This king, having charged his astrologers to make the horoscope of his son, found that the child would be holy, and that he would despise the kingdoms of his father and become a pilgrim; at which the father becoming grieved, resolved to confine his son in some court, and so prevent him from having a sight of anything; he accordingly confined him from his fifth year in walled gardens, and had him brought up in the company of many noble youths of his age, who were kept always near him, in order that no one else might speak to him.

"He was thus brought up till his sixteenth year, without having any knowledge of sickness, misery or death. Having arrived at the years of discretion, and understanding more things than were to be seen about him, he requested of his father that he might be permitted to see the towns and villages of his kingdom. This was granted, with directions that the guards in charge of him should bring him to the city and keep an eye upon him. On his way to the city he was

met by a cripple, respecting whom he inquired as to the cause
of his condition. · His companions said, that the man was
born so, and that it was very common to see such sights, and
that there were also men who were born blind, &c.   At
another time he saw an old man, hunchbacked, leaning on a
stick, his body also trembling. The prince inquired the
reason of this, and they told him that it came from old age.
He also saw a corpse, which was being taken for burial with
much weeping and lamentation, and inquired what it all
meant, and whether he and they should also die?   They
said yes; at which the prince became very sorrowful; and
while in this sorrowful state there appeared to him in a vision
a pilgrim who advised him to forsake the world and lead a
solitary life.

"Being much disturbed by this vision, he determined to
find means to effect his escape, in the guise of a pilgrim, into
uninhabited places.   Concerning his flight and wanderings
the Siŋhalese recount many fables, adding at last, that he
came to Ceylon with a great concourse of followers, and
resorted to this mountain, where he spent many years of a
very holy life, so that the Siŋhalese adored him as they
would a God.   When about to leave the Island for other
lands, his followers implored him to leave them something*
which might cause them to remember and think of him with

---

* This seems to have reference to the legend which describes the
impression of a foot-print made by Buddha in the bed of the Kęlani-ganga,
at the time of his third visit to Ceylon, and before he departed for

reverence; he thereupon kept his foot in this water tank, and left the impression to them for a remembrance. Their historians give this prince many names, but his proper name was Drama Raja;* and after he became a saint, that of 'Budhu,' which signifies the 'Sage.'" †

After referring to what is quoted in the note at page 64, De Couto continues:—"The mountain of Adam has towards its base a marsh from which the four principal rivers of the island have their source. The Portuguese give it the name of the Peak of Adam, but the Siŋhalese name it 'Dewa Gorata,' that is, God's country." The correct term for such an expression in Siŋhalese is 'Deyyangé raṭa,' and it is applicable not so much to the Samanala mountain, as to the whole country from beyond Gílimalé, which is still called by the natives Saman's Country; the shrine of that deity,

---

Samanala to leave behind him the venerated Srí-páda on the summit of that mountain. The two accounts are fused or confused together in almost all the accounts derived from the oral traditions of the natives.

* There is here again a confusion, arising from the mixing up of traditions of Buddha with those of Dhurma-rája. Dhurma-rája-galla is the name given to a mountain about midway between Diabetma and Sítagangulla-hena. Its steepest part is ascended by the aid of 130 steps cut in the living rock; by these steps, on the bare rock, is the outline of a human figure, with an inscription above it. The purport of the inscription is that the steps were cut by order of Dhurma-rája, who died here while on a pilgrimage to the Srí-páda.

†·For the above translation from Valentyn's work I am indebted to Mr. R. A. VanCuylenberg, the talented principal clerk in charge of the Record Office attached to the Colonial Secretariat at Colombo.

almost on the top of the Peak, being fully as much reverenced by the Siṇhalese as the foot-print that is just above it. During the reign of Wimaladharma Suriya II., A. D. 1684—1706, that monarch, who is praised by the historians for his piety, made a state pilgrimage from Kandy " to pay his adoration on Adam's Mount, and to offer a salver (sombero) of massy silver with other presents." *   He was accompanied by a train of nearly 300 tusker elephants, which were kept by him merely for the parade of the Court; most of them being ordinarily distributed among the temples in the neighbourhood of Kandy, where, for purposes of devotion, he was a frequent attendant.

---

* PHILALETHES, p. 130.

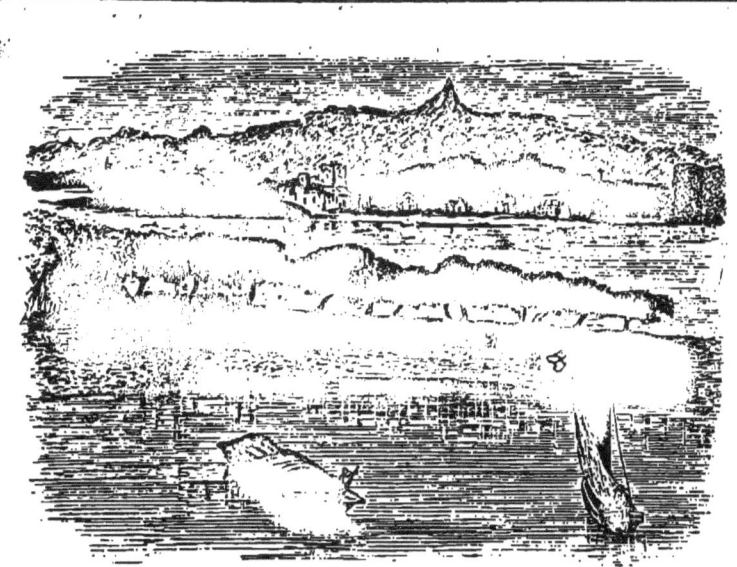

ADAM'S PEAK FROM GALLE FACE, COLOMBO.

THE PEAK AND THE RAINA' SAMANALA FROM THE KALAGUNGA.

Adam's Peak.

~~~~~~~~~~

"The mountains of this glorious land
Are conscious beings to mine eye,
When at the break of day they stand
Like giants, looking through the sky
To hail the sun's unrisen car
While one by one, as star by star
Their peaks in ether glow."

J. MONTGOMERY.

———

CHAPTER III.

THE SAMANALA PEAK.—RATNAPURA ROYAL MAIL.—PANABAK-
KERY.—KELANI.—BUDDHIST TEMPLES.—KADUWELLA.—HANG-
WELLA.—RIVER SCENERY.—AWISSA'WELA.

THE shrine-crowned Samanala is distant in a direct line
from Colombo, the Maritime Capital of Ceylon, about 46
miles,* and rises to a height of 7352·8 feet above the level
of the sea; where, in clear weather, it has been seen at a
distance of thirty leagues.† It forms the crowning point of

---

* 45·9 from the Clock-tower, Colombo.

† It is stated in the Rájawalia, that Wijaya, the Indian invader and
first king of Ceylon, made for the island [B. C. 543] in consequence of
seeing from his ship the large rock called Samanta-kúṭa, whereupon he

L

the south-western range of the mountain zone,* and was for
a long time considered the highest, as it certainly is the most
conspicuous mountain in the Island.† Although not often
visible during the southwest monsoon, (May to November),
it is generally, during the intervening months, more or less
distinctly seen from Chilaw on the northwest to Dondra-
head on the south coast, a distance of one hundred and fifty

---

and his followers concluded amongst themselves that the country would
be a good one to reside in, and accordingly they bore up for it, and
landed at Tammçnna Nuwara, on the northwest coast.

Mohammad Ibn Batuta, in the narrative of his travels, mentions that
being driven from the Maldives, he "arrived at last at the Island of
Ceylon, a place well known, and in which is situated the mountain of
Serendib. This appeared to us like a pillar of smoke, when we were at a
distance of nine days from it."

* "On carrying the eye onwards to the landward horizon, it is seen
to be bounded by a noble mountain range, between thirty and forty miles
distant, culminating, if the voyager has made the Island near Point-de-
Galle, in a conical summit named the Haycock, which in general effect
may be compared with the Schehallion in Scotland, as seen from the East;
and if he make the coast nearer Colombo, in Adam's Peak,—a summit so
eminent, that I do not remember to have seen anything that will bear
comparison with it, except perhaps Monte Viso, in the Maritime Alps,
as seen in the western horizon by the traveller when descending towards
Turin."—Rev. Dr. MACVICAR on the Geology, Scenery and Soil of
Ceylon. *Appendix to Ceylon Almanac*, 1854, p. 26.

† It is, in fact, the fourth in altitude. Pçdurutalágala, the highest,
springing from the Nuwara Eliya plains, being 8,295 feet above the sea
level. The others are Kirigalpotta, 7,836·8, and Toṭapçlla, 7,720 feet in
height.

miles. On the western coast, the low lying champaign région of which reaches from the sea almost to the mountain's base, the range from which it springs forms a magnificent purple-tinted back-ground. The Peak, there lifted high in lonely grandeur, and shrouded at intervals from sight by the mists that rise from the surrounding valleys, or by the low clouds drifting in the monsoon wind, has been associated by the fervid imaginations of Oriental races with legends of the most romantic kind. With some of these, and with descriptions of the mountain, the writer was familiar in early life; and when his lot was cast in Ceylon, he determined, if possible, to make the ascent to the "Srí-páda,"—the Sacred Foot-print,—and thencefrom see what the intrepid blind traveller Holman, who visited it in 1830,* described in graphic terms

* The first Englishman who ascended Adam's Peak was Lieut. MALCOLM of the 1st Ceylon Rifle Regiment, who reached the summit on the 27th April, 1827. The account of his ascent will be found in Appendix C.

Lieut. HOLMAN, R. N. in the 3rd volume of his Travels Round the World, p. 228, thus writes:—"We reached the summit just before the sun began to break, and a splendid scene opened upon us. The insulated mountain rising up into a peaked cone of 7,420 feet above the level of the sea, flanked on one side by lofty ranges, and on the other by a champaign country stretching to the shore that formed the margin of an immense expanse of ocean. I could not see this sight with the *visual* orbs, but I turned towards it with indescribable enthusiasm. I stood upon the summit of the Peak; and *felt* all its beauties rushing into my very heart of hearts." On his return from the Peak Holman mentions that his servant purchased a fowl from a native for 3½*d.* In 1870 the bazaar charge at the same place for a very middling sized fowl was 1*s.* 3*d.*

he felt. But time wore on, and many a wistful glance did
he make towards that Alpine height, wondering when,
if ever, he should be able, from the shrine a-top, to behold
the beauties of the wide-spread scenery below; nor was it
until twenty weary years had passed away that he was at
length enabled to accomplish his long-cherished purpose.
This was done in the Easter-week of 1869 (March 24—31)
in company of Messrs. Larkum, Giles, and Deslandes,
gentlemen connected with the Public Works Department of
the colony; a second excursion was made in the month of
September following,* when the writer was accompanied by
his son, and Mr. Gullett, the talented correspondent at Galle
of the leading Australian Journals; and a third was undertaken during the Christmas holidays, in company of Mr.
E. Gower of Colombo. The narrative of these pilgrimages,
as given in the following pages, will, he trusts, prove not
only interesting to the general reader, but also be useful
as a guide to pilgrim-visitors hereafter.

On the first excursion three of us started from Colombo at
6 P. M., in the Ratnapura Royal Mail, a vehicle constructed
on the char-a-banc principle, and with the addition of another
passenger, with baggage, mails, driver and horsekeeper to
boot, we were somewhat too much of a load for the wretched

---

* Notes of these journeys appeared in the "Ceylon Observer" at the
time; those of the first by the present writer under the signature of
"PILGRIM BROWN," and of the second by one of his companions—an
extract from which is given in chapter I.

animals with which the coach was singly horsed. We did the distance from Colombo to Ratnapura, 56 miles, at the rate of exactly four miles the hour, inclusive of the half-hour we rested at Awissáwela. Starting from Awissáwela at past midnight, already considerably cramped by our six hours' journey, we arranged for sleeping the remainder of the way, if sleep we could, in the following manner: No. 1 coiled on the driver's seat; No. 2 in the well of the coach on the top of the boxes and portmanteaux; and Nos. 3 and 4 on the side-seats parallel with him; their three pairs of legs protruding over the back of the machine, and the whole party presenting a most extraordinary group to the eyes of any who in the bright moonlight might have seen them as they were dragged by each gaunt horse at a funeral pace from stage to stage. Not unfrequently we came to a dead stop on a soft piece of road, or where a length of hill proved an obstacle too much for the animal's strength to surmount:* and certainly had the road not been in very fair order, we should have had to have bivouacked by the way, instead of breakfasting at the bungalow of our excellent host and fellow-pilgrim, whose house was to be our head-quarters, and who was anxiously awaiting us a mile on the road before we

---

* It is only fair to state, that since the time of the excursion referred to, there has been an improvement in both horses and coaches in the Ratna-pura Royal Mail. But a more uncomfortable night journey can still scarcely be made, as the writer and his companion found to their cost on their Christmas journeys to and fro.

drew up in front of the low hill on the brow of which stands Ratnapura Fort.

The morning, a couple of hours before sunrise, was raw, cold, and misty, but as it advanced, and the sun rose behind the mountains, they came out clear and sharp in the rosy golden-tinted sky; and when we saw three small looking pyramidal peaks of apparently just the same level, filling the space formed by a gap in the nearest range through which the Kalu-ganga (black river) winds its way, it was hard to believe that one of them, about twelve miles off in a direct line, but distant nearly thirty by the road, was indeed Adam's Peak itself, the lofty sky-piercing cone seen in the distant mountain view from Colombo and its adjacent Cinnamon Gardens: yet so it was, and to reach the top of that Peak we purposed starting on the morrow's dawn. The peaks we saw, belonged, in fact, to two distinct mountains.* One, the Bęna Samanala, nearly faces the other, and has two summits, the highest of which is called the False Peak. These two being brought into line with the true Peak at the place where we caught sight of them, the intervening distances had the effect of reducing the apparent altitude of the two hindermost to the exact level of the foremost.

This night journey by coach is anything but agreeable;

* "Ptolemy describes, in his "System of Geography," two chains of mountains, one of them surrounding Adam's Peak, which he designates as Malœa, the names by which the hills that environ it are known in the Mahawansó."—Sir J. E. Tennent's Ceylon, vol. i. p. 535-6.

and the traveller who has time at his command would do well to proceed leisurely from stage to stage and make himself acquainted with the places of interest that lie along his route. This—diverging from the Bridge of Boats that leads to the great, but since the opening of the Railway between Colombo and Kandy, now little used highway to the mountain capital,—runs partially along the left bank of the Kęlani-ganga, and forms, as far as Awissáwęła, a portion of what used to be known as the old Kandy road. The extended views and occasional glimpses of river scenery that greet the eye from the road, now skirting and now receding from the flowing stream, here narrow and rapid and there broadened into a placid lake-like bend, are exquisitely beautiful, and go far to justify the phrase that the Island of Ceylon is the "Eden of the Eastern wave."

Distant about three miles from Grandpass (the road leading from Colombo to the Bridge of Boats) the traveller passes by Panabakkery, once an extensive Government brick and tile manufactory, and also the training station for the elephant establishment belonging to the Public Works Department, where every now and again might be witnessed the operations by which the old tamed giants of the forest brought into subjection their newly caught companions, and intelligently, as well as literally by brute force, instructed them in the duties they were thenceforth to perform in the service of their lord and master, Man.

A little beyond Panabakkery, is an ancient Buddhist temple, the Kitsirimewan Kęlaniya vihára, probably

originally built by king Kitsirimewan, after whom it is named,
and who reigned A. D. 302—330.   To visit it the traveller
has to branch off from the main up one of the minor roads.
The resident priest, in lately making some excavations on
the spot, dug up a stone, upon which was a Sinhalese inscription partly effaced, but which, as far as has hitherto been
made out, indicates that the temple had been repaired by or
under the directions of Prákkrama Báhu I., in the latter
half of the twelfth century.   About two miles further from
Colombo, on the north bank of the river, is the village
Kelani, from which place, the river derives its name.
Formerly the capital, and for ages the chief seat of the
worship of the deified king Vibhíshana, the friend of Ráma,
and traitorous brother and successor to Ráwana on the throne
of Lanka [B. C. 2387] it still possesses as a memorial of its
antiquity, a dagoba, which B. C. 280 was erected by the
tributary king Yatalátissa over one asserted by Buddhists
to have been built on the same spot by the Nága king
Mahódara, B. C. 580.   Connected with, and contiguous to
the dágoba, are a vihára and monastery, the Raja-maha
Kelaniya, so-called to distinguish it from the Kitsirimewan
Kelaniya, on the opposite side of the river.   The approach to
this vihára is up a noble flight of broad stone slabs, and
through an ancient gateway; but the steps, gateway and
dágoba, are the only remains of antiquity; the rest of the
buildings are of modern date, the older structures having
been ruthlessly destroyed during the Malabar invasions, as
well as in the wars with the Portuguese, and the intestine

struggles for power among the Siṇhalese themselves. There is also a recently built lofty tower or belfry of a curious composite order of architecture. What the place once was has been described in glowing terms in the "Sẹla-lihiṇi Sandése," written when Ceylon had attained to perhaps its highest pitch of prosperity under native rule, during the reign of Prákkrama Báhu VI.[*]

> Who with the three-score four gemm'd ornaments robed round—
> The state regalia—was, mighty monarch, crown'd;
> Who 'neath one white umbrella's canopying shade
> Had brought the whole of Lanka, one kingdom of her made:
> Who pride of haughty foes had humbled in the dust;
> Who skill'd was in each science; in king-craft wise and just;
> In use of arms proficient, and perfect master in
> The poet's art and dancing; who far had banish'd sin
> By knowledge of the Piṭakas,—the three-fold cord
> That binds the wondrous words of Buddha the adored;
> Who to the people's eyes was like collyrium laid
> When they beheld his form in majesty display'd;
> Who chief of Dambadiva's sovereigns stood confest
> And in his godlike splendour shone like Sẹkra blest.

The sites of the spots then famous are still pointed out by priests and people, who every July swarm thither by tens of thousands; a national pilgrimage to the place made holy by the presence and relics of the founder of their faith. Externally the vihára is a plain and unpretentious tiled

---

[*] A. D. 1410—1462.

building; it contains in its principal apartment a figure of
Buddha in a recumbent posture, upwards of forty feet in
length, and in the vestibule colossal figures of Hindu deities:
the ceilings are painted over with Buddhist symbols, and the
walls with scenes from Buddha's life and various mythic
existences before his latest birth and attainment of the
Buddhahood.

A place of renown ages before the advent of Buddha, its
sanctity in the eyes of his followers is thus specially accounted
for. "At the time of Gautama's appearance [B. C. 588] Kalany
would seem to have been the capital of a division of the
island called Nága Diwayina, and that its inhabitants called
Nágas [serpent-worshippers] were easily converted, and
afterwards zealously adhered to the Buddhistical doctrines,
for which they were rewarded by various relics and a second
visit of the Buddha. In his first visit to Ceylon Gautama
converted the Nágas and settled a dispute between two
of their princes, Chulódara and Mahódara, who made an
offering to him of the throne composed of gold, inlaid with
precious stones, which had been the original cause of their
quarrel; over this throne a dagoba was built, and is encased in the one now standing. At the request of Mini-
akka, uncle of the Nága king Mahódara, Gautama made
his third visit to Ceylon, and left the impression of his foot
beneath the water of the river: a deep eddy in the stream is
now pointed out as the spot; it is near the temple, and the
natives say that the circling of the current here is the Kalani-
ganga descending in homage to this sacred memorial. Having

arranged the disputes of the Nágas and confirmed their faith, the prophet departed for Samanala, Díggánakhya, and the other places which had been sanctified by the presence of former Buddhas."*

The details of a romantic legend connected with the destruction of king Tissa at this place [B. O. 200 will be found in Appendix E. It was here too, that Bhuwanéka Báhu VII., the first native king who allied himself with the Portuguese for the purpose of making war against his brother Máya Dunnai, at Sítáwaka, met with his death, A. D. 1542. The occurrence is thus recorded in the Rájawalia, " Buwanaika Bahu Rajah taking the Portuguese to his assistance, marched out with his Siphalese army to attack his brother, and on his route halted at Kelani, where there was a house built upon the river for his residence, and being in this house with the doors open and walking backward and forward, looking up and down the river, a Portuguese loaded his musket, and shot the king in the head of which he immediately died." The historian adds, "Hereupon it was said, that God only knew what was the reason of this treachery,— that having been so simple as to make a league with the Portuguese, and so foolish as to deliver his grandson to the protection of the king of the Portuguese, this judgment fell upon the said king; and on his account that calamity will be entailed on the people of Ceylon for generations to come."

* Fornes's Eleven Years in Ceylon, vol. i. p. 152. In Appendix D will be found accounts of Buddha's three visits to Ceylon.

Eleven miles from Colombo, at the village Kaḍuwela, is a resthouse, pleasantly situated on the banks of the river. A halt here for an hour will suffice for a visit to an ancient rock temple, supposed by some to be one of those founded by king Walagambâhu, after his reconquest of the kingdom from the Malabars, B. C. 88, or perhaps, as others think, of even a still greater antiquity. The principal object of interest is an inscription on the rock, which has hitherto baffled every attempt made to decipher it, the letters being cut in the oldest type of Nágari, or rather Pali, character, the key to which was first discovered by the late Mr. James Prinsep.

From Kaḍuwela, to Haṇwęlla, the road passes through several villages, the inhabitants of which are potters, who carry on a thriving business with Colombo in the manufacture of the common earthenware of the country. Between the villages lie tracts of paddy fields and topes of cocoa-nut palms. On the rising of the river during the rainy season, portions of the road between Haṇwęlla, Kaḍuwela, and the Bridge of Boats, are more or less flooded. The inconveniences arising from this state of affairs have led to the opening of a new road, which crossing higher ground shortens the route to Colombo by about two miles, and establishes an almost direct communication with the Railway terminus.

A little to the left of the road, on the summit of a bluff projecting tongue of land that overlooks the Haṇwęlla ferry, are the grass-grown remains of a small star fort, supposed to have been originally constructed by the Dutch, in the centre of which is the present resthouse, the keeper whereof, a good humoured obliging old native, is jocularly termed the Commandant. Here good accommodation and very fair quarters can generally be procured. Round the steep flanks of the fort the river flows towards its outlet at Mutwal, a few miles north of Colombo; while landwards a choked up ditch indicates what in bye-gone days formed its protection on that side. From its position, previous to the annexation of the Kandyan Kingdom, it was a point of some importance as commanding the routes both by land and water from the interior to Colombo.

During the campaign of 1803, the Kandians succeeded in taking the fort and village on the 20th August, but their progress was checked by a detachment of troops under the command of Lieutenant Mercer of the 51st regiment, who on the 22nd stormed the battery they had made in a strong position at the bridge of Putchella, near Hanwella, and drove them back with great slaughter; a success which led to the immediate recapture of the fort. In the operations which followed, the British were everywhere successful; although in defending the almost untenable fortress of Chilaw, which the Kandians attacked in immense numbers on the 27th August, the little garrison, consisting of only 25 sepoys and two young civilians, completely exhausted their ammunition,* and for twenty-four hours before they were

---

* CORDINER's Ceylon, vol. ii. pp. 226, 236.

relieved kept the enemy at bay by firing copper coins instead of grape shot.

It was at Hanwella, after the abovementioned occurrences, that Sri Wikrama Rája Sinha, the last King of Kandy, directed an attack in person, on the 6th September, against the British forces; he having resolved, after the treacherous massacre of the troops at Kandy, on Major Davie's surrender on the 26th June, to invade the British territory and attack Colombo. After an engagement which lasted for two hours, the Kandians fled, headed by the king. During his retreat he ordered the heads of his two principal chiefs to be struck off, for their want of success, besides, in his rage at his defeat, indiscriminately slaughtering a multitude of his subjects, whose bodies were either cast into ravines or thrown into the river. A richly ornamented bungalow had been erected for his reception near Hanwella, previous to the engagement, in front of which two stakes were placed, on which, in the event of the capture of the fort, the English prisoners were to have been impaled.

From the ridge that formed the ramparts of the fort the river view is one of the finest to be found in Ceylon. The stream sweeps grandly down in its course in a curve from southeast to northeast—

Where grateful falls the shade upon the fair twin shores,
Where plantains, honey mangoes, yield their luscious stores,
Where the silk cotton tree, with flowering betel twined,
And the tall areka and cocoa palms you find ;

Where asoka, pátali, and domba graceful grow ;
Where champac, kina, sal, and erehindi blow ;
Where rêranga, midell, and iron-wood appear,
And the sweet sugar-canes their slender stems uprear ; *

and an endless variety of magnificent forest trees and palms
and bamboo clumps reflect from either bank their images in
the lucent stream, while in the back-ground rise the purple
hills, their summits veiled in clouds, or sharply outlined in
the clear blue sky.

A break down in our carriage was the cause of a day's
detention here on our second journey. The village smith
was however equal to the emergency, and while the repairs
were being effected we strolled about the place, admiring
the scenery, and listening to the somewhat monotonous if
not doleful chants of the goyiyás† reaping their crops of
kurakkan in the neighbouring fields and hill slopes. A
most refreshing bath in a secluded nook in the river just
below the fort, was not the least pleasant of our enjoyments;
and was moreover an excellent preparative for the capital
dinner which "the Commandant" provided for us as the day
drew to a close.

Between Hapwella and Awissáwela the scenery is bolder
and more varied than that already passed. Noble trees
overarch the road, and plantations of jack, bread- and other
fruit trees, indicate the industry of the inhabitants as well as

---

* Sęla-lihini Sandése.　　　† Peasant women.

the fertility of the soil. In the early days of British enterprise, the cultivation of the sugar-cane and the indigo plant
was attempted on an extensive scale in the neighbourhood;
the results were not however so profitable as were anticipated,
and the luckless speculators soon abandoned the scene of their
operations. A pleasantly situated resthouse on the slope of
a hill, at the foot of which lies the village of Awissáwela,
affords the traveller an opportunity for halting and devoting
a day to the inspection of Sítáwaka, where some interesting
ruins, together with a rock temple on a mountain opposite,
well repay the trouble of a visit. In the clear atmosphere
of the season of the northeast monsoon, a fine view of the
Peak is seen from the road near the resthouse. Twenty-
one miles distant in a straight line, it rises from behind a
range of mountains, which, when the southwest winds prevail, bounds the prospect on the horizon to the southeast.
The hills on either side the road converging to this point,
there is an apparent gap on the sky-line, save when, as on
the occasion of our catching a glimpse of the Peak during
our September excursion (the only one we had except when
on the Peak itself,)

> "a thousand cubits high
> The sloping pyramid ascends the sky."

It then forms the central and most striking object in the
scenery there beheld.

ANCIENT BUILDING AT THE SAMAN DÉWALE, NEAR RATNAPURA.

RUINS OF BERAINDE HOWILA, AT SITIWAKA.

Adam's Peak.

"At last a temple built in antient days
Ere Æa was a town they came unto;
Huge was it, but not fair unto the view
Of one beholding from without, but round
The antient place they saw a spot of ground
Where laurels grew each side the temple door."

MORRIS.[*]

CHAPTER IV.

AWISSA'WELA. — SI'TA'S BATH. — SI'TA'WAKA. — THE BERE'NDI-
KO'WILA. — ROCK TEMPLE. — PUSWELLA. — KURUWITA WATER-
FALL. — EKNELIGODA DISA'WA. — KATUTIYAMBARA'WA
VIHA'RA. — WERALUPE. — SAMAN DEWA'LE.

THE village of Awissáwela, "a field not to be trusted,"—
so named from the character of its adjoining paddy lands,
which were liable to sudden inundations,—is situated at the
foot of bluff hills of black rock which rise almost perpendi-
cularly from 900 to 1000 feet in height. From the time of
the Portuguese to the annexation of the Kandian kingdom
by the British, it was a post of importance; the territories

---

[*] "The Life and Death of Jason."

of the European and Native powers there joining each other
on the principal route that led direct to the interior from
Colombo.* On the top of a low but steep hill, a picturesque
cantonment was formed by the British, of which the ramparts and surrounding ditch yet remain.† This is now the
site of the house occupied by the resident Magistrate.‡ Being
almost isolated, extensive panoramic views of the surrounding mountain ranges are here obtained. The Court-house
is at the foot of the hill near the Sítáwaka ferry. The
jurisdiction of the Court extends over a considerable area of
country; and a few lawyers, the leader of whom is a Sinhalese gentleman, ever on hospitable thoughts intent, seem

---

* "In his fifth volume, p. 352, Valentyn mentions the escape of two
Englishmen, after a captivity of twenty-two years, from the capital of
Kandy to the Dutch fortress of Sítáwaca."—Philalethes, p. 10.

† In the Kandyan Campaign of 1803, the natives obtained possession
of the place, and commenced building some rude fortifications; but they
were speedily dislodged by a military party under command of Captain
Hankey.

‡ In the year 1851 the writer, while staying a few days at this house
with the then resident Magistrate, Mr. N. Robertson, was witness to
what seemed to him and others at the time an extraordinary phenomenon.
About 5 P.M., there commenced to issue out of the wall, near the ceiling,
from a hole not more than a quarter of an inch in diameter, countless
myriads of flying ants; in a very short time they so completely filled
the house that every one was compelled to leave it. A dozen large
bonfires were lighted round the building; and attracted by the blaze,
the ants poured into these in dense clouds for the space of two hours.

to have a fair amount of practice provided them by a people whose love of litigation is an all-absorbing passion. A walk of about 250 yards in the rear of the resthouse leads to a romantic glen, down which runs and leaps a brawling rivulet. Here is what is called by the natives Sítá's bath, and an adjacent cave, her dressing room; the popular belief being, that while the disconsolate wife of the hero of the Rámayana was confined in a neighbouring grove by Ráwana, she was permitted, as often as she desired, to come here with her attendants to bathe. It is also, we were informed, called Bisówala, or the Queens' bath, the King's consorts using it as a bathing place when the Court resided at Sítáwaka.

In the olden days Awissáwela formed a portion or suburb of the adjoining city, Sítáwaka, Sítá's city on the winding stream—so named after Sítá, and the river on the banks of which it stood; the spot being rendered famous, according to Hindu traditions, because it was there that Indrajit the son of Ráwana, caused a magic figure of Sítá to be beheaded, in

---

When the flight was over, the servants collected from the rooms basket after basket full of ants' wings, as well as bodies, the former appearing to serve but the one purpose of aiding the insects to escape from the earth, since they drop from their bodies immediately after. It was not until nearly 8 o'clock, that the house was again habitable. The birds from the adjacent forests left their roosting places, and came in flocks to feed upon the ants that thus made their appearance. Their incredible numbers made it evident that the hill was an immense breeding place, of which they had held undisturbed possession for a length of time.

the hope that Ráma, who was waging a destructive war
with Ráwana for the recovery of his consort, would in the
belief of her death be induced to return to India.

"Sítávaca was the ancient residence of kings or rájas.
The kings of Sítávaca were rulers of all the low lands, and
were of such paramount importance, that the kings and
chiefs of the hill and wood country were their tributaries.*
The kings of Sítávaca boasted that they were of nobler
blood and finer descent than those of the high lands. They
asserted themselves to be genuine descendants from the
legitimate stock of a Prince of Tanassery, and a daughter
of the royal race of Madura, whilst the Kandians kings
were only bastards and of less honourable extraction. But
it is certain, that when the king of Sítávaca was conquered
by the kings of Kandy and U'va, they found it requisite to
pay so much deference to the people, in favour of the high
claims of the extinguished dynasty, as to undergo the

---

* "In more early periods, when the island was under the domination of
no less than sixteen kings, the one who reigned at Sítáwaka was acknowledged as supreme, on account of his descent from the legitimate stock
of a prince of Tanassery, in token of which he was presented every year
with a gold arm ring, on which were engraved sixteen heads; and a
meeting of the kings was also held at the capital to celebrate a great
festival which lasted sixteen days corresponding with their numbers. In
after times, however, this mark of homage on the part of the other kings
fell by degrees into disuse, and a spirit of independence began to prevail
among them, though they made no objection to the king of Sítáwaka
bearing the nominal title of emperor."—S. C. CHITTY's Ceylon Gazetteer.

ceremony of inauguration in the ancient palace of Sítávaca. This practice was still observed on the arrival of the Portuguese. Valentyn mentions, p. 229, that the palace at Sítávaca had been repaired by the Dutch, and that the gates, walls and architectural embellishments attested its original magnificence; though he adds, it was not to be compared with the ruins of the buildings left by Malabar sovereigns."*

From its proximity to the outposts of the Portuguese and Dutch, the city underwent a variety of vicissitudes; it was made a royal residence by Máya Dunnai, about 1534, and became the capital of the kingdom, under his warlike son, in 1581; but after its abandonment as the seat of government by Wimala Dharma A. D. 1592, it rapidly fell into decay; the inhabitants indeed seem to have forsaken it for the preferable situation of Awissáwela. Its ruins are now overgrown with jungle, but can still be traced, as well as the foundation and walls of a Portuguese fort, on a projecting tongue of land formed by the confluence with the Sítáwaka-gauga of a small stream, in the bed of which rubies, sapphires, and other gems have been found. This fort was once a place of some strength, and is described by Dr. Davy, who explored the place in 1817, and visited it on two subsequent occasions in 1819.†

Situated on a commanding eminence on the right bank of the river, opposite the site of the Portuguese fort, are the

---

* PHILALETHES, n. p. 146.
† DAVY'S Account of the Interior of Ceylon, pages 352—354.

very interesting ruins of the Bęrędi-kówila,* a temple built,
or commenced to be built, by the "lion-king," Rája Siŋha
I., so named by his father, the king Máya Dunnai, but
known and execrated in Buddhist annals as "the Apostate
Rajah." This king, renowned as a warrior from the time
he was eleven years old, to the day of his death, when
he had attained the age of 120 years, resolved upon the
building of this temple, to be dedicated to the worship
of Káli, as an atonement for some atrocious acts of cruelty
committed in the course of his life. The approach of
death seems to have terrified him. "Oppressed by the
recollection of his monstrous barbarities, he sent for some of
the leading Buddhist priests to attend him, and when they
had come into his presence, he interrogated them as to the
hope of pardon for his sins. The priests, whether emboldened
by the sight of the sunken form of their aged persecutor, or

---

* Bęrędi is the Siŋhalese form of the Hindu term Bránḍi. The
derivation of the term is doubtful; probably it is a corrupt form of one of
the names of the goddess Káli, the consort of Sivá; and assuming, with
FORBES, the tradition to be correct which states that this kówila or temple
was erected by Rája Siŋha on the advice of the Aandiyás, who were
worshippers of Sivá, the attributes of Bránḍi, or Káli, were such as
would peculiarly attract and suit the constitutional temperament of the
king. He would believe that by her aid he could destroy his enemies,
since in sacrificing to her "An enemy may be immolated by proxy,
substituting a buffalo or goat, and calling the victim by the name of the
enemy through the whole ceremony, thereby ' infusing by holy texts,
the soul of the enemy into the body of the victim: which will, when

impelled by the workings of conscious rectitude, replied,
'that they could hold out no hope of forgiveness in a future
state.' Sipha, in whose nature the stern will of absolutism
had been too deeply implanted to depart but with the soul
that enshrined it, raised his eyes lit up with a scarcely
human fire, and in his rage at their presumption, and as he
deemed it, disloyalty, ordered them all, with the exception
of the chief priest, to be shut up in a house and burnt alive.
After incurring in this manner the vengeance of heaven, he
sent for the priests of another temple: these, warned by
the fate of their brethren, responded in a more soothing
tone to his question, declaring indeed that so great a sinner
could not hope for absolution but by repentance, but that as
his majesty felt contrition for his enormities, they would
endeavour, by the force of their prayers, to procure a sojourn
for him in some intermediate region between heaven and
earth, instead of an abode where he would be tormented by

---

immolated, deprive the foe of life also.'"—Moon's Hindu Pantheon,
p. 83. Edit. 1864.

Kówila is the term applied in Ceylon to a temple dedicated to an
inferior Hindu god or goddess, in contradistinction to Déwála, which is
applied to a temple dedicated to a superior deity. The two words
however are similarly derived, and have the same signification. The one
is Tamil, and the other Sanskrit; the Sinhalese apply the Tamil term to
Hindu temples built by Tamils, and use the Sanskrit word for the
temples to Hindu deities built by themselves. The officiating priest of a
Déwála is generally called a Kapurála, while that of a Kówila is called
a Pattinehami.

devils. This answer seemed to compose the inquietude of
the dying king, and he not only saved their lives but loaded
them with presents, which they refused to receive. He
requested them also not to take to heart the massacre of
their brethren, which he had ordered in a paroxysm of rage.
On receiving an assurance of forgiveness, he soon after gave
up the ghost." * Some of the native traditions however aver,
that the priests he sent for on the second occasion were the
Aandiyás, to whom, for the consolatory answer he received
from them, he gave the custody of Adam's Peak; that he
recovered from his sickness, and under their advice set about
the building of the Berendi-kówila, which was left incom-
plete at the time of his death.

Whichever of the preceding statements as to the origin
of the Berendi-kówila is correct, is perhaps a matter not now
possible to determine, but the ruins themselves, although of
no great antiquity, are unquestionably amongst the most
interesting in Ceylon, and are moreover of easy access to
the traveller. Dr. Davy and Captain Forbes both notice
them, but at the times of their visits the overgrowing jungle
had more or less concealed them from view. In this respect
we were more fortunate, for the owners of the property, the
priests of the Daladá Máligáwa, or Palace of the Tooth† at

* PRIDHAM's Historical, Political and Statistical Account of Ceylon
and its Dependencies, vol. i. p. 96.

† For an account of this temple-palace, and its worshipped relic, see
Appendix F.

Kandy, had leased the grounds for a term of 99 years to the incumbent of a Buddhist vihára at Cotanchina, near Colombo; and the lessee was making the most of his bargain. The jungle was nearly all cleared, and the crops of grain we saw growing seemed to indicate considerable fertility of soil. Our visit was greatly facilitated by the courtesy of Mr. J. W. Gibson, the Commissioner of Requests and Police Magistrate of the District, who obligingly accompanied us, although the drenching showers which fell were the cause of no small discomfort at the time. We crossed the Sítúwaka-gaṇga at the ferry, also used as a ford when the water is low, the track of which is paved with broad flag stones, said to have been brought from the kówila; and after proceeding a short distance along the Yaṭiyantoṭa road, turned to the right, the ground gradually rising, until we came to a ravine which forms a kind of base to the triangular knoll, on the summit of which the ruins are seen. Across this ravine a singular bridge permits access to the precincts of the kówila. It consists of five huge stones, admirably dressed on their upper surface, each fifteen feet long, varying in width from two feet to three feet and a half, and in thickness from twelve to eighteen inches. One of these is broken through the middle, and a native legend by way of accounting for the fracture, states, that owing to a woman crossing it when affected with a natural infirmity, the goddess to whom the place was dedicated became so incensed, that she caused the stone to split in two, and thereby precipitated the offender to the bottom of the ravine.

The surface of the hill, or slope of ground, at some distance beyond the bridge, is scarped and levelled into a series of terraces or platforms. The first and lowest is a parallelogram about 280 feet in breadth; the second about 180; on and near the northern end of this is the third, a square of 80 feet, and on this again, perhaps twenty feet from its northern side, the fourth, a square of 20 feet. The sides of each face the cardinal points, those of the north overlooking what may be called the apex of the triangle, round which the river makes a sharp curve. Retaining walls of massive carved and moulded granite stones surround the first, third and fourth platforms; and from the angles of the walls of the fourth, which is wholly paved with broad flags, rise the handsome clustered pillars which formed the temple. A narrow groove or channel is cut through one of the carved blocks at the southwest angle, the use of which is not very manifest, unless it was to carry off the blood of animals slaughtered in sacrifice to the goddess.* Flights of steps lead to the platform from the centre of each side, and corresponding steps are placed in each of the walls of the terraces below. Traces of such steps are also seen down the steep face of the hill to the brink of the river, from which, in its windings above and below, the Bęręṇḍi-kówila must

---

* All Hindu altars, I am informed, have a passage to let out the water which the Brahmans pour upon them for the purpose of purifying them from the defilement which they are supposed to contract when the gods feast upon the offerings which are there placed.

have presented a noble appearance. Captain Forbes is of opinion, that the temple was about 30 feet in height from the topmost platform; and that it consisted of pillars supporting a cornice, the plan appearing to be as if eight ornamented pilasters projected two on each side from a plain square pillar. Excepting as to the height, which, including the basement wall, now scarcely exceeds fifteen feet, the description he gives of the plan of the temple is correct. The carvings in the stones are deep, and the mouldings project out boldly. These are all covered with delicate floral tracery, which must have required great manipulative skill on the part of those who had to execute it. The walls of the two terraces below harmonise with that on which the temple stands; the whole having evidently been designed by an architect of no mean ability. It is however questionable whether it was ever finally completed. Between the two lower walled terraces an unwalled one intervenes, and from the number of blocks of stone lying about, some in a rough, and others in a half finished state, it seems probable that the work was stopped when near its completion, owing to the struggles with the Portuguese and the domestic wars in which the king was engaged previous to his death,* and the determination of his successor

---

* The local tradition is, that the works were stopped at the time when Kunappu Bandara raised an army, and advanced against the king with a view to his overthrow. This happened while Rája Sinha was engaged in besieging the Portuguese in Colombo, he having determined upon

to remove the seat of Government to Kandy. The new
king, moreover, being a Buddhist, would not be disposed to
promote the interests of an opposing and persecuting faith.
The conjecture that the temple was destroyed by the Portuguese, is not borne out by the general appearance of the
place; but from the time of its abandonment up to within a
very recent period, the natives have made free with its
stones for buildings of their own.*

Higher up the river, on the opposite side, is the Mániyaŋ-
gama vihára, a rock temple, the route to which is through a

---

their expulsion from Ceylon. Kunappu Bandara was one of the royal
family who escaped destruction at the hands of Rája Siŋha, when he
resolved upon removing every obstacle to his claims to sole sovereignty
throughout the island. He had made his way to Colombo, and adopted
the Christian religion, and was subsequently baptized at Goa under the
title of Don John.   To aid the Portuguese, by whose means, if successful,
he hoped to gain the Kandian throne, he now made his way from Jaffna to
Kandy, and increasing his adherents at every step, ere long threatened
Sitáwaka itself.   Raja Siŋha was thus forced to raise the seige of
Colombo in order to relieve his capital.   Don John, retiring to the south
and east, was pursued by the king, when the Portuguese, watching their
opportunity, captured Awissáwela. A desultory warfare followed, which
lasted for some years.   At length, in a final battle at Kadugannawa, Don
John routed the forces of Rája Siŋha, and that monarch, wounded by a
thorn in the foot, could no longer take the field.   This wound, combined
with his chagrin at being defeated, caused his death in a few days; but,
according to the Rájn-walia, his end was hastened by the treachery of
some of his attendants.

* For an account of the ruins at Sítáwaka, in the times of the Dutch,
see Appendix II.

number of paddy fields intersected by nullahs or small ravines, to cross which we had, at the time of our visit, either to wade knee and thigh deep in water or be carried over by natives. At one place, through which a pretty broad stream was flowing, my weight proved almost too much for the two men who were my bearers for the occasion, and we were nearly toppling into the water together. In about half an hour we began to ascend the base of a mountain, and after a considerable rise, and making our way over a lengthy flight of steep steps formed of rough blocks of stone, we came to an enclosure within which was the temple. This was made out of the recess below an immense overhanging boulder, which had probably been artificially hollowed in parts.* A long wall built up to the rocky roof, and divided so as to form one main hall, wherein was a recumbent figure of Buddha thirty or more feet in length, with several smaller apartments for the use of the priests; and wing walls at each end, forming a large open verandah; was the rude architectural device for constructing a temple here. The situation was nevertheless very picturesque; above and around, the rocky mountain; streams and small waterfalls running and murmuring and leaping in mimic cascades as they pursued their course over and among the rocks: immediately in front a broad level

---

* King Walagambáhu, after his recovery of the throne, "caused the houses of stones, or caves of the rock in which he had taken refuge in the wilderness, to be made more commodious."—Upham's Rájawalia, p. 224.

platform, on which was erected a bana-maduwa,* where
several old men and women and young children were as·
sembled to listen to the priest reading bana; beyond this a
stretch of cultivated paddy fields, bordered by forest trees,
or topes of cocoa-palms, and mountain ranges rising in the
distance on the other side of the valley through which the
Sítáwaka-gaŋga wound its way. It was a scene to which
might be well applied the following lines by the author of
"Pleasures of Memory:"

> "Above, below, aërial murmurs swell,
>   From hanging wood, brown heath and bushy dell!
> A thousand nameless rills, that shun the light
>   Stealing soft music on the ear of night."

In addition to the colossal figure of Buddha, there were
several smaller ones, many of bronze, not an inch in height.
The principal priest, Dhammadassi Maha Terunwahansé, paid
us every attention; honouring us in the presence of the
people by spreading white cloths on the chairs he brought
out for us to rest on.† We learnt from him that the temple
was one of those founded by king Walagambáhu; that one
of its chief benefactors had been king Kírti Srí, the same

---

* A pagoda-like building, generally temporary, in which the priests
read or preach Bana, i. e. the word of Buddha.

† White is the royal colour of Ceylon; and the reception of strangers
with the spreading of white cloths is one of the highest compliments a
Siŋhalese can offer.

who restored the custody of the Srí-páda to the Buddhists, and who had given this temple the handsome pair of
elephant's tusks, each six feet in length, which were displayed
in front of the recumbent figure of Buddha. In an outer
hollow he pointed out to us a small shrine dedicated to
Mahasen, the divinity to whose temple at Kataragama,
Hindus from all parts of the East flock with fanatic enthusiasm during the annual pilgrimage in the months of June,
July, and August; at which time Moors and Veddahs also
take a part in the processions held in his honor. We could
not however make out whether there was any particular
connection between this place and the temple at Kataragama.

The internal decorations of this temple, the appearance of
the priests, and the colossal image, so closely correspond
with the description given by Captain T. A. Anderson,
formerly of the 19th Regiment, in his now rare poem "The
Wanderer in Ceylon," that I do not hesitate to quote him.

> "The vaulted roof is studded o'er
> With various hieroglyphic lore:
> Touch'd by the artists' glowing hand
> Flow'rs of all colours here expand!
> There some wild legend lives portray'd,
> Here, all the zodiac stands display'd;
> While every vacant space between
> Some uncouth form or shape is seen.
> With yellow robes and shaven head
> The priests around that altar tread,
> Near Buddha's giant figure stand
> And incense shed with lavish hand,

> Then bending at his hallow'd feet
> Their wishes, wants, and vows repeat.
> Tho' painted robes the figure screen,
> And but the countenance is seen,
> You may a due proportion trace
> Throughout his giant form and face;
> No lion look, no eagle eye,
> But that serene philanthropy
> Which plainly indicates a breast
> With every milder virtue blest!"·

Returning to Awissáwela, it may be noted that the road
so named terminates at the Sítáwaka ferry, which forms the
link between it and the Yaṭiyantoṭa road from the north.
A short distance below the resthouse is the junction with
the Ratnapura road, which trends away in a south-easterly
direction. On this road a traction engine* has just been
placed, to run between Badulla, Haputale, Ratnapura, and
Colombo. If successful in its operations, about which
there can scarcely exist a doubt, it will be speedily followed

---

* The "ENTERPRIZE," manufactured by Mr. R. W. Thomson, C. E., of
Edinburgh; imported by Mr. John Brown, for the Ouvah Coffee Company:
landed in Colombo, on the 22nd January, in charge of the engineer
Mr. James Westland. This engine is of 6 horse power, but can be
worked up to 12, and with a load of 12 tons, in a train of four waggons,
will travel on level ground 8 miles an hour, and on the inclines in the
interior at from 2½ to 4 miles an hour, according to the nature of the
gradients. The first trial trip in Ceylon was made at Colombo on the
17th February, 1870.

by others elsewhere, and the traffic on the main lines of
communication throughout the island will be as completely
revolutionized in the course of a few years, as has already
been the case with that between Kandy and Colombo, by
means of the Railway.

The first stage for halting at, after leaving Awisséwela,
is Puswella.* The road undulates along the base of forest-
clad hills, or through tracts of paddy lands, and presents
nothing remarkable, beyond the paintings on the walls of
a way-side Ambalama,† which represent, among other things,
Buddha striding from the top of Adam's Peak, after in-
denting there the print of his left foot, to Siam, where he in
like manner left the impression of his right foot ‡ The resthouse at- Puswella is perched on the summit of knoll, a
little distance off the road, and affords a fair amount of
accommodation. A secluded pool, a stone's throw behind
the resthouse, at the foot of a small and shady glen into
which a rocky stream pours its crystal waters, is a capital
bathing place, a desideratum not always obtainable at a
roadside resthouse in Ceylon.

---

* ' Pus,' a kind of jungle creeper; ' wella,' a tract of sand.

† A native resthouse.

‡ " The Siamese," says Baldæus, " exhibit a footstep impressed upon
a stone on a mountain, which is an ell and a half long and three-fourths
broad. The sides of it are covered with silver; and a magnificent temple
is erected in the neighbourhood, round which many of the priests of the
country, and other people dwell."

P

Beyond Puswella, and near the 48th mile post from Colombo, is the river Kuru-gaṇga, a principal tributary to the Kalu-gaṇga. By diverging to the left of the main road at the village Higgaha-héna,* about half a mile before reaching the bridge, a walk for a mile and a half through alternating paddy fields and cocoanut plantations will bring one opposite the Kuruwita waterfalls, which are well worthy of inspection. At the time of our visit the waters were high, and the Kuru-gaṇga was rushing along its bed with a dangerous velocity. From a gap in the rocky ridge that faced us, and which formed an almost mountainous embankment to the river, a broad volume of water thundered down and leapt in broken masses of ever-changing form from rock to rock, until, after a fall of a hundred and fifty feet

> " the torrent with the many hues of heaven "

that   .

> " flung its lines of foaming light along,"

surged against and mingled with the stream that hurried past to swell the waters of the Kalu-gaṇga.

Besides the waterfall there are in this and an adjacent range, two remarkable caverns, or grottoes, or subterranean passages, six or seven miles apart from each other, the

---

* Héna, or chena, a high jungle ground, cultivated at intervals, upon which originally grew the Hik, or Hulaṇhik trees, *Chickrassia tabularis*, AD. Juss.

KURUWITTE FALLS.

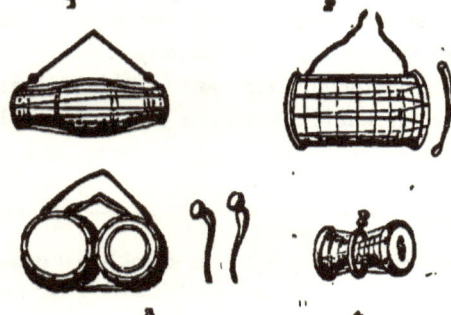

MUSICAL INSTRUMENTS:—1. THE BERRIGODEA. 2. THE DOOLAH. 3. THE TAM-A-TAM. 4. THE UDIKKA.

terminations of which have not been explored. The Ratómahatmayá* of the district told us he had examined one for a distance of two hundred fathoms, and might have gone further but for the annoyance of bats; and that the natives believed the other could be traced for at least two miles; but they had a dread of both, fearing serpents, &c. Possibly the author of Sindbad the Sailor had heard something of these, and fancying the streams which ran by them to have gone through instead, worked them up in his hero's experiences of Ceylon; for he speaks of rivers flowing through mountains; and declares that by one such he was floated on a raft into the interior of the Island.

There is a route through the jungle from this place to the pilgrims' path to the Peak, much frequented by those who make the pilgrimage from the immediate neighbourhood; but the usual route being from Ratnapura, we turned back to the main road, and shortly after crossing the bridge, saw on our left, the Kaṭutiyambaráwa vihára. We found it to be of modern date, having been built by Eknęligoḍa Diśáwa, the daring chief who seized the person of the last king of Kandy, and delivered him, a fettered captive, into the hands of the British;† an act which greatly facilitated,

---

* 'Ratómahatmaya,' the chief native revenue officer of a Kandian District. The corresponding officer in the Maritime Provinces has the rank of Mudaliyar.

† "On the 14th February 1815, the British forces entered the Kandian capital unopposed. The king having awoke too late from his

if it was not the actual immediate cause of the annexation
of the Kandian kingdom, and for which, as also for other
eminent services, he received a gold medal and chain from
the then Governor, General Sir Robert Brownrigg, together
with the more substantial though not more prized rewards

delusive dream of security, had fled on their approach into Dumbera,
accompanied by only a few Tamil adherents; leaving the females of his
family, with a considerable treasure to the mercy of the victor. Driven
by heavy rain from a mountain where he concealed himself during the
day, he descended and took shelter in a solitary house in the neighbourhood of Medamahanuwara, not aware that there was a force at hand
lying in wait for him. The retreat was soon discovered by some of
Ehelépola's adherents, under the orders of Ekneligoda, who surrounded the house in which he had hid himself with two of his wives.
The door was strongly barricaded, but they battered down the wall of
the apartment in which the tyrant was concealed; when he was exposed
by the glare of torchlights to the derision of his enemies. Their abrupt
entry,—the first time for fifteen years since he became king that he had
been approached without servile humility,—for a moment seemed to
confound him; but as the party pressed forward, he dared them to touch
him. The chief urged on his followers, and the orders to seize the king
were soon obeyed. Ekneligoda had ventured too far to indulge any
hopes of safety, unless the downfall of the tyrant could be accomplished.
If the king should regain authority, he felt certain that he would have
been added to the list of forty-seven headmen, many of them friends of
his own, who in the previous year had been brought from Saffragam,
and impaled by the tyrant's order. Wikrama Sinha, was soon after
conveyed to Vellore, in the Madras Presidency, where he died of dropsy
in 1832."—HISTORY OF CEYLON, published by the Sinhalese Tract
Society.

of grants of lands, and the high native rank of Disáwa.* There is an inscription on a stone, set upon a pillar, recording the piety of the builder, who is also buried here. The image of Buddha is sedent, and some of his relics are here preserved in a karandua or case carefully covered over with cloths, in order to preserve them from the profanation of the gaze of vulgar or heretical curiosity. The grounds about the vihára are kept in very neat order, bordered with laurels and flowers, and the pansala or priests' residence is of two stories, the upper one having a balcony in its front, from which was hung a representation on white cloth of the Srí-páda, with the hundred and eight signs, marked in vermilion, that indicate the possessor of them to be a Buddha. These correspond with the embossments and ornaments on the cover of the sacred footstep kept at Palúbaddala. The signs consist of devices formed from the appearance of the lotus flower in its various stages of development, the lotus being, throughout the East, the emblem of beauty and perfection.

The expression "lotus feet" or "lotus-footed," is one

---

* Governor of a Kandian Province, under the native kings. This title is now either extinct, or in abeyance; its last holder, Eheliyagoda Dasanáyaka Ranasiyha Mudiyanse, Disáwa of Three Kórules and Lower Bulatgama, having died in September 1869. The grandfather of the highly intelligent and influential Kandian Chief, William Alexander Abraham Ekneligoda, or Ekneligoda of that ilk, the present Ratemahatmayá of the Kuruwita Kórale, was the Disáwa referred to in the text.

commonly used when speaking of Buddha's person; and the idea that

"flowers upsprang where'er his feet were placed" *

is repeated again and again in the legends and poetry of the Sinhalese. To realise this idea, and indicate the appearance of flowers as actually marked upon his feet, was but to obey the tendencies of the Oriental mind. The same or a cognate idea is conveyed in purer form in the well-known language of the inspired Hebrew prophet, "How beautiful upon the mountains are the feet of him that bringeth good tidings, that publisheth peace, that bringeth good tidings of good, that publisheth salvation."† The doctrines of Buddha, when first promulgated, were good tidings in comparison with those of the Brahmans; and whosoever received them, secured to him or herself, according to his teachings, peace and salvation —the perfect bliss and absolute never-ending repose of Nirwana. Perhaps this was referred to by the original symboliser in the full-developed lotus flower in the centre of the ball of the foot. At any rate this mode of symbolisation is more poetical than that adopted by Burmese

---

* This is an idea firmly impressed upon the minds of Buddhists, who have a singular method of perpetuating the belief, in the manufacture of a peculiar kind of sandal, from the upright peg of which, gripped between the great and second toe, each time a step is taken, a spring causes a metal-shaped lotus to start up.

† Isaiah lii. 7.

Buddhists; who, while they demand the same number of a
hundred and eight marks, depict them in a different form,
each form, no doubt, symbolising perfection: thus, the toes
are each marked underneath with a chank with right handed
whorls,* and the ball of the foot has circles of alternating
hanzas,† and other animals and figures; which signs the
orthodox Buddhists of Burmah now-a-days believe were
actually marked upon the feet of the founder of their religion, when he lived and moved and had his being upon earth.

The senior priest of this vihára, Delgamuwe Terunwahansé, is a friendly hospitable old gentleman, well pleased
with the visits of Europeans, of whom he never fails to
inquire concerning Major Skinner. He evidently entertains
an enthusiastic regard for the great Road-maker and ex-
Director of Public Works in Ceylon.

The village through which the main road passes at this
place is called Tembiliyana, or Eknęligoḍa, the ancestral
domain of the Eknęligoḍa family. From thence to within

---

* In the ordinary *Turbinella rapa*, the whorls run from left to right;
but those called by the natives *Wallampory*, have the whorls reversed,
running from right to left. These were regarded with such reverence
that formerly they sold for their weight in gold. Even now specimens
can scarcely be procured for less than four or five pounds sterling.

† The sacred hanza, or Brahmance goose, is the national emblem em-
blazoned on the standard of Burmah; it has been from time immemorial
an object of veneration there, as well as throughout all parts of India,
including Ceylon.

a few miles of Ratnapura, the character of the country is much the same as that already passed through from Awissá-wela. The hills perhaps assume more of a mountain character; their slopes may be are bolder, their sides more rocky, their altitudes greater; and the forest timber with which they are clad or crowned is possibly of a heavier growth.

The tract of paddy lands, for about two miles before reaching Ratnapura, is called by the natives 'Weralupe,' the cat's-eye district. It is also famous for rubies and sapphires. This circumstance, and the richness of the beds of the immediately adjoining streams in similar precious products, gave to the city its name,—'Ratnapura,' the city of gems. A large amount of money, we were informed, had recently been made by some speculating Moormen from Kalutara, in extensive gemming operations here, the principal of whom, owing to the excitement caused by a too sudden acquisition of wealth, had unfortunately lost his reason. Gold is also found in the beds of these streams, but not in sufficient quantities to pay Europeans for the expense—irrespective of the risk to health—of washing it from the soil; and washing or digging for gold is not so attractive to the native mind as the search for gems.

A minor road branches off from the main one to the right near to an iron bridge about a mile from Ratnapura. This leads to the Maha Saman Déwálé, distant about two miles from the city, and close to the right bank of the Kalu-ganga. To this place a pilgrimage is made by large bodies of natives every July, when the festival of the Perahera, lasting

fifteen days,* with processions of elephants, &c. is held.
At this time a temporary town is erected for the accommodation of the pilgrims. This consists principally of two
streets, 260 yards long by 45 feet broad, on either side
of which is a continuous row of huts made of bambus and
jungle sticks roofed over with cadjans, or the plaited leaves
of the cocoanut palm. These roads lead straight up to
the eastern side of a quadrangular enclosure (80 ft. E. &
W., by 200 ft. N. & S.), which forms the outer courtyard
to the temple. An inner quadrangle (150 ft. by 200 ft.) is
approached from this by a flight of 25 stone steps.† Both
quadrangles are enclosed by dwarf walls five feet high, above
which are rows of palings alternating with pillars, the whole
protected by a tiled roof to shoot off the rain. The gateway to the first consists of two brick pillars, on the top of
each of which a bo-tree is growing. On the top of the steps
leading to the second is a narrow verandah, with four carved
wooden pillars, two on each side the doorway. This is of
stone, with rudely carved lintel and jambs. The inner

---

* For an account of the great Perahçra festival at Kandy, to which
that at Ratnapura is very similar, see Appendix I.

† Captain PRIDHAM, in his work on Ceylon, describes these steps as well
as those which lead up to the temple from the river, as made of marble.
This is a mistake. The steps, which are very roughly dressed, are of the
ordinary stone of the neighbourhood, gneiss or hornblende, with here
and there a carved block apparently brought from some overthrown
building, probably from the Portuguese church which once stood here.

quadrangle seems originally to have been a low mound,
the sides of which were artificially raised, so as to form the
foundation platform for a fortification.   There is reason to
believe that this was the site of a Déwálé from very ancient
times,* and that upon the capture of the place by the Portuguese, its strategical importance led them to convert it into a
stronghold for themselves.†   In the centre of the quadrangle

---

* "The earliest mention I have seen made of the Saffragam temple of
Saman (which is either this or the one on the Peak) is, that in the reign
of Dappoola A. D. 795, a statue of Rámachandra, (an incarnation of
Vishnú) formed of red sandal wood, was sent from Dondra to be placed
in the temple of Saman at Saffragam."—Forbes's Eleven Years in Ceylon,
vol. i. p. 185.   The inclemency of the weather for nine out of the
twelve months of the year being such as to prevent any one living on the
Peak, and the shrine there, dedicated to Saman, being open on all sides,
and only about three feet high, the probability is that the statue referred
to, was sent to the temple at Sabaragamuwa, where it would be better
cared for and preserved.   During the season of the pilgrimage to
the Peak, it might have been taken thither from Sabaragamuwa, and
returned when the season ended.

† Captain Ribeyro, in the chapter of his work which gives an account
of the regular troops and militia which the Portuguese maintained in the
Island of Ceylon, says, that besides the camp at Manicavary, where, in
times of peace, at least 4000 men were always stationed, "there was a
second camp in the Saffragam country, near the kingdom of U'wa; it
comprised four companies of Portuguese infantry, amounting to 150
men, and from 4000 to 5000 lascorins; these were under the command
of the Disáwa of the Province, who had with him an adjutant and a
chaplain.   In these two camps consisted the chief strength of the
country, especially in time of peace."

they built their Church, a portion of which is probably included in the existing Déwálé. Opposite the doorway, in the centre of the quadrangle, is a colonnade fifty-four feet in length, and twenty in breadth. This consists of two outer dwarf walls, five feet high, with openings near the west end, and five pillars rising at irregular distances five feet above the walls; inside these are corresponding rows of five brick or cabook pillars, with a passage ten feet wide between. On each side of the colonnade, at the west end, between the last two pillars and the walls, is a kind of raised dais, intended probably for the accommodation of priests or musicians. At the end of the colonnade, a doorway gives access to a hall, about sixty feet long, dimly lighted by two small windows, and having in its side walls two central doors facing each other. A row of seven wooden pillars, three feet distant from each wall, leaves an avenue in the midst of the hall of about fourteen feet width, which leads to five semicircular steps at the foot of the door of the sanctum, a two-storied building, occupying an area of 20 by 30 feet, the top of which, viewed from the outside, has a very pagoda-like appearance. Plaster statues of Hindu deities flank this door, and on either side of the second step is placed one of a magnificent pair of elephant's tusks, each seven feet in length. We could not gain admittance to this part of the building; but Captain Forbes states, that it contains what is called by courtesy, the golden bow and arrow of the god. We heard that it also contained a silver-stemmed umbrella, which in former times used to be spread above the shrine

of Saman, on the summit of Samanala, indicating his divine
supremacy in the District. Inside the hall were several
large long-handled fans, and other articles used in processions,
besides six antique looking gingalls, some of which we found
to be of but very rough and modern manufacture. They
were eighteen inches long, with an inch thickness of metal,
and a bore an inch in diameter. Each was firmly fixed
upon a three-legged carriage raised about eighteen inches
from the ground.

In the open quadrangle, north of the sanctum, is a well,
enclosed by four old massive walls (15 ft. by 24 ft.), each
wall having a narrow arched doorway in its centre. This
is the most archæological feature of the place; the walls are
undoubtedly those originally built by the Portuguese, and
the arched doorways differ from anything of the kind to be
seen elsewhere. At the east end of the quadrangle, facing
the two openings in the colonnade, are two Buddhist temples,
each on a raised platform 16 ft. by 24, with four pillars on
each side, forming narrow verandahs round a central room,
in which is an image of Buddha, and a karandua containing
some of his relics. These relics hold an important position
in the processions at the Perahera in the month of July.
Against the walls of the quadrangle are several lean-to
buildings, either occupied by the temple attendants, or
used as stores.

Cordiner, in his description of this Déwálé, says, at the
time of the Kandian campaign in 1803, "the apartments
of the Pagoda"—(by which he evidently meant the whole of

the buildings in this quadrangle)—"afforded excellent shelter for the troops; who found in several chests, a greater quantity of silver and copper coins than they were capable of carrying away. The Malays, probably from motives of superstition, refused to receive any share of them: and almost all the indigent coolies [camp followers] disdained the sacrilege of either entering the Pagoda, or touching the coin. The idols had been removed, but a great many beautiful elephants' tusks, and other curious articles remained, which could not be brought away." *

Scattered about the ground are sundry fragments of slender gothic pillars, which clearly formed a part of the church that once stood here; and near to one of the Buddhist temples stands what looks most suspiciously like a baptismal font. It consists of a stone pillar rising two feet three inches from the ground, square at the base for twelve inches, and octagonal above. This supports a font eighteen inches square on the upper surface; the outer edges of which are moulded, and carved with delicate tracery; and the sides rounded from the top to the base. The inside is hollowed into a circular basin fifteen inches in diameter, and four in depth.

Let into a deep niche in the basement of the raised quadrangle, a little to the north of the flight of steps leading from the outer courtyard, is a mural stone of some

---

* Description of Ceylon, vol. ii. p. 252.

historic value, and of singular interest from the strange and
unexpected position in which it is found.   On it, sculptured
in bold relief, are two figures, about half the size of life.
They represent the closing event of a mortal combat between
a Portuguese, armed cap-à-pie, and a Siŋhalese warrior.
Conquered in the encounter, the latter has been stricken
down; his sword and shield are cast despairingly aside; and
his antagonist, trampling under foot his prostrate form, is
now with one final blow about to deprive him of his life.
The inscription below, partly in Roman, and partly in
Siŋhalese characters, is so much effaced as to be only very
partially readable; some portions of the figures are also
damaged, seemingly from the action of the weather upon
the stone.   The whole is, however, most spiritedly executed,
and enough of the inscription remains to shew that the name
of the Portuguese soldier was Gomez.   The Siŋhalese say,
the prostrate warrior was their champion, one Kuruwiṭa
Bandára, a dreaded enemy of the Portuguese, whose soldiers
he had repeatedly cut off, and that some fifty had fallen by
his hand ere he himself was slain.   The sculpture was no
doubt executed in Europe by royal or vice-regal command,
and sent hither to do honor to the soldier whose valorous
deed it commemorated.

   At the north and south sides of the outer courtyard are
raised platforms, with high canopies, which are profusely
decorated during the pilgrim season.   The backgrounds
are then filled with paintings of the gods, and in front of
these, gazed at by admiring multitudes, the dancing girls

in the service of the temple, perform their parts in the annual festival in honor of Saman. On such an occasion one can realize the description given by Srí Ráhula of similar scenes in honor of Vibhíshana at the temple at Kẹlani, four centuries and a half ago.

> Yet linger for awhile and note the dancing fair
> Whose charming, handsome ears, bright shining gold plates bear;
> Whose eyes, long, lustrous, dark, wash'd with collyrium, seem
> With deeper, darker lustre, beneath their lids to gleam;
> Whose tresses, twined with flowers their beauty to enhance,
> And fragrant odours flinging, beholders' hearts entrance.
> Upon their dancing stages, in gala garb array'd,
> Each vestment strew'd with jewels, gems dazzlingly display'd,
> At every agile motion and lissom action light
> They scintillate in splendour, seem lambent lamp-flames bright:
> Aloft, alow, their arms, tossing, waving in the dance
> And around them casting many a swift-sped sidelong glance,
> Their narubaras' * end-falls they from their broad hips fling,
> The full-folds op'ning, closing, at each elastic spring,
> While bells from zones gem-spangled their slender waists girt round
> In unison chime sweetly, as o'er the scarce touch'd ground
> They clink their golden anklets and flash their lotus feet
> And step in time responsive to music's measured beat.†

A flight of fifty steps leads up from the river to a path in the outer temple grounds; and on the sides of the quadrangles,

---

* The *narubara* is a graceful kind of waist cloth, the wide end of which, about a foot in length, falls from the girdle over the hips in a number of thickly gathered folds or plaits.

† Sẹla-lihini Sandése.

Bó, Temple,* and other trees spread their umbrageous
branches over the enclosing walls. Kapurálas and temple
officers and tenants perform a daily service within the walls,
with the harshest of pipings and the noisiest beatings of tam-
a-tams. A dozen or more elephants are attached to the place,
their chief duty being to take a leading part in the annual
processions. The temporalities are large, and the revenue
is collected, and all the affairs of the temple regulated by
the Kandian Chief Iddamalgoda Abayakón Atapattu Mudiyanse, himself a Buddhist, but the Basnáyaka Nilamé, or
lay incumbent of the great Hindu Déwálé, which, with a
kind of mutual toleration, Buddhists and Hindus alike agree
to consider one of their most notable places of holy resort.†

---

* The *Ficus religiosa*, and the *Michelia Champaca.*

† Saman is generally believed to be an incarnation of Vishnû, (see
ante, p. 13). With reference to this deity I am indebted for the following
note, to the learned Tamil Advocate, Mr. C. Baïro, "During the domination of the Tamils, the elastic faith of the Siphalese had to be extended
so as to include a large number of the gods of the rulers. And every
vihára had to receive a number of images of these uncouth gods. But
they were not received indiscriminately. And if I do not greatly err,
Vishnû was the only god who was received without reluctance. His
shrine is the Déwálé we meet with everywhere attached to Buddhist
temples." The adoration of Vishnû under the forms of Rama and
Lakshamana, or Saman, was the old traditionary religion of the Siphalese
before the Vijáyan invasion. Buddhists moreover believe that this god
is the tutelary divinity of the island; that he is a candidate for Buddhahood, and will, in some future kalpa, be manifested as a Buddha; hence
the readiness with which they allowed his worship at the time referred to.
But at the same time many Hindus maintain that Buddha himself was only
an avatár or incarnation of Vishnû.

Adam's Peak.

~~~~~~~~~~

"Amidst the grove that crowns yon tufted hill
Which, were it not for many a mountain nigh
Rising in lofty ranks, and loftier still,
Might well itself be deemed of dignity,
The convent's white walls glisten fair on high:
Here dwells the caloyer, nor rude is he
Nor niggard of his cheer; the passer by
Is welcome still; nor heedless will he flee
From hence, if he delight kind Nature's sheen to see."

BYRON.

CHAPTER V.

RATNAPURA. — MOUNT KARANGODA. — GODIGAMUWA. — GILI'-MALE'. — ELLAPITA TOTUPOLA. — GURULUWAN, KALU, AND HATELA GANGAS. — BANDA'RA MAHATMAYA'. — TUNTOTA FERRY. — MASKELIYA GANGA. — BRIDGE AND FORD. — ALI-HA'NTENNE. — "ESTUARY OF REEDS." — BATAPOLA. — ROCK-CAVE. — MAPANAN-ELLA WATERFALL. — PALA'BADDALA.

THE city of Ratnapura, like the "lang toun o' Kirkaldy," consists principally of clustering rows of houses on either side of the main road. On the left of the road, approaching from Awissáwela, picturesquely situated in an arborescent dell, is the residence of the Assistant Government Agent of

R

the District, near to which is the small episcopal place of
worship, called by courtesy, the church.   On the right of the
road is the gaol; beyond which, receding towards the bank
of the river, are the resthouse and the Government Hospital.
These are both newly erected, commodious buildings; and
at the back of the former, fringing the high river-bank, is a
luxuriant grove of nutmeg trees.   Within the walls of the
small fort, surmounting a rocky hillock, about 114 feet above
the level of the sea, are the Government Kachchéri, in which
a meteorological observatory has lately been established, the
District Court, and other official buildings.   This fort was
formerly a military station; but the troops have been withdrawn; and the Police, who have a station and barracks
further on, now guard the Kachchéri, and discharge the
duties formerly entrusted to soldiers.   The situation of the
city is considered healthy; there is an excellent bazaar; and
a Roman Catholic chapel in a very central position.   In the
suburbs there are many pleasantly detached bungalows, the
residences of the Judge, the lawyers, and other leading
inhabitants.   An ancient mosque, indicates that the faith of
Islam is no very recent profession amongst a section of the
community, the majority of whom it may be presumed, from
the neighbouring vihâras, and the great Saman Déwâlé, are
Buddhists and Hindus.   Strings of bullock bandies con-
tinnally pass up and down the road; either on their way to
planting districts Badulla-wards, or with coffee to Colombo;
or to and from the stores of an enterprising British Colonist,
the depôt for the traffic on the river, the southward rival of

the road; taken altogether, the city has an aspect of busy thriving industry, which may be considered an index of the prosperity of the District of which it forms the capital.

Many lofty mountain groups and ranges tower around, and radiate from the point where Adam's Peak is seen. Amongst these, a few miles to the northeast of Ratnapura, is Mount Karangoda, the view from the summit of which is magnificent. Bennet, in chapter xlvii. of his work on Ceylon, gives the following description of its temple and scenery.

"The ascent to the first landing is by some hundreds of broad steps, hewn in the solid rock, which is covered with jungle, and pine apple plants, whose leaves are from five to six feet in length, a proof of the effect of shade upon that plant. Upon the first landing is the residence of the priests, an extensive and substantial stone building, having a large interior square, with wide and covered verandahs, into which the dormitories open.

"A similar but less inclined flight of rock steps leads to the second landing place, where a rock 'vihára displays Buddha's recumbent image, surrounded as usual with Hindu deities, and having an oblong table before it profusely covered with flowers. But the chief attraction to the European is a well of the purest water, of so very cold a temperature, that in five minutes a bottle of claret was cooled as well as if an experienced *Hopdar* [butler] had iced it.

"From hence the approach to the summit is extremely rugged, and covered with the gigantic groundsel (*Senecio*

giganteus) exceeding twenty feet in height, jungle and grass;
both well tenanted with snakes and land leeches; but one
is amply rewarded for toil, trouble, and even danger, by the
magnificent panorama which, on gaining the crown of the
mountain, bursts upon the view.   Here, castellated Ratnapura, and surrounding country, interspersed with every
variety of champaign, undulating, and hilly land, intersected
by the meandering and (for boats) navigable Kalu-gaṇga;
there, the Peak towering high above the clouds to the
northeastward, and the various villages dispersed upon the
banks of the river and its tributary streams, bordered by
extensive areka, kettule, and cocoanut topes, with occasional
patches of intervening jungle, scattered among verdant
tracts of pasture land, as if by way of contrast to the golden
glare of paddee and mustard fields in their approaching
maturity; and everywhere teeming with abundance; the
nearest plains covered with innumerable herds of bullocks
and buffaloes, and the distant ones with deer and elephants."

The route from Ratnapura to the Srí-páda commences
near the 57th mile-post, in a path which strikes to the north
just before the road crosses the Ratnapura bridge—a three-
span iron latticed structure, each span 140 feet in length,
with a roadway 18 feet in width.

Our arrangements having been completed overnight, we
thought to have started by daylight on the morning of the
26th March.   But our interpreter, and chair-bearers, and
commissariat coolies and other servants, were by no means
so anxious as ourselves for the trip, and it was not until

8 A. M. that we were all fairly off. A rather ludicrous occurrence took place immediately before. Our host's appu,
who went by the name of the Angel Gabriel, hearing his
master (our commissary general) inquire about the supply of
tea, in order that nothing might be wanting to ensure every
requisite for making that refreshing beverage while on the
road, detained one of the coolies until he had boiled a large
kettlefull of water, with which he made a final addition to the
man's load, and it was just a chance that it was discovered, and
the boiling water emptied out, before the man set off.* Descending from the road (a pretty stiff embankment forming
the approach to the bridge) we struck briskly across the field
and were soon into the jungle, where we mounted our
chairs,—arm-chairs with stout bambus tied to the sides, each
one borne by four coolies. The chair that fell to my lot,

---

* On our two subsequent journeys our start was here delayed. The
cause of the first I give in the words of one of my companions:—" We
made our start from Ratnapura in rainy weather, and with about fifteen
or twenty coolies to carry our baggage, we headed up towards the Peak.
A trick of one of the coolies just after starting caused us some amusement. We had some difficulty in getting the number of men we wanted,
and this one was the last whom we obtained. As he came last, he found
a load awaiting him which many of the others had tried the weight of,
and left as being rather too heavy for their tastes. He trudged along
behind us with his box, still lagging more and more in the rear, and soon
after we turned off on to the pilgrims' track, we lost sight of him altogether. The interpreter was sent back to hurry him on, and some-
time after returned with another coolie carrying the load, and told us the

however, soon gave way, my weight cracking the bambu which
supported it; and not being accustomed to such means of
progression, we found them so uncomfortable in rounding
sharp rocky corners, and in going up and down ascents and
descents, and we had to make such frequent dismounts at
the frail bridges placed across watercourses and ravines—
"edandas," i. e. logs of trees, many of them half rotted, with a
loose swinging bambu or length of jungle creeper for a hand-
rail,—that when we had proceeded about five miles, and came
to a bend of the Kalu-ganga, which we had to cross, we sent
them back to Ratnapura, and performed the rest of our
pilgrimage on foot.

The footpath passes through a considerable, well-cultivated
tract of paddy lands, until it reaches Godigamuwa, when it
skirts the base of a range of hills which abuts upon the Kalu-
ganga, here called the Ratmone-ella.   On the opposite side
are the mountains Batugedarakanda and Katugala.   The
river runs rapidly down the narrow intervening valley, and at

---

first one had left the box in the road and had bolted. Evidently the
fellow, on finding that our way turned off towards Adam's Peak, had,
with a sagacity and discrimination that did credit to his intellectual
powers, determined to run all risks rather than carry his box to the top
of the Peak, and had set down his load and 'made tracks.' " On the third
journey, the coolie we had despatched from Colombo with provisions,
four days previously, failed to make his appearance, and after waiting for
him in vain for twenty-four hours, we had to proceed with such provender
as we could procure at the bazaar.

this place the processions of the Perahẹra terminate, the elephants marching thus far, when the Kapurála proceeds to cut the waters of the running stream.* Beyond this is the small village Koskolawatta, and opposite it, the mountain Kirigala,†—so named from a conspicuous patch of white rock near its summit. A narrow track near this leads to . a ford, which in dry seasons enables the traveller to make a short cut, and save a quarter of a mile's walk. Our guide took us down this track, but we found the current running . too strongly, and the water apparently much too deep, to warrant the risk of an attempt to cross it; we therefore returned, and soon after, descending a ravine, came to the Irihadepána-çlla, or dola,‡ a broad brawling mountain stream, considerably swollen by late rains, but passable without much difficulty, with the assistance of large rough stepping stones laid at irregular distances across. This . stream is the boundary between Goḍigamuwa and Gilímalé. Near the 61st mile is the village Malwala, or, as its name . indicates, "the flower village," a place where flowers are or

---

* The Kapurála strikes the water with a golden sword. At the same instant a brazen vessel is dipped into the river while the water is yet disparted, and a portion is taken up, which is kept in the vessel until the following year. The water which was taken at the previous festival is then poured back into the river.

† 'Kiri,' white, milky; 'gala,' rock.

‡ 'Ella,' a stream free from stones. 'Dola,' a stream, the bed of which is full of stones and rocks.

were cultivated for offerings to the temples. From thence, the path leads across the Doḍankanewe-ęlla, and the Búdola, beyond which the Kajuwatta, a native roadside tavern is reached, where a short halt is usually made. We here procured some kurumbás,* and some of our coolies refreshed themselves with arrack, obtained at the primitive bar of fence and bambu sticks where it was retailed in the hut. Leaving this, we shortly after reached Dimbulwitiya; and to cross the ęlla had to balance ourselves cautiously over an ugly édanda. The road from this point to where the Kalu-gaŋga. is crossed, was being cleared and widened when we last travelled upon it; on the two former occasions it was pretty well overgrown with jungle. Here, at the Ęllapita Toṭupoḷa, or ferry, we dismissed our chair-bearers.

Just before reaching this point we observed a remarkable species of fungus, of a kind which none of us had ever before seen. The stem was about nine inches long, and an inch in diameter at the ground. From the top, where the stem had narrowed to about a quarter of an inch, a cap loosely hung like a cup-shaped bell, covered with a fine white raised reticulation, the interstices of which were filled with a viscid liquor of an olive brown colour. From the neck, below the cap, and surrounding the stem to the ground, was a globe-shaped mantle, as if an outer skin had been blown

---

* Young cocoanuts, containing half a pint or more of the refreshing cocoanut milk.

out bladder-wise, and then pierced through and through until it became patterned into inimitable lace-work, of a white colour above and piuk below. Nothing of the kind could be more beautiful.

The banks of the river, on either side of the ferry, are somewhat abrupt, and require care to avoid a slip down the steep slope of stiff mud of which they consist, when the weather is at all damp. In the dry season the natives usually ford the stream, which is then not more than from two to three feet in depth; but when the rains have been heavy and continuous, the passage is by the ferry-boat, a small frail looking double canoe. Past the 64th mile-post is the Yaṭowiṭa ella, and beyond it the Mahá-dola, both which are crossed by édanḍas. Between the 65th and 66th mile-posts, lies the plain of Gilímalé, and here, on each of our journeys, we halted. For, although from the point at Goḍigamuwa, where the road undulates along the base of the valley through which the Kalu-gaṇga runs and flows and eddies its seaward way, ferns and slender battalees* overhang the path, while mosses of an infinite variety beautify the untrodden ground, and shrubs and flowering plants enliven the scenery, agreeably shaded here and there by gigantic forest trees or clumps of tall bambus, and every now and again diversified by patches of open plains and level tracts of paddy-fields,—the pleasure all this affords the eye

---

* The *Bambusa stridula.*

and mind, does not counterbalance the feeling of fatigue that begins to make rest and refreshment longed for, and heartily welcomed as soon as they can be obtained.

Gilímalé, famous for its betel leaves, is, in this particular portion of it, a level fertile plain, about a mile in circumference, fringed and skirted with belts of cocoanut and areka palms, and clumps of jack, shaddock, orange, plantain, and various other fruit trees, which flourish in luxuriant abundance at the base of the lofty hills which surround it, and amongst which clusters of native dwellings and nestling villages may be seen half hidden in their grateful shade. The spot, and the singular shrinking sensitive plant* which here abounds, reminded us of old James Shirley's lines in his poem " Narcissus."

> "From hence delight conveys him unawares
> Into a spacious green, whose either side
> A hill did guard, whilst with his trees like hairs
> The clouds were busy binding up his head.
> The flowers here smile upon him as he treads,
> And but when he looks up hang down their heads."

It was here, or in the immediate neighbourhood, that Prince Dutugemunu, son of Kávantissa, king of Róhuna, concealed himself when threatened with punishment for

---

* A plant of the genus *Mimosa*, so called from the shrinking and contraction of its leaves on being touched.

the insult offered to his father, after failing in his endeavours to induce or provoke him to make war against the Malabars, then ruling in the Northern kingdom, and whose expulsion from the island it was his great ambition to accomplish; an object which he succeeded in effecting soon after his accession to the throne, B. C. 164.[*]

The name of the place, Gilímalé, signifies "mountain immerged," the Samantakúṭa not being here visible, although

---

[*] "This prince Gámini, who was skilled in the elephant, horse, and bow exercises, as well as in stratagems, was then residing at Mahágámo, and the king had stationed his (second) son Tisso, with a powerful and efficient force, at Díghnwápi, for the protection of his dominions, (against the invasions of the damilos.)

"After a certain period had elapsed, prince Gámini, having held a review of his army, proposed to his royal father, 'Let me wage war with the damilos.' The king, only looking to his (son's) personal safety, interdicted (the enterprise); replying, 'Within this bank of the river is sufficient.' He, however, renewed the proposition, even to the third time; (which being still rejected) he sent to him a female trinket, with this message: 'It being said my father is not a man, let him therefore decorate himself with an ornament of this description.' That monarch enraged with him, thus spoke (to his courtiers); 'Order a gold chain to be made, with which I shall fetter him; not being able to restrain him by any other means.' He (the Prince) indignant with his parent, retiring (from his court) fled to (Kútta in) the Malayà district [Kotmálic]. From this circumstance of his having become ('duttha') inimical to his father, he acquired from that day the appellation, 'Dutthagámini.'"— Turnour's Mahawansó, p. 145. The Rájawaliya, narrating the same event, adds that the prince first "fled to Gilímalé, and having hid himself there for several days, fled from thence to the place called Kotmulic."

the two summits of the Bęna Samanala are. This is
owing to the lowness of the level, which is probably not
more than seventy feet higher than the sea. On the way from
Godigamuwa, at the points where the road rises by the bank
of the Kalu-gaŋga, all the three peaks are distinctly seen
when the sky is clear; but the lower the path descends, the
more the Peak of the Holy Foot-print seems to shrink out
of sight, until it is wholly hidden by the mountains that
begirt the Gilímalé plain.

The bungalow where we breakfasted on our first excursion,
and where, notwithstanding we brought all our supplies with
us, we were most hospitably entertained, and made to
partake of the owner's abundant fare, was the Walawwa
or mansion of Laksha Mudiyanseláge Punchi Bandúra,
Mahatmayá of Gilímalé. It lies a short distance to the
east of the road passing through the plain, where it is

> " Well set with fair fruit bearing trees and groves,
> .   .   .   .   . all populous with doves,
> And watered by a wandering clear green stream,"—

the Guruluwan-gaŋga,—which flows in a northerly direction
to join the Hatula, a tributary of the Kalu-gaŋga. While
breakfast was preparing we adjourned to the adjacent river
for a bath; the stream was broad and rocky, and in some
parts deep; the water cool, clear and most refreshing; and
abounding with numerous small fish, of two kinds in particular;—one, apparently a species of perch, from two to four
inches in length, with red mouth, tail, and fins, and banded

vertically with alternate stripes of black and silver from head to tail; the other smaller and more slender, of a dusky brown colour with a longitudinal black stripe on either side. Both were bold and fearless, and swarmed about us when we rested, pecking at our limbs with their mouths, and producing a sensation as if we were being pricked with a multitude of blunt pins. Their elegance of form and beauty of colour should make them valuable acquisitions to aquariums, as much so as the Chinese gold and silver fishes, to which one kind seems to be allied.

On the opposite side of the plain, running south, and forming its western boundary, flows the Kalu-gaṇga,—here, at the Gilímalé Parapa-toṭupola, very picturesque and sylvan, with a fine shelving sandy bed,—a stream altogether to be preferred to bathe in; with its gentle windings, shady banks o'erhung with trees, and placid waters, which

"to their resting place serene
Came freshening and reflecting all the scene
(A mirror in the depth of flowery shelves:)
So sweet a spot of earth, you might, (I ween)
Have guessed some congregation of the elves
To sport by summer moons had shaped it for themselves."

CAMPBELL.

The Bandára family came originally from the Maritime Provinces. The cause of their settlement in Gilímalé, we were informed, was as follows.—The grandson of Rája-Siṇha II., King Srí Wíra Prákrama Neréndra Siṇha, the

last of the Sinhalese born sovereigns of Ceylon, who reigned
A. D. 1685—1707, was considerably addicted to drinking,
and apt, when in his cups, to resolve upon strange freaks.
He was nevertheless, from a Buddhist point of view, a pious
monarch, who devoutly repaired and endowed vihárus, and
otherwise benefited Buddhism and Buddhist priests. One
day, when on a visit to Sítáwaka, he took it into his head
to wish for a light to be exhibited on the universally
supposed inaccessible summit of the mountain Kunudiyaparvate. None of the Kandians would make the attempt,
whereupon one Bandúra, from Púgoda, a village near Cotta,
undertook the task, and after spending much time and
overcoming many difficulties, succeeded. The king saw the
light, and royally rewarded Bandúra with grants of land:
these lands his descendants still retain.

After breakfast, to which our liberal host added plantains,
oranges, curdled milk, and a variety of curries, we indulged
in a few hours' rest, and did not resume our journey until
3½ P. M. Then, divesting ourselves of sundry articles
of dress, such as coats, waistcoats and neck-tyes, and
grasping light tough sticks some five feet long, courteously
presented to us by our host, we went on our way, as light
hearted and merry—and I may add, in our purple, plaid,
crimson and grey woollen shirts, varied-shaped pith and felt
head-gear, and dissimilar cut and coloured nether garments—as picturesque a quartette of pilgrims as ever trode
the pilgrim's path in that or any other direction. One of our
number, armed with a double barrelled gun, was to sporting

tastes inclined, but the number of pilgrims journeying to and fro had made both bird and beast shy of the road we were taking, and sport we had none; an occasional shot or two, however, awoke the echoes of the woodland wilds, and reverberated amongst the mountains that rose on either side of us with a grand and sometimes startling effect.

From Gilímalé to Palábaddala, where we purposed sleeping, a distance of six miles, the country begins to assume a more rugged and mountainous appearance; the ascents becoming higher and steeper, and the descents deeper and more difficult; the route in fact traversing some of the outlying spurs of mountains, into a chain of which we were penetrating.

Shortly after leaving Bandára Mahatmayá's Walawwa, we came to the Tuntota ferry, which crosses the Hatula-ganga; here, at its junction with the Kalu-ganga, a broad and rapid, but somewhat shallow stream, overhung with clumps of the tall gracefully waving feathery bambu, and the wide-spread branches of many a noble forest tree. Proceed-ing onwards through a well wooded country, we crossed the Pahalewala édanda, and the Saman watte ella,—so called, because the land through which the ella flows belongs to the Saman Déwálé. Four low hills followed, from 60 to 100 feet in height, at the bases of which flow 'dolas' of various names. We were now upon the bank of the rushing Maskeliya-ganga.* A bridge was being constructed over

---

* 'Maskeliya,' playing of the fishes.

the river in lieu of the old rocky ford,—a difficult passage
at best, and at times decidedly dangerous.   The site of
the bridge was some distance above the ford; a huge
precipitous boulder formed a natural abutment on one side,
and a masonry one had been built to correspond on the other.
The river, rushing from the north down a mountain gorge,
strikes and ponds up against a mass of rock that causes it to
make an abrupt bend to the west.   In making the bend,
close to the right of the bridge, it swells into a deep lake-like
pool, the waters of which swarm with plump, inky coloured
fish, about 18 inches long, with large well defined scales.
They were called by the natives *oropulle*, and were said to
be unfit for food; this however is not the case, unless it be at
special seasons; but it is certain they are not held in estimation, and are but rarely eaten.   This particular part of
the river is called Nána-wala, the king Srí Wikrama Raja
Sinha, the last of the Kandian sovereigns, having used it as
a bathing place.

The bridge was about 60 feet in length, in two spans
of 30 feet each, supported in the centre by wooden piles:
its height above the water was about 30 feet.   Coming up
to this, and observing that in its then state one half consisted
of but two round untrimmed trunks of iron wood trees,
between two and three feet apart, and the other of two
similarly placed trees, roughly squared; and that the only
side support was a loose swinging hand-rail of jungle cane,
I paused in dismay, not perceiving the ford, about a hundred
yards lower down, and not at all relishing the necessity for

venturing along so perilous looking a path. On the opposite side however, numbers of pilgrims were assembled, who had all crossed in safety, and my companions, all more or less accustomed to such matters, encouraging me to make the attempt, on I went, hardly daring to lift one foot after the other, until I reached the squared timber, when I breathed more freely, and in a second or two felt myself wonderfully relieved, as I again trod the solid earth. From the bridge a short ascent led to a patch of comparatively level ground, perhaps 100 feet above the level of the sea, where we were overtaken by a smart shower, and gladly availed ourselves of the shelter of a boutique on the wayside, until it had passed away.

The characteristic features of the scenery from the right bank of the Maskeliya-ganga, where we crossed the stream, differ considerably from those we left behind us on our way from Gilímalé. There, it was open, undulatory, park like; and "from the many jessamines, from the various orange flowers, from the citron and lime, from the areka, from innumerable plants and flowering trees arise divers perfumes, which blended in the morning dew and wafted on the early breeze, afforded the most delicate and exquisite fragrance."[*] Here, it was the rising base of a mountain range thickly clothed with magnificent forest trees, straight as pines, and from fifty to seventy feet in height. Gigantic creepers

---

* Major Forbes' Eleven Years in Ceylon, vol. i. p. 167.

T

twined about the .trunks, and with serpentine convolutions
spread from tree to tree; orchids and mosses and lichens
overgrew their bark; while a floral undergrowth breathed
rich odours and scented the air with sweets of a different
but not less fragrant perfume. . Passing through the forest,
and cresting several hills that rose each higher than the one
behind, we came to Ali-hántenne,* a tract of dense canes
or battalees, crossed in all directions by numerous elephant
tracks. This was evidently one of the favourite feeding
grounds of that monarch of the forest, as the name it bore
plainly enough indicated.   Beyond this is an extensive
marsh, thickly covered with large reeds,—"the estuary of
reeds" of Ibn Batutá,—a swampy district, not at all pleasant to pass at any season, wet or dry, owing to the swarms
of leeches that infest it: and further on is Batapola, a part
of the domain of the Bandára family.   Here temporary
bungalows are put up for the accommodation of pilgrims.
On the right of the path in the upward ascent, is one of the
caves which Ibn Batutá refers to in his narrative.   It is
formed by a straight fissure, in shape like an immense
inverted v, Λ, running longitudinally through a huge
boulder forty feet in length, from twelve to fifteen feet in
height, and proportionally broad.   In a distant range in the
same direction is seen the Mapanan-ella water-fall, leaping
down the mountain side on its way to join the Maskeliya-
ganga.

---

* The elephant chena plain.

> " There was the river heard in bed of wrath
> (A precipice of foam from mountains brown),
> Like tumults heard from some far distant town ;
> But softening in approach he left his gloom
> And murmured pleasantly, and laid him down
> To kiss those easy curving banks of bloom
> That lent the windward air an exquisite perfume."
>
> CAMPBELL.

A steep and rough ascent, for a considerable distance from Batapola,—midway in which a stone tumulus has been erected on the spot where the remains of an old priest were burned,—brings the pilgrim to Palábaddala, "the house of the old woman," according to Ibn Batutá, "and the farthest inhabited part of the island of Ceylon," that is, when he travelled through it, about five hundred and thirty years ago.

Although fatiguing, the walk from Ratnapura to Palábaddala, from the rich variety of scenery one passes through, is very enjoyable, especially if the weather be fine: and in this respect our first excursion was all that could be desired. It was not so on the two subsequent occasions. Opportunity serving, a second trip was resolved upon in the usually fine and dry month of September; but the cycles of the seasons are undergoing a change, and the month turned out an exceptionally wet one. It was not the pilgrim season, and as Colombo coolies' were averse to undertaking the journey further than Ratnapura, it was possible that our progress might be delayed for want of assistance along the uninhabited districts; owing however to the good offices

most readily rendered us by Mr. F. R. Saunders, the Assistant Government Agent, and the directions given to their
subordinates by the Chief priest of the Peak and the Ratemahatmayá of the Kóralé in which the Samanala is situated,
we were put into communication with the Ganárachchies
(petty headmen) of Godigamuwa, Gilímalé, and Haghapolla,
(a village near Palúbaddala), and through them were enabled
to hire, at different stages, as many coolies as we desired,
at the rate of 9d. a day. Eknęligoda Ratemahatmayá also
placed at our service one of his retainers, a man who knew
every inch of the route, and was in every respect a valuable
acquisition to our party.*

---

* The services of such a man are invaluable on any similar journey in
the jungle in Ceylon; he was a capital shot, and never at a loss for resources; and I heartily agree with the following tribute paid him by one
of my companions:—"If ever there was a right man in the right place,
Francina was the man.¹ Ready, willing, active, inexhaustible in expe-
dient, and cheerful under all difficulty, he never failed us. He always
was ready to time, always came up smiling, and if under trying circumstances, in positions sometimes that would have reduced Mark Tapley to
the brink of suicide, we were enabled to bear discomforts which vex the
spirit of even a good man, with a jolly philosophy—and we certainly
did—why it was to Francina's dinners in a large measure that we owed it.
Fortified by those dinners we defied obstacles, the adverse spirits of the
Peak, the evil genii of the way, and the clerk of the weather." Our
interpreter, Mr Solomon Justin Rebera, also proved a useful intelligent
assistant to us; but the pilgrimage knocked him up, and he returned to
Ratumpura, more fatigued than either of his European employers.

It was late in the afternoon when we started, and we did not reach Ellapita Ferry until the sun had set. The rest of the way to Gilímalé was in the dark; and as a drizzling rain was continually falling, the "chules" or torches that we lighted were of no great use. Punchirála, and Mudalihámi, the Ganárachchies of Godligamuwa and Gilímalé, met us on the road, and the latter provided house-room for us in his bungalow on the plain, where white cloths were spread above and around the apartment allotted to our use; our train of servants and coolies finding shelter in the neighbouring huts. Our first care was to get rid of the leeches which had swarmed over us while tramping along the slumpy paddy fields, or through the dripping jungle.* The

---

* No description will convey to the reader's mind a better idea of these pests, than the following by worthy old Robert Knox.—" There is a sort of leeches of the nature of ours, only differing in colour and bigness; for they are of a dark reddish colour like the skin of bacon, and as big as a goose quill; in length, some two or three inches. At first, when they are young, they are no bigger than a horsehair, so that they can scarce be seen. In dry weather none of them appear, but immediately upon the fall of rains, the grass and woods are full of them. These leeches seize upon the legs of travellers, who, going barefoot, according to the custom of that land, have them hanging upon their legs in multitudes, which suck their blood till their bellies are full, and then drop off. They come in such quantities, that the people cannot pull them off so fast as they crawl on: the blood runs pouring down their legs all the way they go, and it is no little smart neither; so that they would willingly be without them if they could, especially those that have sores on their legs; for they all gather to the sore. Some, therefore, will tie a piece of lemon

night was boisterous, and the rain fell in torrents; and at day-
break we learnt the Maskeliya-gnuga was impassable. We
were in the position of Jason of old on his way to Iolchos,
when

> "...lightly through the well-known woods he passed,
> And came out to the open plain at last,
> And went till night came on him, and then slept
> Within a homestead that a poor man kept,
> And rose again at dawn, and slept that night
> Nigh the Annurus, and at morrow's light
> Rose up and went into the river's brim;
> But fearful seemed the passage unto him,
> For swift and yellow drave the stream adown
> 'Twixt crumbling banks; and tree trunks rough and brown
> Whirl'd in the bubbling eddies here and there;
> So swollen was the stream a maid might dare
> To cross, in fair days, with unwetted knee."

We were not, like him, fortunate enough to find a goddess
to help us across; the torrent raged furiously over and

---

and salt in a rag, and fasten it unto a stick, and ever and anon strike it
upon their legs to make the leeches drop off: others will scrape them off
with a reed, cut flat and sharp in the fashion of a knife; but this is so trouble-
some, and they come on again so fast and so numerous, that it is not worth
their while: and generally they suffer them to bite, and remain on their
legs during their journey; and they do the more patiently permit them,
because it is so wholesome for them. When they come to their journey's
end, they rub all their legs with ashes, and so clear themselves of them
at once; but still the blood will remain dropping a great while after."

among the rocks and boulders, and the bridge had, months
ago, been swept away. Shortly after the burst of the monsoon, in the month of May, the floods from the mountains,
checked by the bend of the river, rose rapidly to a height of
forty feet, and completely submerging the banks, whirled to
destruction every impediment they met with. On their
subsidence it was found the bridge was gone, the masonry
abutment on the right bank destroyed, and only a few logs
of the entire timber work of piers and pathway, left stranded
here and there on either bank.*

We at first thought the natives were trying to frighten
us from going further, but on ascertaining the state of
affairs for ourselves, we returned to Gilímalé, and waited
to see what another day would bring forth; in the meantime a few pigeons, kingfishers, orioles, jungle crows and
other birds, were shot, and a little taxidermy practised with
a view to the preservation of their skins. Starting early
the next day, we with some difficulty effected a passage;
although in crossing the Hatula-ganga, we found that that
river had fallen four feet during the previous twelve hours.
The ford, where we crossed, was fully a hundred and fifty feet
wide from bank to bank, and we had occasionally to make a

---

* A bridge has again and again been put up here; but only to be swept
away as often as erected. It is understood to be the intention of the
Chief priest of the Srí-páda to erect a suspension bridge of a single span;
raised sufficiently high to ensure it against destruction from catastrophics
similar to those which destroyed its predecessors.

jump from one rock to another, in places where a slip would
have been followed by inevitable destruction; unless one
had the good fortune to be caught by or against a length of
cable-ratan* which had been partially stretched across the
bed of the river, apparently with a view to rendering assistance in case of possible accidents. The worst place was near
the right bank, where a mighty tree had been overthrown, the
trunk of which stretched diagonally over the deepest channel
of the river, a chasm down which the waters were rushing
and tumbling in tumultuous foam. A large limb of the tree
was jammed between the rocks on one side of the channel,
while the roots were stuck fast in the other. Up this limb,
and along the wet and slippery trunk, and down the roots,
each one had to pass ere he could gain the opposite bank.
It was a nerve trying operation, and under such circumstances heavy nailed boots certainly do not give one a feeling
of security. Here the shoeless natives had a decided advantage over us. Several of these indeed declined trying
the tree; and slinging their loads on bambus, waded two and

---

* This ratan is a species of *Calamus*, occasionally found 300 feet in
length, an inch in diameter, and with scarcely any difference in thickness
throughout its entire length. From its lightness, strength and toughness,
it has been employed by the natives with striking success in the formation
of suspension bridges over water-courses and ravines. Descriptions of
these bridges are given by both Sir J. E. Tennent, and Major Forbes.
In the work by the latter a wood engraving is given of the one which
crossed the Dedru-oya, on the Trincomalee road.

two among the rocks above where we crossed, probing the
depth of water with long sticks as they went, sometimes
sinking to their armpits, but always so zigzagging as to find
the shallowest part of the stream. They knew the river
and we did not; and after all had passed, they declared that
but for our determination to go on, and the number we had
to render help to each other, they would not have ventured to
try the passage. Happily no accident occurred, and we
reached Palábaddala with no further damage than that of
being wet through; with the exception of what happened
to one of the coolies, who, carrying a nitrate of silver bath,
the top of which was fortunately screwed on, in shifting his
load turned it upside down; a slight leakage followed, which
not distinguishing from the rain, he took no notice of; the
consequence was, that the brown skin of his back and chest
become covered with stripes and streaks of black, which,
when a glimpse of sunlight broke through the clouds, shone
with a bright metallic lustre, and he was very nearly believing he had been bewitched, or was undergoing punishment
from Saman for venturing through his territories at so unwonted a season. It was a sort of satisfaction to our minds
to find, on the third excursion, that the natives themselves
are not without feelings of apprehension, sure-footed as they
are, and nonchalant as they seem to be. At this same ford,
although the water was lower, and nothing near so foamingly
boisterous as on our second journey, one of our coolies became
completely panic-stricken. He stood trembling on a rock in
the middle of the stream, perspiration pouring out at every

pore from sheer dread: move he could not; and we had to
send two men to relieve him of his load, anything but a
heavy one, and help him over: but he would go no further,
he had had enough of the pilgrimage, and we were obliged to
proceed without him.

Palábaddala,—or according to same authorities, Pulá-bat·
dola,—stands on an elevated plateau, 1,100 or 1,200 feet
above the sea. It consists of a village or hamlet, containing
several small irregular streets, with sundry spacious open
bungalows for the accommodation of pilgrims passing to and
from the Peak. Its ordinary population, according to Baba
Sinho, the intelligent Ganárachchi of Haghapola, was about
250; but thousands throng into it during the pilgrim season,
especially in the months of February, March and April.
In August 1866, the place was nearly all burnt down by an
accidental fire; but wattle and daub huts, with cadjan roofs,
are soon run up again, and one good has perhaps resulted
from the fire, in that several of the bungalows are now
substantially roofed with tiles.

The following legend is connected with the place, and
accounts for its name. Long, long ago, a very poor woman
was desirous of performing the pilgrimage to the Srí-páda,
but, owing to her extreme poverty, could take nothing with
her except some common jungle leaves, which in times of
distress the natives occasionally resort to for food; these she
boiled, and rolled up in a plaintain leaf; and having arrived
thus far, when about to partake of her food, she found
the boiled leaves had been miraculously turned into rice.

Thenceforward it was called Pala-bat-dola, "the place of rice and vegetables," a name which it has ever since retained. The fact that rice was substituted for the leaves, is, no doubt, correctly enough recorded; but the change was one which it needed no miracle to effect; although if miracles were needed at the time, the supply, as a matter of course, would be created to meet the demand.

To the south of the hamlet, separated from it by a field a few hundred feet in breadth, is a quadrangular platform about 90 feet long and 72 broad, raised three feet from the ground, and approached by six roughly hewn steps. On this is placed the Vihára, a small modern building, adjoining which is the Dágoba, formed of brick, about 12 feet in height and 70 in circumference. In front of the dágoba is a stone slab, 3ft. 6in. by 1ft. 8in., raised 3ft. 6in. from the ground: faint traces of an inscription are observable upon it, and it is carefully roofed over; it is used as an altar, on which the Buddhists make their floral offerings to the dágoba. This is apparently of considerable antiquity, but much dilapidated; it was partially grown over with a shrubby vegetation, the roots of which were penetrating through and threatening to destroy it.

The vihára contains a facsimile in copper of a former golden and gem-adorned cover and representation of the Srí-páda, long since lost, or destroyed. Engravings, and embossments in silver, represent the 108 marks upon the sole of the foot, which indicate their possessor to be a Buddha. In this instance these are all represented by lotus buds and

flowers, in various stages of development. A brass rim was
lying by it in pieces, richly chased and engraved, and at
one time adorned with precious stones; but the sockets they
once filled were now either empty, or filled with imitations
in glass. There was also an image of Buddha, in a standing
position, about two feet high, made of an amalgam called
"lokade," consisting of copper, brass, and three other metals,
the names of which the priests did not know. A silver
dágoba-shaped karandua, with a golden top, containing an
image of Buddha in bronze; and a shrine, covering a sedent
Buddha, about six inches high, made of a stone called
"kirigarunde," stood in front of the copper Srí-páda. This
shrine was filled with dead flowers, and had certainly not
been looked into for some time; for when the priest opened
it, to give us an opportunity of examining the figure, out
jumped a rat, and a family of young ones were discovered
left behind in their nest. The two officiating priests,
Rattembe unanse, and Hatwelle unanse, reside in the central
street of the hamlet. We were, on each of our visits, much
beholden to them for accommodation and information. They
are literally worshipped by the people, (and so, in fact, are
Buddhist priests, by Buddhists,* in all other places), to a

---

* ' The Buddhas, sacred books, and the priesthood, are regarded as
the three most precious gems. They are all associated in the three-fold
formulary repeated by the Buddhist when he names, as an act of worship,
the triad to which he looks as the object of his confidence and his refuge.''
—HARDY's Eastern Monachism, p. 166.

greater extent even than the Sri-padá, and the dágoba; and it was painfully pitiable to see men, women and children, making their offerings of flowers, oil, money and valuables; and bowing down in adoration before them.

It being nearly sunset when we arrived, and every corner apparently occupied, we were for a while puzzled where to find a resting place. At last having told the interpreter to make known our wants to the principal priest, he was good enough to allot to our use an unfinished house, which, although its walls were of undried clay, and one side was minus both door and door-frame, was, happily for us, roofed in, and gave us all the shelter we were actually in need of. In a few minutes two rude bed-frames were also supplied, as well as a small table; and while our servants were preparing dinner, we strolled out to observe what was going on around. The pilgrims came and went, in a continuous stream of companies of families, or villages, some of them in regular procession, headed by a party bearing an ornamented shrine, and accompanied by a band of shrill horanawa, tam-tam and doula* players, blowing and beating, and tormenting one's tympanums with their noisy discords. All found quarters, any where and every where, as best they could. Amongst

---

* The horanawa is a kind of clarionett; the tam-tam a small pair of kettle drums slung in front of a man, and beaten with two slender sticks, the extremities of which are bent into circles; the doula is an oblong drum, generally beaten at one end with a stick, and on the other with the hand.

them were a few Hindus, and a sprinkling of Moormen.
Some of these latter, with an eye to business, had extempo-
rized a bazaar, where almost everything in a small way could
be bought by those who were so disposed.

"The place afforded a very interesting view.* Situated
just at the commencement of the upward slope, the altitude
was scarcely sufficient to command much of a view of the
low country, but the prospect given of the mountain range
before us was fine indeed. A long barrier of mountains,
covered with dark forests, lay in our front, and it was up
one of the passes of these that our to-morrow's route would
lie. About half way up the slope a long wall of perpendicular rock stretched along the mountain front, and over this
cliff, many torrents were streaming in far resounding waterfalls, on which the evening sun-light was pleasantly playing.
At the extreme left of the range a noble mountain erected
its head to the clouds. The mountain I refer to is called
Kunudiyaparvate. It extends from the low country in
one sheer, unbroken slope, to a height of upwards of 5,000
feet, like an enormous buttress to the mountain range behind.
Towards its top it rises in precipitous rocks, and the black
shining surface of these lofty cliffs were on the evening
that I watched them, all glowing in the last rays of the sun,

---

* The above extract is from a sketch of our second excursion published
by one of my companions. It will be understood that all similar matter
distinguished by marks of quotation, but to which no name or authority
is given, is from the same pen.

then setting behind the western hills. Shortly afterwards
the clouds lowered on the mountain, and the beautiful view
became lost in the night."

Our appearance rather excited the curiosity of the people,
and when we dined, we ate our meal in state—a state which
we would have dispensed with had it been possible, for we
were gazed upon the whole time by as many fellow pilgrims as
could crowd their heads in at the open doorway. They were
not however otherwise rude or uncourteous; but did all that
lay in their power to assist us in our wants. As the moon
rose, it being nearly full, and the sky clear, the appearance
of the place was animated enough;—here, companies of men,
women and children, clustered round their cooking fires,
eating their food, or chanting Buddhist legends;—there,
lighted by the glare of numerous torches, throngs intently
listening to men reading aloud from olas;—in one place, a
number looking on and applauding the musicians, as they
danced an accompaniment to their music;—in another, devotees surrounding a portable shrine, worshipping the small
image it contained, and depositing their offerings in a cup or
basin placed before it. We did not escape the notice of the
tam-tam beaters, who formed up before, and treated us to
their best performances; and the way in which the two
dancers, each beating a pair of kettle-drums slung before
him, rattled away with stick and elbow and palm, and kept
time with the seated doula, or big drum beater, and the
horanawa blower, was marvellously strange and grotesque.
Rewarding them with a few rupees, by way of getting rid

of them, we laid down to try and sleep; but the continual
noise occasioned by fresh bands of pilgrims arriving and
departing, was of so disturbing a nature, that we no sooner
dozed off than we were again awakened, and were only too
glad at last to hail the rising of the sun as a signal to proceed ourselves. It must be owned, our beds were not of the
most sleep-inducing kind. Two of us lay on frames, the
canes of which were at least three inches apart; a couple of
rough planks, and a door taken off its hinges, served the
other two: but we had not expected luxuries; we had provided ourselves with rugs, and for the rest supposed we
should have to rough it; and we found our suppositions here
and there fully realised. The unfinished house we occupied
was one being built for the priests, and on our subsequent
visits we found the rooms pleasant quarters enough. The
worthy unanses gave us a hospitable welcome, and the best
accommodation the place afforded, and we were abundantly
satisfied.

Adam's Peak.

"Where'er we gaze, around, above, below,
What rainbow tints, what magic charms are found!
Rock, river, forest, mountain all abound,
And bluest skies, that harmonize the whole:
Beneath, the distant torrent's rushing sound
Tells where the volumed cataract doth roll
Between those hanging rocks, that shock yet please the soul,"

BYRON.

CHAPTER VI.

PALA'BADDALA.—MOUNTAIN RANGES.—KALUGANGA BRIDGE.—
UDA PAWANELLA. — NI'LIHELA. — GETANETUL-GALA. —
DIYABETMA.— IDIKATUPA'NA.— DHARMA-RA'JA-GALA. — KU-
NUDIYA-PARVATE'.— BE'NA SAMANALA. — TELIHILENNA.—
GANGULA-HENA. — SI'TA-GANGULA, — HERAMITIPA'NA.

AFTER performing our morning ablutions in the presence
of a number of persons, who watched our proceedings intently, if not admiringly, we took, from a stand point near
the vihára, and while waiting for coffee, a rapid survey
of the scenery around. To the north of Palábaddala rises
Kunudiya-parvaté, the monarch of all the mountain ranges
within view. Running south and shouldering against it, as

it were, is a range consisting of the Kondagala, Nílihela, and Kękillagala mountains. To the southwest are
the mountains Dewanagala, Morangala, Nawemeneagala,
and Kanugala-kanda. In the distance, southwards, beyond
Ratnapura, are the two high mountains Amhuldeniakanda
and Kanugala-kanda;* and through the valley between
them, is seen another high range one of the mountains of which appeared to have a double summit, not
unlike that of the Bęna Samanala. Our path lay up by
Kondagala and over Nílihela. Passing out of Palábaddala
by the east, a glimpse of the top of the Peak is caught
above the mountains, and is hailed with shouts of " Sádhu!"†
by all true pilgrims, both going and returning. As the
crow flies, the distance between the two points is not more
than three and a half miles; but the height to be surmounted was still 6,250 feet above where we stood; and by
the pilgrims' path, the distance to be traversed was at least
eleven miles. The intervening country forms a part of
what is known as the " wilderness of the Peak." A walk
of a furlong and a half, partly through paddy fields, brought
us to an upper branch of the Kalu-gaṇga, which is crossed
by a well-constructed rustic bridge, about thirty feet in span,
and three feet wide, floored with short mopas (sticks an inch in

---

* Quære "Gallenakanda." It is sometimes difficult to catch the exact
names of places when spoken in a language not familiar to the listener.

† 'Sádhu!'—a joyous exclamation. Well-done! Good! In a religious
sense, equivalent perhaps to Hallelujah!

diameter). The river here runs down a steep and somewhat gloomy looking rocky ravine, and from this point, about a hundred feet higher than Palábaddala, the difficulties of the journey may be said to begin. Immediately after passing the bridge, the ascent is by a steep climb up the mountain side, here called Pawaneli-hela; after half an hour of this work, and passing a huge overhanging rock, we came to the village Uda Pawan-ella, consisting of a few bungalows on narrow plateaux, rising one above another. They belong to the Bandára family; and are of essential service to pilgrims, who generally halt at them for a while. Just below, there is a small plantation of coffee, growing under the shade of tall forest trees, among which some specimens of the cotton family are conspicuous. This is the last regularly inhabited station, the elevation being about 1,500 feet above the sea. When we first passed it, the bungalows were crowded, and as we did not care to stop, we pushed along up the path, which is simply the not always dry rocky bed of a mountain torrent, with here and there a few ladders of jungle sticks to assist the traveller up a more than ordinary precipitous piece, elsewhere with notches cut in the rock to afford a foot-hold;* and for the rest an ascent on and over gnarled and

---

* "The walk from Gilimalé to Palábaddala is by no means an easy one, although much inferior in difficulty and steepness to that immediately succeeding......This part of the road is by far the most difficult and precipitous; in fact, much more so considering the extent, than anything I could have supposed possible. I had ascended Ben Lomond and

interlacing roots of trees, and stones and steps of every size and shape, from three inches to three feet in height, the average gradient being one in two—some parts of which can scarcely be overcome otherwise than by crawling up on all fours.

Two wearying miles of this kind of toil brought us to the Nilihela ambalama, a welcome halting place on a level of a few yards length; and a station celebrated for the loud and reiterated echoes thrown back from its surrounding mountain walls and stupendous precipices. Here we rested, and while partaking of a roughly prepared breakfast, entered into conversation, through our interpreter, with some of our fellow-pilgrims. One old man, leading his family, told us this was his 51st trip; another, that he was returning from his 52nd; and a third, whom we subsequently overtook, old, feeble, and tottering, and supported by son and grandson, was making his 56th journey.

Not far from the ambalama, near a bend of the path, a small patch of cleared jungle leads to the ledge of a terrible precipice; where it is said a fair and sprightly girl having carelessly stepped aside, fell over and was dashed to death in the abyss below. Her name was Nilihela, and her fate is

---

Snowdon, the latter after a hard day's walk, which I considered no ordinary achievement; but anything like the ascent from Palábaddala to Diyabetma, I had never before dreamt of. It was a constant succession of the most precipitous hills to be climbed, one after the other, with wearisome uniformity and unvarying difficulty."—History of Ceylon, by W. KNIGHTON, 1845, p. 391.

commemorated by the place being named after her. It is customary accordingly for the pilgrims as they pass to shout out Nílihela-akké! "sister Nílihela!" and in a second a distinct double echo comes back,—a voice they think, from the spirit of the girl, in answer to their call; the fancied answer being 'eññá!'—coming. The elevation here is about 2,700 feet. "The precipice is almost hidden by the vegetation which grows on its face. Looking over it you view a valley of immense depth, all filled with lofty forests, and on the opposite side of the chasm you are fronted by the long lofty precipice visible to us the previous evening from Palúbadalla. Here we had a splendid view of the [8] waterfalls, which now ran full and strong, from the effects of the night's heavy rain. One was a broad deep stream, which leaped at two long bounds into the chasm below, where its roar was deepened by the reverberations reflected from the surrounding walls. Others were thin gauzy films of foam, others long drawn threads of silver, and each had a tone which contributed to the loud deep harmony of the whole." *

" The evening mists, with ceaseless change,
Now clothed the mountains' lofty range,
Now left their foreheads bare,

---

* "To show how these streams depend on the immediate rains, I may here mention, that on visiting the same place the next day, on our return, we saw that nearly all of the falls had disappeared, and the place of the largest one was now only marked by the bare dry rocks over which it roared on the preceding day."

And round tho skirts their mantle furled
Or on the sable waters curled,
Or, on the eddying breezes whirled
   Dispersed in middle air.
And, oft condensed at once they lower,
When, brief and fierce, the mountain shower
   Pours like a torrent down,
And when return the sun's glad beams
Whiten'd with foam a thousand streams
   Leap from the mountain's crown."*

The next object in the ascent to which our attention was drawn was a stone or pebble tumulus, which we at first supposed marked the last resting place of some pilgrim who had died on the road; we were however mistaken in our surmise. It seems it is the practice for each pilgrim to deposit a small stone here, and to pray to Saman-Dewiyó to grant him a renewal of strength and enable him to proceed and finish his pilgrimage. These small mounds are of frequent occurrence further on. A long pointed jutting slab of rock was next pointed out to us, called Uruhoṭa, "the pig's snout." Not very long ago, our informant said, the resemblance between the rock and a hog's snout was remarkable, but from some cause,—probably to facilitate the ascent,—the end had been broken off by some one, and the name is no longer applicable. Beyond this is the site of the Geṭanetul-gala ambalama. This no longer exists, but on a rock below where it stood, is

---

* "The Lord of the Isles." By Sir WALTER SCOTT.

a rough inscription after the opposite fashion;
what the characters meant we could not learn.
The elevation was about 3,100 feet.

Proceeding onwards, the mountain still rises
for five or six hundred feet, when there is a dip, and in a
nearly level hollow, of the length of about a hundred and
eighty yards,—a part of the pilgrims' path in fact,—is the
Kalu-ganga-dówa,* the source of the Kalu-ganga. At this
elevation, 3,500, or 3,600 feet above the sea, we duly halted
at the spring which here welled out its crystal waters, in
order to quench our thirst, and otherwise refresh ourselves.
Near the point where we entered this small dell or ravine,
the dówa, a mere rill of water, runs down a channel to the
southwest. The headman and the natives all agreed in calling this the source of the Kalu-ganga,—its highest, or head
waters. Baba Siñño said he had himself traced its course
down to Gilímalé, and he was therefore quite certain about
it. From this 'dówa' a toilsome half mile of uphill walking
brought us to the top of the well known mountain Diyabetma.

We were now on the summit of the water-shed of this
part of the country. The streams we had hitherto crossed
ran in a south or southwesterly direction; flowing more or
less directly towards the main branch of the Kalu-ganga.
East of Diyabetma, "the division of the waters," they took a
northwesterly course, to be ultimately absorbed by the

---

* 'Dówa,' the source of a river.

Kuru-ganga, as it winds its way through the Kuruwiṭi
Kóralé.   The small plain on the top of the mountain is about
3,800 feet above sea-level. The first object that catches
the eye upon entering this plain on a clear day, is the Peak.
Shouts of reverential salutation are then chorussed by the
pilgrims as the object of their journey thus bursts upon
their sight.   Its appearance reminded us of Milton's description of the eastern gate of Paradise.   True, it was no
"rock of alabaster," yet was it, and the pilgrims' path, and
the shrine, surmounting all

> .   .   .   · "piled up to the clouds
> Conspicuous far, winding with one ascent
> Accessible from earth, one entrance high;
> The rest was craggy cliff, that overhung
> Still as it rose, impossible to climb."

On the south of the plain stands a dilapidated bungalow,
once a good substantial rest-house, built, the Gaṇ-árachchi
told us, for a lady, by Dasanáyaka Nilamé, in the Rajakáriya*
times.   This lády, we understood, was the universally
esteemed wife of the Governor, General Sir Robert Brownrigg.   Our informant seemed to take an interest in the
place, and added that his father was one of those who were
obliged to assist in its construction.   Roofless, doorless, and

---

* A royal or Government service; under which system works were
executed by the compulsory labour of the inhabitants.   This system was
abolished in 1832.

windowless, it is now utterly abandoned, the interior being choked up with rank vegetation.*

* Mr. KNIGHTON, who visited the Peak about 1844, and stayed a night in this building, thus notices it. "The Ambalam at Diyabetma, is a large uncomfortable tiled building, having two rooms surrounded by a kind of walled verandah of peculiarly forbidding aspect. The interior of it, as may be easily imagined, is a damp, close uncomfortable cell, the floor being of earth, and so thoroughly saturated with the heavy dews of the district, that the guide informed me, it was never known to be dry. The ambalam stands in the corner of a small plain, cleared of its brushwood for a short distance round the building . . . The temperature of the place was so refreshing, that I felt comparatively little fatigued by my exertion, whilst the poor coolies who accompanied me, sat upon the damp cold earth the very pictures of misery and chilliness. Two of the number were busily engaged in endeavours to obtain a spark from the flint and steel, in which however they did not succeed; and seeming utterly unconscious of any other way of warming themselves, they huddled together in a corner and lay down to sleep. Having dined upon a little bread and cold bacon, which we had fortunately brought with us, washed down with libations from the brandy flask, I wrapped my blanket round me, and endeavoured to compose myself to rest upon the bamboo platform supported by four rugged sticks, that served me for chair, table, couch and sideboard. This was a vain attempt however; for what with the noise of elephants, cheetahs, monkeys, jungle cats, jungle fowls and crows, it was utterly impossible even to doze, beside the pleasant expectation of having some of the former as visitants (for our mud edifice was without doors) during the long dark night that was approaching. I lay with my walking stick in my hand during that tedious night, listening hour after hour to the roar of the elephants, and the screams of the cheetahs, which were often, to all appearance, within a very short distance of

A descent of about forty feet brought us to Diyabetma Bépata, a rocky streamlet, when we again commenced an ascent, crossing ridge after ridge on our upward route. Between these ran streams, the most remarkable of which is the Idikaṭupáne,* a broad water-course, fifty feet in width, of bare, smooth, slab rock. This name was given to the place because of a legend which asserts that Buddha, on one his visits to Samanala, stayed here awhile to mend his robes; while so occupied, his terrible opponent, the great demon Wasawaṛti-máráyá, first caused the rock to rise to bar his way; finding that to be useless, he then caused a torrent of water to rush down upon the spot where he was seated. Buddha, seeing the flood approaching, merely traced a semicircle before him with the needle he was using, when the waters parted right and left, and the malice of the demon was again defeated. On our second excursion, a sheet of water was rapidly rippling and running down the smooth rocky bed, and close to the place where we crossed, the stream

---

the house. However, 'it is a long lane that has no turning,' and a still longer night that has no end.—morning dawned at last, and the mists which had encircled the mountain on which I stood the whole of the preceding evening, like a vast sea of quiet foam, gradually wore away, and a magnificent view rewarded us for the tedium of the preceding night To the south and west was a long succession of irregular hills, terminated by an extended plain, which appeared fading off in the distance, till terminated by the sea, whilst in the north a high range of hills abruptly ended the prospect."

* The needle rock.

divided in two, one branch running north, and the other northwest, uniting again a little distance lower down. The islet thus formed was pointed out to us as the spot where Buddha sat, and was alleged to be a convincing proof of the truth of the miracle recorded in the legend. The spot is considered sacred by Buddhists, who upon reaching it, ceremoniously bore their ears over a hole near the middle of the river bed. The height above the sea is about 3,900 feet.

A few yards further brought us to the foot of the Dharma-rája-gala,* an all but perpendicular mountain mass, with three flights of in-cut steps to enable pilgrims to surmount it. Counting these, we found 21 at the bottom, 9 a little further on, and 100 leading to the top.† From the morticed holes by the side of the top flight, it is evident stanchions and chains were once intended to be, and probably had been, placed. But there is nothing of the sort there now, and on a gusty day the ascent or descent of this particular spot must be one of some little hazard, if not of actual danger. To the left of the steps, ascending, is cut in outline, on the face of the rock, the figure of a man with his hands joined above

---

* Rock of the righteous king.

† Buddhists believe that these steps cannot be counted. A hundred different people may count them, they say, but their numbers will always differ. A similar belief is held by some people in England, in regard to Stonehenge—the remains of the Druidical temple on Salisbury plain.

his head, pointing towards and in adoration of the still
afar-off Foot-print. Above this figure is an inscription in
Siṇhalese, very much obliterated and weather-worn, but
said to record the death of him, a king, whose figure is
carved below, who there died, and whose name the rock now
bears.

There is a very curious tradition connected with the
mountain range of which the Dharma-rája-gala forms a
portion. It is to the following effect.* To the left of the
Dharma-rája-gala, some distance in the jungle, is a tree,
round the roots of which three serpents are continually twin-
ing; about the distance of five bowshots from this tree is
another, contact with which produces instant death.† Surrounding the place are quantities of the bones of those who
have in this manner met their death. An exploration of the
neighbourhood might lead to interesting results. Possibly
this Golgotha of the hills may be one of those places to
which the elephants retire to die. The whole of the surrounding country is marked by their presence, and we had
seen their spoor and other indications of their presence, all
along the route since we left Palábaddala. "It is certain"
says Sir J. E. Tennent, "that frequenters of the forest,
whether European or Siṇhalese, are consistent in their as-

---

* The tradition is given in full, I am informed, in a native work, an
old and rare ola, but my informant could not recollect the name of the
work.

† This is probably an allusion to the deadly Upas tree.

surances, that they have never found the remains of an elephant that had died a natural death."*

On a fine clear day, the view from the small platform where the steps on the Dharma-rája-gala terminate, is very striking. To the north the towering Kunudiya-parvaté; its square rocky summit like the fracture on a mighty pillar from which, in a convulsion of nature, the capital had been broken off; its western face a steep, tremendous, appalling-looking precipice: there it stands, the frowning tempest-battered warden of that amphitheatre of rock and mountain, caves and waterfalls and rushing streams, and legends, mystery and awe. To the south, of a nearly equal altitude, is the Béna Samanala, with its alleged demon-haunted double summit. Circling round between both lie a multitude of

* " The Singhalese have a further superstition in relation to the close of life in the elephant: they believe that, on feeling the approach of dissolution, he repairs to a solitary valley, and there resigns himself to death. A native who accompanied Mr. Cripps, when hunting, in the forests of Anarajapoora, intimated to him that he was then in the imme-diate vicinity of the spot ' to which the elephants come to die,' but that it was so mysteriously concealed, that although every one believed in its existence, no one had ever succeeded in penetrating to it. At the corral which I have described at Kornegalle, in 1847, Dehigame, one of the Kandyan chiefs, assured me it was the universal belief of his countrymen, that the elephants, when about to die, resorted to a valley in Saffragam, among the mountains to the east of Adam's Peak, which was reached by a narrow pass with walls of rock on either side, and that there, by the side of a lake of clear water, they took their last repose. It was not without interest that I afterwards recognised this tradition in the story of *Sinbad of the Sea*, who in his Seventh Voyage, after conveying the

mountain tops of minor elevation. In front, below, facing
westwards, is a mighty chasm, from whose depths, and from
the valleys between the smaller mountains, rises the ceaseless
roar of the rush of many waters. These were the most
striking features of that wide-spread mountain panorama,
Concerning Kunudiya-parváté, there is the following legend.
Buddha, struck by its singular appearance, at first intended
to leave the impression of his foot on the summit of its
crowning rock. Suspecting this, Wasawarti-márayá placed
there the carcass of a dead rat-snake; whereupon Buddha
turned from the place in disgust, and ever since the waters
from the mountain have run foul and dirty—whence the
name, Kunidiya, "dirty water." The upper part of the
mountain also bears the name of Unudiya, "hot water."

---

presents of Haroun al Raschid to the king of Serendib, is wrecked on his
return from Ceylon, and sold as a slave to a master who employs him in
shooting elephants for the sake of their ivory; till one day the tree on
which he was stationed having been uprooted by one of the herd, he fell
senseless to the ground, and the great elephant approaching wound his
trunk around him and carried him away, ceasing not to proceed until
he had taken him to a place where, his terror having subsided, he
found himself amongst the bones of elephants, and knew that this was
their burial place. It is curious to find this legend of Ceylon in what
has, not inaptly, been described as the 'Arabian Odyssey' of Sinbad;
the original of which evidently embodies the romantic recitals of the
sailors returning from the navigation of the Indian seas, in the middle
ages, which were current amongst the Mussulmans, and are reproduced
in various forms throughout the tales of the Arabian Nights."—Natural
History of Ceylon, by Sir J. E. Tennent, pp. 235—237.

It would be interesting to ascertain whether there is a hot mineral spring here; if so, the name it bears would be much more rationally accounted for, than by the tale Buddhistic lore has handed down to present days.

Respecting Bęna Samanala, the highest of whose summits overhangs its base, and is sometimes called the False Peak, from being visible when intervening mists or clouds hide the Samanta-kuṭa from view, it is alleged that no human being has ever yet succeeded in scaling its topmost height. The name of this is Dęyáguháwa, or cave of the God. Major Forbes states, that once a priest, confident in his sacred character, ascended so far that the light was observed which he had kindled at night beneath this overhanging summit of the haunted mountain, but that next day he returned a confirmed maniac, unable to give any account of what he had seen. He adds, " There is nothing incredible in this story, for the dreaded mountain is apparently easier of ascent than Samanala; and we need not be surprised at the melancholy fate of the priest, if we take into consideration how strongly the mind of a native (nurtured in the belief of demons) would naturally be acted on when alone in an untrodden solitude, haunted by vague terrors of superstition, and the just dread of savage animals."*

An ascent of some fifty feet brings the pilgrim to the crest

---

* In 1857 a company of Buddhist priests resolved to make the attempt. The hearts of some failed when they reached the foot of the mountain, and they went no further. The rest proceeded, and found the ascent

of the ridge of which the Dharma-rája-gala forms a part.
On the other side there is a rapid descent of some hundred
and twenty feet, to the Gangule-héné-ella, midway to which
is the Telihilena, a rocky cave, where tradition says an
ancient king who had forsaken his throno for an ascetic life,
took up his abode.* After crossing the ella, and ascending
about a hundred and seventy feet, a few posts on the top of
the ridge point out the site of a former rest-house, known as
the Gangule-héné ambalama. An elevation of about 4,100
feet is here attained, from which a steep descent of fifty feet
leads to the Hita or Sita-gangula—"the cold water fall,"—
across a portion of which, and carried a short distance up the
precipitous gully from which we had just debouched, was
the first of the chains, which from this point are slung at
intervals to assist the pilgrims in the most difficult parts of
their journey. From the length of this chain, made of stout
half-inch iron, with links a span long, we imagined it might
have originally been slung on the site of the hundred steps,
very likely before, those steps were cut, since after their
formation, the necessity for such aid would, to a considerable
extent, be done away with.

---

by no means difficult; but terror seized them when on or near the top,
and they swooned away. While in this state one believed that he saw
revealed to him a magnificent temple, adorned throughout with gold and
precious gems, and in the interior, resplendent beyond all else, a Srí-páda,
to which that on the Samanala was not in any way to be compared.

  * This is probably the cave referred to by Ibn Batúta, as that of the
king Síbak.

Large irregular masses of rock, filling a span of perhaps two hundred feet in breadth, form the bed through which the river stormily forces itself at the point where it is crossed. The rapid waters seem to rush out of space as they leap from the brow of a high rocky ridge above, and are quickly hurried off down the steep ravine below, which carries them on their way to the Kuruwita Falls, where at their junction with the Kuru-ganga, they bear the name of Dapat-ella. There is a stern grandeur in the scene, the effect of which is heightened by the dark forest banks on either hand, and the high background in the distance, an immense mountain wall, —a sheer bare precipice many hundred feet in depth. The rocks and boulders are piled about one another in strange confusion, and form a number of cavernous dens, which indentifies the spot as that named by Ibn Batúta, the "place of seven caves." When crossed at the dry season, the appearance of these rocks is more likely to attract attention than that of the river itself.

Pilgrims of all classes here make a halt; their special object in doing so being to bathe in the stream, and to put on clean clothes; since any neglect in these matters would nullify all the merit of their pilgrimage. Much worship is also at the same time paid to the dewas or guardian spirits of the rock and stream, and many were the prostrations we saw made by young and old alike; for large numbers were congregated, of both sexes and of all ages, from the babe of a few months old, to the tottering age of seventy, and the ancient dame of even riper years.

A variety of reasons have been assigned for this practice.
Some consider that the name of the stream refers to Síta
the wife of Ráma, who in the course of her captivity was
detained in this part of the country ;* and that it is owing to
her having performed her ablutions in its waters that they
possess the peculiar sanctifying powers attributed to them.
This corresponds with the belief in India, where we know
that the mountain springs in which she bathed, when
she and her brother-in-law accompanied her husband in his
exile, are to this day objects of veneration among the
Hindus.   It is to this fact that Kálidása alludes, in the
opening lines of the Megha Dúta :†—

> " Where Rámagiri's cool dark woods extend
> And those pure streams, where Síta bathed, descend."

Others again believe in the tradition, that somewhere in
the mountains near, Saman possessed a garden, watered by
the sources of the river, which teemed with all precious fruits
and delightful products; while a third party, holding to another tradition, fix at its source either the site of the garden
of Eden, or of a garden cultivated by Adam after his expulsion from Paradise.   Both have their faith confirmed by

---

* The place where Queen Síta was hidden was called Asoka-wane.
The precise site of this place has not been determined.

† The Megha Dúta, or Cloud Messenger, written in Sanskrit about
56 B.C. Translated into English by Professor H. H. WILSON, 2d
edit. 1843.

the alleged fact, that fruits,—king-cocoanuts, oranges, limes, &c.—are occasionally brought down by the stream, the place of whose growth they consider is inaccessible; and moreover believe, that any one venturesome enough to explore it would never return. At any rate, one could almost imagine, that it was from the spot where we stayed awhile to admire the peculiar features of the scenery, and with a knowledge of the traditions last alluded to, that the Bard of Sheffield wrote the following lines, so truthfully does the latter portion describe what we saw on our second visit.

> "There, on Euphrates, in its ancient course
> Three beauteous rivers roll'd their confluent force,
> Whose streams, while man the blissful garden trod
> Adorn'd the earthly Paradise of God;
> But since he fell, within their triple bound,
> Fenced a lone region of forbidden ground.
> Meeting at once where high athwart their bed
> Repulsive rocks a curving barrier spread,
> The embattled floods, by mutual whirlpools crost,
> In hoary foam and surging mist were lost;
> Thence like an Alpine cataract of snow;
> White down the precipice they dash'd below;
> There, in tumultuous billows broken wide,
> They spent their rage, and yoked their four-fold tide,
> Through one majestic channel calm and free
> The sister rivers sought the parent sea."*

---

* "The World before the Flood." The Síta-gangula, the Bapat-ella, and the Kuru-ganga, add their streams to and unite in the Kalu-ganga, before it reaches the sea.

in prose as truthful, my companion wrote, "The bed of
the river is of the wildest character. Overshadowed by
lofty forests, and flanked on each side by towering mountain slopes, the flooded stream roared and blustered, as it
tore its foaming course over and amongst the enormous
angular masses of rock by which its bed is obstructed:" and
if ever the injunction was needed, as regarded mere phy-
sical actions, to "walk circumspectly," we found it to be
so when crossing the Síta-gangula, in the state described.

> "Huge terraces of granite black
>   Afforded rude and cumbrous track;
>   For from the mountain hoar,
>   Hurl'd headlong in some night of fear
>   When yell'd the wolf and fled the deer,
>   Loose crags had toppled o'er;
>   And some chance-poised and balanced lay
>   So that a stripling arm might sway
>   A mass no host could raise,
>   In nature's rage at random thrown
>   Yet trembling like the Druids' stone
>   On its precarious base." *

The bed of the river being passed, we found ourselves at
the base of a shoulder of the Béna Samanala, from which
rose an ascent as steep, as rugged, and as difficult, as any
portion of that up which we had already toiled since leaving
Palábaddala, even if it was not more so.   Again and again

---

* "The Lord of the Isles." By Sir Walter Scott.

we were on the point of succumbing to fatigue, but as often, after a halt of a few seconds, we again strode on—"Excelsior" our cry,—until, after passing the Yakkahattawegala, an immense perpendicular rock frowning above the path on the left of the ascent, we stood on the summit of the ridge, and entered Heramiṭipána, where we purposed resting our wearied limbs. The heat was excessive, and some of us almost vowed never to undertake such a journey again; but six months later the experience of perhaps the most fatigued of the number was as follows:—

From the Síta-gangula to Heramiṭipána, " we had before us a long series of high rough steps of rock, winding up the gorge. But owing to the heavy drenching rain then falling, a mountain torrent was now rushing down, and each step was a small waterfall. Consequently, in forcing our way up this gorge, we had to plunge through a shower bath at every step. Not that we cared for the wetting. In fact we were always wet. It would be hard to say which would be most wetted by the contact—we or the torrent. Dry clothes we had long looked upon with scorn, as tokens of effeminacy and luxury. But even disregarding the wet, it was not very easy to make head against that water. However we at last reached the top, where we took possession of the bungalow buildings of Heramiṭipána."*

---

* On this journey, and on the subsequent one as well, from the time of our leaving Ratnapura, it rained more or less the greater part of every day. After once getting drenched, our plan was to strip off our wet clothes

It was past mid-day when we reached this spot on our first
excursion, and we had not accomplished more than about
eight and a half miles in more than six hours, and there were
yet perhaps two and a half to be traversed ere we "the sacred
impress of the lotus foot could see," in its temple-shrine at
the top of the Samanala, which stood full before us in all the
sublimity of its majestic height and size.   To attempt to
go further was out of the question, and besides, our coolies
with commissariat supplies had not yet come up, and we
were hungry as well as weary.

The station, built in the shape of a quadrangle, 70 feet
by 30, in its inner square, was filled to overflowing, and as
we could obtain no room under any sheltering roof, we were
fain to do as hundreds of others were doing, and bivouac
in the open, with umbrellas to screen our heads from the
sun's burning rays—the intensity of which was little less
than in Colombo, although we were now 4,350 feet or more
above the level of the sea.   Casting ourselves down on mats
courteously spread for us, we watched the animated scene

---

at each halting place, and wring them as dry as we could, and while we
rested or stayed, to enjoy the comforts of warm dry suits, which with
our rugs, were carefully packed in a large water-proof wrapper.   When
we proceeded, we again got into our damp suits, but the active exertions
which immediately followed, prevented any inconvenient or evil results.
The chief difference in our two journeys was, that in September we had
much mist and little sunshine with the rain; in December we had more
sunshine and scarcely any mist.

around. Huge copper and brass and iron caldrons were
seething their contents over dozens of fires inside and outside the bungalows on each side of the quadrangle; thousands
of natives were busy eating, or arranging themselves in
their best for the final ascent; companies were continually
coming and going; singing or chanting on their way stanzas
of the Samanala-hella;* the noise of the tam-tam and doula
and horanęwa was incessant, and ever and anon arose the cry
of "Sádhu! Sádhu!"—the shout of many voices saluting the
sacred shrine above, the outline of which was perfectly
distinct, as also was that of the long and many-coloured string
of natives, winding up and down the mountain side, eager to
attain the end of their journey, or as eager to return, now
the great object of their pilgrimage had been attained. We
had not lain long however, before we attracted the notice
of a kind motherly looking Sinhalese lady, who sent each of

---

* The Samanala-hella is one of the popular ballads of the Sinhalese,
having about as much poetry in its composition, in the estimation of
educated natives, as the street songs of London, the productions of the
bards of the Seven-Dials, have in comparison with the songs and ballads
of the classic poets of England. But for all that they catch the attention,
and are rivetted in the memories of those for whom they are specially
written. The Samanala-hella consists of forty-eight four-line stanzas,
each of which contains a recitation of an attribute of Buddha, or of an
incident connected with his visit to the Samanala, or an allusion to Saman,
or the features of the country, the usual occurrences on the journey, &c.,
and concludes with the determination of the singer to worship the 'Sirí-
pa Samanala'—the sacred foot of Samanala.

us a brimming bowl of hot rice conjee, boiled in cocoa-nut milk, a dish we found by no means unpalatable, and certainly very refreshing in its immediate effects. For this she would accept nothing more than thanks; and we subsequently ascertained that the whole of the accommodation of the place as well as the food distributed, was given gratis by a Headman of the District;—a very meritorious and charitable act on his part, which we, with all the other pilgrims there assembled, most gratefully accepted.

By the time our servants had arrived, (and it was a marvel to us how they came at all with such heavy loads upon their heads) an exodus of a part of the pilgrims had taken place, and we took possession of the quarters they vacated, a space in a cock-loft of loose planks immediately below the tiles of the principal ambalama or bungalow. This ambalama (a building about 60 ft. by 30, with lean-to's at each end), is unwalled on three of its sides; the roof is supported by six rows of pillars, on the four inner rows of which is laid the planking that forms the upstairs apartment; a clear open space of about five feet all round this planking, enables those above to see nearly every thing that is going on below; the staircase leading to the cock-loft is the notched trunk of a 'tree. Here we spread our rugs and lay down awhile to rest, some fifty of our dusky coloured brethren sharing the apartment with us. Breakfast, tiffin, dinner, or whatever the meal might be called, was ere long served, our boxes doing duty for tables, and our rugs for chairs; and however rude the accessories might be, the viands were good, and the cooking excellent; the only drawback to our enjoyment being the discovery that we had exhausted our stock of beer and brandy; we had however ample supplies of tea and coffee, and except that they took longer in getting ready, they were perhaps quite as good, if not better, than the more ardent beverages. Refreshed by rest and the meal we had partaken of, we amused ourselves, for the remainder of the day, in watching the proceedings of our fellow pilgrims,—who appeared to be equally as much amused with ours,—and in admiring the grandeur of the surrounding scenery; the most attractive feature in which was the Samanala mountain, broad and huge and high, from the centre of whose long stretching ridge rose what here presented the appearance of a bell-shaped conic mass, the venerated shrine-capped Peak, to visit which we had joined the pilgrim throng.

> "There stood in that romantic clime
> [The] mountain awfully sublime;
> O'er many a league the basement spread,
> It tower'd [oe'r] many an airy head . . .
> Pure in mid-heaven that [worshipp'd] cone
> A diadem of glory shone;
> Reflecting in the night-fall'n sky
> The beams of day's departed eye;
> Or holding, ere the day begun,
> Communion with the unrisen sun." *

---

* "The Reign of Summer." By JAMES MONTGOMERY.

The sunset was magnificent, though our horizon to the
west was bounded by the tops of the hills we had just surmounted, but the wooded slopes and the high towering cone
of the Samanala, as well as the rugged precipitous sides of
Kunudiya-parvaté, were aglow with brightest tints of green
and purple, brown and red; and no sooner had "he of the
thousand rays" sunk beneath the bounding sea-line of the
west, than the temple above us was lighted up, and looked,
as it was, a mighty Pharos in the blue serene. As the
shades of evening rapidly advanced, suddenly "the silver
moon in splendour shone," rising just above and eclipsing
with its brilliant glory the lamp-lit temple that had just
attracted our attention; then sparkling up and down and
zigzagging on the mountain's side, came the flaring torches
of parties of ascending and descending pilgrims: while
light, fleecy clouds gathered round the "shining monarch of
the night "* to be wondrously illumined by the lustre of his
rays; and in the concave vault above, now thick besprent
with flashing stars,

> " Unnumber'd orbs of living fire appear
> And roll in glittering grandeur o'er the sphere."

Altogether, the beauty of the night excelled anything that
any of our party had ever either witnessed or imagined.

---

* The moon in oriental poetry is always spoken of in the masculine
gender, while night is personified as a female.

But soon the mists from the valleys crept up the mountains' sides, and gradually veiled from our eyes the enchanting scenes upon which they had been gazing.

> . . . . "Sweetly sail
> The twilight shadows o'er the darkening scene,
> Earth, air, and ocean, all alike serene.
> Dipt in the hues of sunset, wreathed in zones,
> The clouds are resting on their mountain thrones;
> One peak alone exalts its [cone-like] crest
> A golden paradise above the rest;
> Thither the day, with lingering steps, retires,
> And in its own blue element expires."*

Feelings well nigh akin to awe had by imperceptible degrees stolen upon our souls while contemplating the sublimities of nature above and around, and in this mood it was that we sought in our respective resting places, "tired nature's sweet restorer, balmy sleep."

But when we wrapped our rugs round us and lay down in our quarters, the wish was father to the thought, that

> Somnus soon would o'er us steal,
> Our eyelids in soft slumbers seal,

for while the noise continuously kept on, the smoke from the greenwood fires underneath us ascended through the chinks between, and clung about the planks along which we were stretched; and its obnoxious pungency, mixed with the

---

* "Greenland." By James Montgomery.

other mal-odours that arose from the densely stowed throngs
below, and the utter neglect of sanitary measures around,
gave grievous offence to the eyes and nostrils.   Looked at
from our platform, the natives on the ground below were
literally packed together as close as herrings in a barrel;
and we certainly felt that, where we were quartered, we were
undergoing the process of being cured like flitches of bacon.
Despite every drawback, exhausted nature at last fell under
the influences of the drowsy god, and we had enjoyed a tolerably sound two hours' rest, when the arrival of a fresh
party, either coming or going, produced such a hubbub and
commotion in the place that we were thoroughly roused.

Such rest and accommodation were, however with all their
drawbacks, infinitely to be preferred to our subsequent experiences.   On our September journey "when we stopped at
the top, we soon began to discover that we had arrived at a
far cooler climate than that we had left at the bottom of the
mountain.   A thermometer we had with us indicated 64° and
afterwards went down to 59°.   The bungalow was streaming
wet ; the roof leaked at every joint ; it seemed considerably
wetter inside than out ;" the planks forming the floor of the
central loft dripped heavily, and every drip was like liquid
soot; "and a green damp growth that coated the walls and
the sodden floor did not tend to make the place look any more
comfortable.   Outside, a cold penetrating mist was driving
past, and enveloped every thing, altogether obscuring the
prospect.   Certainly not a nice place to spend a night in.
We thought that on the whole we might indulge ourselves

in the luxury of dry clothes, but had to wait almost an hour
for the portmanteau to arrive in which they were packed.
We spent the time in walking up and down, and laughing
at the decidedly unhappy look of the coolies. Poor beggars,
they felt the cold very much. Their attire was not calculated for such a climate. There we had an advantage over
them, and they would no doubt gladly have exchanged the
primitive simplicity of their rig for the trousers of civilisation.
We told them to light up some fires, and they made some
attempts, but these natives do not appear to possess the fire-
making instinct, and some of their trials were very unsuccess-
ful. However they at last succeeded in filling the place with
damp and smoke, which had the most pungent action on the
eyes and nostrils. If they could not extract heat from the
wet wood, they seemed pretty satisfied to get smoke, and
began to look somewhat more contented. The couches
which we had that night would not have satisfied a Sybarite.
Our accommodation altogether was rather defective. The
mist drove right through the building, and the only advantage we possessed by being inside instead of out, was that
we were nearly stifled and blinded by the smoke." We lay
on some damp rough planks placed on the muddy floor, over
which we spread our water-proofs and rugs; and although
sleep visited the eyelids of some, the rest were thankful
enough when the dreary night had passed. For—

> "Loud the gusty night wind blew,
> Many an awful pause between . . . .

And the moon's bewilder'd bark
By the midnight tempest tost,
In a sea of vapours dark
In a gulf of clouds was lost."*

In December, the bungalow was dry; although rain fell
heavily during the night; but there was no dense driving
mist, or gusty squalls, and that was about all that could be
said in its favour.

* "The Wanderer of Switzerland." By JAMES MONTGOMERY.

Adam's Peak.

" Emerging from the cavern'd glen
. From steep to steep I slowly climb,
   And far above the haunts of men,
   I tread in air sublime ;
   Beneath my path the swallows swoop,
   Yet higher crags impend,
   And wild flowers from the fissures peep,
   And rills descend.
   Now on the ridges bare and bleak,
   Cool round my temples sighs the gale ;
   Ye winds ! that wander o'er the Peak,
   Ye mountain spirits I hail !" *

CHAPTER VII.

Heramitipa'na. — Ascent of the Peak. — Aandiya-mala-tenna. — Menik - lena. — Ehela-kanuwa. — Maha-giri-dan-kapalla. — Shrine of Saman Dewiyo'. — The Sri'-Pa'da. — The Ranhili-ge'. — The Kudamita. — Scenery of the Skies. — Sunrise. — The Shadow. — The View.

The moon was still high in the heavens when we woke on the night of our first visit, and shining with unusual brilliancy (or so it seemed to us in the pure atmosphere of

---

* "The Peak Mountains." By James Montgomery.

so unusual a height); and bright was the sheen of the many stars of magnitude whose rays the larger orb paled not in stellar space. Scarcely a cloud was visible; and feeling invigorated by our short rest, we resolved forthwith to resume our journey.

> "With strengthened confidence, the march began. . . .
> A vista-path, that through the forest led,
> The pilgrims track'd, till on the mountain's height
> They met the sun, new-risen, in glorious light;
> Empurpled mists along the landscape roll'd,
> And all the orient flamed with clouds of gold." *

Heramitipána which signifies "the rock of staves," or "the lamp of walking sticks," was, we were also told, "the place for the lighting of the torches;"† and we, who had been wondering what the narrow eighteen-inch or two-foot rolls were, which we had noticed most of the pilgrims carried with them, now saw that they were torches,—tubes filled

---

* "The World before the Flood."

† A friend who made the ascent some five and twenty years ago, informs me, that iron rods, to be used as walking sticks, used to be sold to the pilgrims at this station, at the rate of a rix-dollar, or 1s. 6d., each: and that on the arrival of the pilgrims at the foot-print, they made offerings of these sticks to the Srí-páda. When as many as fifty were thus collected, they were sent back to Heramitipána, by an agent of the priest, to be re-sold; and this would happen three or four times a day, or even more frequently, according to circumstances. The revenue from such a source must have been pretty profitable, as long as it lasted.

with a resinous substance,—here first brought into use, and giving out a strong flaring blaze when lighted. Speedily providing ourselves with a supply of these, and leaving our heavy baggage in charge of a kangani,* we set out accompanied by our interpreter, and a few servants to carry up our overcoats and rugs, which, for this part of the journey, they rolled up and slung upon their backs.

A small valley with a steep dip, but not more than fifty feet below Hęramiţipána, separates the Samanala from the mountain of the False Peak, or that ridge of it from which we were descending. The first portion of the opposite ascent is through several gullies seven or eight feet in depth, and extremely narrow, cut through the soil at the base of the mountain by the torrents which pour down in the rainy season; these alternate with steep rocks on whose faces broad iron ladders are clamped, or with angular boulders, up and over which the traveller must scramble the best way he can. The ascent, nearly the whole of which lies through a densely wooded forest, may be divided into four parts, —1, the face of the mountain, as steep as anything we had yet surmounted;—2, the shoulder, somewhat easier travelling ;—3, the cone, the Akasagauwa, or "sky league," an awful steep climb ;—and 4, the Peak, an all but absolute precipice.

As we wended on our way, taking great heed to our steps, especially when a descending party seemed to block

---

* A responsible head coolie.

the path, we were much struck by a peculiar and incessant clacking sound which came from the woods on either side; and we arrived at the conclusion that it was produced by swarms of some insect or other, just as the "knife" or "scissor-grinder"—the Cicada—fills the air in the lowlands with its shrill ear-piercing notes. Very weird-like was our procession, as the torches flashed down their light into the gullies, or glinted on the cliffs which frowned above and about us; and nervous was the clutch with which we held on to the chains that helped us up some ugsome rock, with steps cut here and there in its adamantine face; or gripped the ladder whose sloping irons gave but a slippery hold to the soles of our boots, admirably adapted although those irons were to the naked feet of the natives, whose toes are trained to all the uses of fingers, as far as mere holding is concerned. Thus on and on we went, until we arrived at a mound which we were told by our guide was the grave of the first man who made a pilgrimage to the Srí-páda, and who became a Saint in consequence; but he was not able to inform us whether the party canonized was a Buddhist, a Hindu, or a Moham-madan.* It is more than probable that the mound is the

---

* Capt. PRIDHAM writes, (p. 614 of his work on Ceylon), "On the summit of the continued ridge, called Aandiyamalle-tenne, is the grave of an Aandiya or mendicant priest, now a Mahommedan saint, who closed his pilgrimage, doubtless to his great content, so near the place at which the father of mankind and the first of Mahommedan prophets, had, in his belief, been compelled, *stans pede in uno*, to perform so long and uncomfortable a penance. After his body had lain for three months on this

place of interment of one of the last named religionists, who
are somewhat apt to revere us saints such notabilities of their
faith as happen to die whilst on their journey, when led to
undertake a pilgrimage. Immediately after, we entered
Aandiya-mala-tenne, "the plain where the Aandiya died,"
a small plateau where once stood a two-roomed bungalow,
now only a ruinous mound. This place no doubt obtained
its name from the fakeers whom Rája Sinha the Apostate
made custodians of the Peak. Here we made a short halt,—
adding one more group to the many already there, the whole
forming a picture such as Salvator Rosa would have been
delighted to transfer to canvass,—all pausing at its immediate
foot

> . . . . . "to view that towering Peak
> That eastwards rears his regal brow
> And shadows half the vale below :
> One moment basking in the blaze
> His majesty of form displays
> Then with a robe of splendid clouds
> His giant bulk again enshrouds.
> With filial awe the Indians still
> View that mysterious holy hill.

spot, resisting the most inveterate causes of decomposition, it was discovered by a hermit from the wilds below, who had undertaken, as an
additional penance, the task of reaching the Peak, through trackless
deserts, thorns, rocks, under caverns, and over barriers of every kind,
where man had never trod before; and he it was who came upon the
dead body, and performed the last office of humanity over the sainted
dead."

> With them thrice hallow'd is the sod
> That Buddha's sainted footstep trod,
> Their priest, their prophet, and their god !
> Upon the mountain's rocky crest,
> The sacred mark yet lies imprest,
> Hence every rank, and sex, and age,
> Perform the pious pilgrimage
> And yearly flock from far and wide
> To climb the dark rock's rugged side,
> Defying danger, want and toil,
> To worship on that sacred soil."*

Again bracing ourselves to the task before us, we set out, and cold as the night was in those upper regions of the air, we were all soon in a streaming perspiration from the violence of our exertions in surmounting the difficulties of the path, which consisted of nothing but a series of chains, ladders and rocks, and rocks, ladders and chains, until all but breathless we reached what may be termed the neck of the Peak itself. In this part of the ascent one comes every now and again to the edge of a precipitous cliff, from whence a magnificent view is obtained of the country below. At first, the suddenness of the opening, as it were on to space, the extent of the prospect, and the height one is conscious of having attained, is apt to produce a sensation of giddiness ; which a few moments in general suffices to dispel. When about forty yards from the neck of the Peak, a divergence

---

* "The Wanderer in Ceylon." By Captain T. A. ANDERSON.

from the upward path for about the same distance, leads to a rocky cave called Menik-lena, where it is supposed gems of great value may be found.* The top of this so-called cave is a large projecting horizontal slab of rock, in size about 20 feet by 10, of considerable thickness, and about eight feet high from the ground. When seated underneath this, should the possibility of its falling in occur to the mind, a feeling of nervousness may result, which it is as well, at once, resolutely to shake off.

In the neck of the Peak, a temporary shed of bambu and thatch had been put up. This we found crammed choke-full of pilgrims who had preceded us, either going or returning, the latter halting for a short breathing space before attempting the final and most trying part of the pilgrimage. Here once stood the Ehela-kauuwa, or post of the Ehela tree, where the pilgrims were accustomed to register vows, marking them with chunam† on the post, before they made the final ascent. As this post is no longer there, it having either fallen, or been thrown over the precipice, they now content themselves with marking a piece of rock which has been substituted for it.‡

---

* The name Menik-lena, signifies "the cave of gems."

† Chunam, a fine kind of shell-lime, eaten with betel leaf and arekanut, as a masticatory.

‡ A story goes among the natives, that some seventy or eighty years ago, one of the Ilangakkon Mudaliyars of Matára, went on pilgrimage to the Srí-páda, and proceeded as far as the Ehela-kanuwa, when looking up the perpendicular ascent he was struck with fear, and would go no

Passing out from this, we at once came to the Maha-giri-dam-[or dan]-kapala,—" the great-rock-chain-narrow-pass"—a ledge with a scant foot-hold and a jutting corner, then a small bare sloping slab, and then the chains, and the ladder, which more than all else affect and test the pilgrims' nerves. This constitutes the final ascent, and is divided into five portions; the sloping slab just mentioned; lengths of chains to assist one up a well nigh perpendicular flight of sixty steps cut in the living rock; another sloping slab of rock, with here and there a few built-up stones; a further flight of forty in-cut steps, still steeper than the last; and a third slab rock immediately outside the wall that encloses the Srí-páda. On either side of the steps several lengths of chains, ten on one side, and the same number on the other, each from six to eight fathoms long, and formed of various large oblong and triangular fashioned links, hang clustering down flat against the side of the nearly vertical cliffs; and by their aid, and, on the topmost flight, the additional assistance of a chain on stanchions forming a low iron balustrade, all are bound to drag themselves up or let themselves down the precipitous wall of rock that forms the pathway to the pilgrims' goal above. Those who prefer it,

---

further, but returned, cursing Buddha in the most reproachful manner, for being so cruelly unkind as to place his foot-print on so dangerous a place; remarking at the same time, how much better it would have been had he left the impression of his foot on a stone at the field of Batugedara, the village next to Ratnapura, on the opposite bank of the Kalu-gagga.

may indeed, at one spot, take a slightly different but more awfully perilous route, up a broad iron ladder close by, fixed neither straight on, nor at an angle in front of, but at a slant falling to the right, sideways from the rock; the slightest slip from which will hurl the pilgrim to destruction in the abyss below. And up this ladder one of our party actually made the ascent. I did not see him, being in the rear, and too busy on my own account to pay much attention to the proceedings of others; but when I saw the ladder, its bang to one side made me shudder, and I gladly turned to the chains. When about half way up the final flight, down came a company of returning pilgrims. To proceed onwards was impossible, and to recede I dare not; so clutching firm hold of the chains with both hands, with the toes of one foot hitched on to a step, and those of the other pressing against the bare vertical rock, I swung aside until all had passed, and then swarmed up with an alacrity which made me wonder at myself. Arrived at the top, I was heartily congratulated by my companions as I entered the opening in the southern angle of the wall which surrounds the platform, from the midst of which springs the mass of gneiss and hornblende that bears on its top the far-famed impress—the "SRI'-PA'DA"— to behold which we had thus far toiled and won our way.

We now had time to look about us and mark the novelty of the scene. The platform or terrace round the central rock is enclosed by an irregular hexagonal wall, five feet high, and about seventy feet in length from the north-eastern to the southeastern angle, by forty-five feet across

at its greatest breadth.   Gigantic rhododendrons overhang
the wall on the eastern side of the Peak.   Their bending
trunks seem, to the Buddhist mind, to bow to the foot-print;
and to offer, in homage and adoration, their wealth of crowning crimson flowers to the pedal impress of the founder of
their faith.   The area within the walls, as well as the central
rock itself, was crowded with devotees.   Numerous streamers,
and flags of quaint and strange device, flaunted in the breeze,
suspended from the chains which serve as stays to support
and protect the temple roof against the violence of the monsoon winds; and many additional ones were hung on ropes
temporarily rove here and there.   On a jutting point of rock,
a few paces from the entrance gap in the wall, was a shrine
three feet in height, dedicated to Saman Dewiyó, the tutelary
deity of the district, at whose request Buddha came hither
and stamped his foot-print on the pinnacle immediately above;
and thither every pilgrim rushed to fall prostrate in adoration, as soon as he or she had gained the level of the terrace,
as well as to deposit certain offerings brought with them for
the occasion.

Behind, and a little above this shrine, is the Kudamita,
a large iron stanchion let into a crevice in the rock, on
which, in former times it was customary, during the pilgrim
season, to fix the silver-handled umbrella which is now kept
at the Saman Déwálé in Ratnapura.

Standards, supporting from a series of spreading iron
branches circle above circle of big tin lamps, each threw
their cumulated glare in front of the shrine, and of the steps

which led to the foot-print; and these were constantly being fed with oil, and grease, and incense, the fumes of which filled the air with a heavy and almost sickening odour. Before these standards, tam-tams and doulas, and horénawas were beaten and blown without pause; and a more demoniacal-looking personage than one of the leading horénawn players we never saw. One of his eyes protruded from disease; his whole face was pitted and seamed with scars from small-pox, and his cheeks were puffed out like bladders blown to almost bursting tension. If, as an ancient writer* has declared, the foot-print is that of none of those to whom it is usually attributed, but Satan's own, then in sober truth the Arch-fiend could not have chosen a worse or more truculent-looking piper to render due musical honors to his mundane mark.

Just below the temple, two large bells are suspended together, between short heavy beams. One of these is cracked, but the other was continually being rung by pilgrims, who thereby intimated the number of their ascents, as well as proclaimed their purity; the legend being that the bell refuses to sound if attempted to be rung by an unclean person. Ten rough blocks of stone lead up to a kind of altar-table of wood, fixed outside the temple, in front of, but a little below, the toes of the foot-print, on which are placed what may perhaps be termed the honorary

---

* Moses of Chorene, who, in his History of Armenia, and Epitome of Geography, writes concerning it, " ibidem Satanæ lapsum narrant."

offerings of the pilgrims. These are chiefly floral, and at the time of our visit consisted almost entirely of the unbroken or just-burst flower spathes of the areka palm. Above and overlooking all, was the pagoda-shaped Swiss-cottage-looking shrine that screened the hollow in the rock, —the so-called Sacred Foot-print,—worshipped alike by Buddhists, Hindus, and Mohammadans, as the impress there left of the foot of Buddha, Sivá, or the Father of Mankind.

The Srí-páda rock, the Samanta-kúta, the pinnacle or apex of the Samanala, is of an irregular pyramidal form, very considerably steeper to the south and west, than to the north and east. Its base is about a hundred and twenty feet in circumference, its greatest length being about forty, and its breadth about thirty feet. We estimated its height to be ten feet above the level of the surrounding terrace or platform. The Raphili-gé,* or temple, is a small quadrangular build-ing, twelve feet by ten, and is, in fact, nothing more than a tiled canopy supported on pillars, between each of which is a small balustrade,—balustrades and pillars alike shewing signs of age and the effects of the weather;† and neither the one nor the other at all improved by being carved all over with the names and initials of visitors and pilgrims. The roof was ceiled with white cloth, and similar cloths were

---

* " The golden covered house."

† This is about to be taken down and a new one put up in its place. It is understood that the old one will be preserved in the grounds of the Assistant Government Agent's house at Ratnapura.

stretched between some of the pillars. The entrance to the interior is on the north-west, and close to this is a great iron bowl, two feet in diameter, which is kept filled with water from the well below. The indentation of the foot-print is to the west of the centre of the interior. The heel is much higher than the toes, and the artificiality of the whole is palpable. A thick raised edging of cement marks the rude outline of a foot, five feet seven inches long, and two feet seven inches broad at the point where the heel begins to curve. The interstices between the toes are also formed of cement, and the whole of the markings of the foot every now and again need repair.* The inner portion of the heel and instep are the only parts that are clearly natural rock. But as there are none so blind as those who will not see, the marks of the artificer's hands are invisible to the thousands who come to worship the venerated relic, which is just about the size of the foot of the colossal images they adore in their principal vihāras. A white cloth concealed the Srí-páda from view, except when the pilgrims were about to present offerings in the shape of money or valuables. These they were allowed to deposit in the foot-print itself, from which however they were at once carefully swept out by the attendant unanse.

---

* This edging of cement, as well as the artificial markings between the toes, is perhaps rendered necessary, in order to make the foot-print correspond with the description given of it in the Samanta-kúṭa-wannaná, where it is said to be as clear and well defined "as a royal seal is, impressed on wax."

After due prostrations and the repetition of the prescribed Buddhist formulas, the priest bestowed his benediction, and the devotees joyfully withdrew to make room for others ; when, returning to the terrace, they collected around small fires, into family groups, while they rested to recruit from their fatigues, previous to attempting the homeward descent ;* for

---

* Dr. DAVY thus describes a scene he witnessed on one of these occasions:—"The party of pilgrims that had just arrived consisted of several men and women, all native Singhalese of the interior, neatly dressed in clean clothes. They immediately proceeded to their devotions. A priest, in his yellow robes, stood on the rock close to the impression of the foot, with his face to the people, who had ranged themselves in a row below ; some on their knees, with their hands uplifted, and joined palm to palm, and others bending forwards, with their hands in the same attitude of devotion. The priest, in a loud clear voice, sentence by sentence, recited the articles of their religious faith, and duties ; and, in response, they repeated the same after him. When he had finished, they raised a loud shout ; and, he retiring, they went through the same ceremony by themselves, with one of their party for their leader.

"An interesting scene followed this: wives affectionately and respectfully saluted their husbands, and children their parents, and friends one another. An old grey-headed woman first made her salams to a really venerable old man ; she was moved to tears, and almost kissed his feet: he affectionately raised her up. Several middle aged men then salamed the patriarchal pair ; these men were salamed by still younger men, who had first paid their respects to the old people ; and lastly, those nearly of the same standing slightly salamed each other, and exchanged betel-leaves. The intention of these salutations I was informed, was of a moral kind,—to confirm the ties of kindred,—to strengthen family love and friendship, and remove animosities."—Account of the Interior of Ceylon, p. 345.

although the moon-lit night seems to be the favourite time for making the ascent, few or none care to sleep till day-break on the Peak, the belief being that only priests and Europeans can do so with impunity.

It was pointed out to an attendant priest by a visitor some years ago, that as there is a hollow under the instep of a man's foot, so there should be a corresponding height in any impression made by that member of the body upon any yielding non-elastic substance; and that in a foot sixty-seven inches long, there should be a proportionate rise in the centre of the foot-mark, which is not the case in the Srí-páda. The priest admitted that ordinarily it should be so; but that the ascent to the top of the Samanala was in places over soft and sticky soil, and that the hollow of Buddha's foot had been clogged with mud or clay as he came up, so that such a rise could not be shewn when the yielding rock was moulded by the pedal pressure of the All-supreme. The answer was by no means bad, as an off-hand reply to the objection of an unbeliever. But the priest either forgot the declarations in sacred olas about Buddha's power of passing through the air whenever he pleased, or of his mode of pro-gression when moving ordinarily from place to place; or he may have presumed upon the ignorance in regard to such subjects of the individual he was speaking to. Now, according to Buddhistic legends, the manner in which the Great Teacher walked, excited universal admiration.* If

---

* HARDY's Manual of Buddhism, p. 366.

there were thorns, rocks, or other obstructions, they removed
themselves spontaneously; if there was mud it dried up; if
holes they disappeared; if elevations 'they melted away like
butter that sees fire; and the air was filled with choice and
delicate perfumes.　If he passed any body in pain, the pain,
however intense, ceased in an instant: and when his foot
touched the ground, a lotus sprang up at every step!　His
foot came to the ground as lightly as cotton wool!　He
could walk in a space not larger than a mustard seed; and
yet with as much ease as a man may cross his door-step, he
on one occasion placed his foot on the earth, then on the
rock Yugandhara, then on the top of Meru!　Of the height
of Meru an idea is to be gathered from the statement, that
a pebble would take four months to drop from the top to
the base!

The Kusa Jataka* describes the way Buddha walked as
follows:—

> "At once from off the couch he rose
> And on the earth that did, well-pleased, his happy advent greet,
> He sought in majesty to place his ever-sacred feet!
> Ere he, the Lord Supreme, who is with every merit graced,
> His shining feet upon the ground majestically placed,
> To bear that ever-sacred twain ere they on earth had trod,
> A seven-budded lotus burst all blooming from the sod! "†

---

* K. J., stanzas 56, 57.

† The *Kusa Jataka* was written A.D. 1610, by ALIGIAWANA MOHOTTALA,
an author who occupies in Sighalese literature the position held by Pope
in that of England.　It is a poem of 687 four-line stanzas, descriptive

THE SAMANTA-KUTA AND THE SHRINE OF THE SRI-PADA.

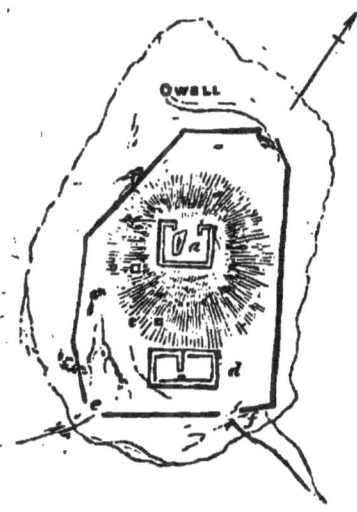

GROUND PLAN OF THE ABOVE.

Thinking over the strange incongruities of the scene before us, we ensconced ourselves in a sheltering angle at a corner of the terrace wall, not far from the small hut occupied by the resident priests, one side of which rests on the base of the terminal rock of the Samanala; and glad of our over-coats, and the thick rugs with which we were provided as a protection against the cold, we endeavoured to compose ourselves to rest, if not to sleep.*

---

of one of the existences of Buddha previous to his final birth and assumption of the Buddha-hood; and in the opinion of competent judges "the unity of its plan, the steady progress of the narrative, and a certain unaffected display of genuine feeling in its principal characters, entitle it to rank as a poem of the highest merit." A brief account of the author and his writings is given in pages ccvii.—ccxi. of the Introduction to the Sidat Sangaráwa, by JAMES D'ALWIS, Esq., Advocate of the Supreme Court, Ceylon, whose untiring researches and manifold writings on the language, literature, history and religion of the Sinhalese, have won for him a reputation among Occidental scholars that has never before been attained by any of his countrymen, and placed him in a foremost rank amongst the highly distinguished Orientalists of the present day. An elegant English metrical translation of the *Kusa Jataka* was published in the *Ceylon Observer*, in the year 1865. It is understood to have been from the pen of T. STEELE, Esq., of the Ceylon Civil Service; and it is hoped that ere long it may appear in a more permanent form, with the author's latest touches to add to its value. To the kindness of this gentleman I am indebted for the extract in the text.

* In the accompanying sketch of the ground plan of the Samanta-kúṭa, *a*, is the Raṇhili-gé, or temple; *b*, the bells; *c*, the shrine of Samán-dewiyó; *d*, the priests' house; *e*, the entrance from Ratnapura; and *f*, the entrance from the Kandian Districts.

But our interpreter and servants were not so well screened
from the cold as we were, and it was not long before they
sought out and obtained permission for us to occupy a
two-roomed house on the southeastern slope of the mountain,
to which we descended by some rough steps, which terminate
the road to the Peak from the Kandian Districts—a route so
comparatively easy, that a man may almost ride to the door
of the building we now took possession of.* Here we found
a Police Constable, and a Priest; the latter attached to the
temple, and the former placed on duty to represent the
majesty of the law, and to protect the offerings made to the
Srí-páda from the depredations of a litigant party, who claim
them on behalf of a former chief-priest. This priest it seems
had been deposed from office, and another elected in his
stead; but the deposed, although he had vacated the office
and allowed his successor to take possession, had been persuaded to dispute the validity of his deposal; and in the

---

* It was up this road that, in 1814, Molligoddé, the newly appointed
first Adikar and Disáwa of Sabaragamuwa, entered the Province, when
Eheylapola his predecessor, rebelled against the last king of Kandy.
Upon receiving the order to suppress the rebellion, Dr. DAVY says
"Molligoddé obeyed with alacrity; he entered Saffragam over the loftiest
point of the island, and the most difficult pass—the summit of Adam's
Peak. The hearts of the natives failed them on his approach; and he
met with but little opposition. Eheylapola, with some of his adherents,
fled to Colombo, and Molligoddé returned to Kandy with a crowd of
prisoners, forty-seven of whom were impaled."—Account of the Interior
of Ceylon, p. 321.

previous season, he, or his supporters, had made a foray upon the temple, and succeeded in carrying away the offerings, which are, in the aggregate, of considerable value. To prevent a similar procedure this season, the law had been appealed to, and by order of the District Judge, the value of all the offerings must be paid into Court, until the right to them of one or other of the claimants has been legally decided.*

Notwithstanding all our wraps and rugs, the cold was so intense that we shivered again, and our teeth rattled together like castanets: so that we joyfully welcomed the appearance of a fire, and watched with an unwonted interest the preparations made for boiling a caldron of rice conjee. Priest, policeman, pilgrims, interpreter, coolies, and all connected with our party, crowded into the small rooms, whose bare mud walls and low roof reminded one of an Irish cabin; a resemblance heightened in its effect by the crooning way in which, with coat collars turned up about our ears, and rugs drawn over our heads, we huddled together over the difficult-to-be-kindled and slow-burning embers, and stoically endured the eye-smarting, sneeze-exciting, larynx-irritating, cough-causing smoke they emitted, for the sake of the warmth which gradually began to temper the biting keenness of the surrounding atmosphere.

---

* Through the obliging courtesy of the learned Advocate of the Supreme Court, Mr. C. L. Ferdinands, one of the leading Counsel engaged in the case, I am enabled to give, in Appendix J, some interesting documents relating to the mode of appointment, and succession to the office of Chief-priest of the Peak.

The water for the cooking was brought from the well—
(some say spring, but I doubt the possibility of there being
a spring at such an elevated point far above all immediate
surrounding mountain tops)—a little distance northwest of,
and about thirty feet below the terrace wall. This water is
said to possess many and peculiar properties, and is held in
as much repute by pilgrims as is the precious water from the
holy well Zem-zem at Mecca by every hadji amongst, the
faithful and turbaned Islamites. In due course the conjee
was ready and handed round: and what with it, and the
fires, about which we sat and stood, and the smoke which
filled the rooms, we at last regained something like our
natural warmth, and began to feel ourselves again.

We had just resolved upon lying down, as best we might,
for a sleep, when a messenger came to say that the house
was wanted for the accommodation of the family of the
Ratémahatmayá of Kuruwiṭí Kóralé, who had just made the
ascent; and out we had to turn, which we did willingly
enough, for ladies, young and old, were now the parties to
be accommodated. This Ratémahatmayá, an able, active
and intelligent Kandian Chief, was educated at the Colombo
Academy, and is believed to be a Christian, although his
family are Buddhists; his presence therefore appeared more
that of the natural protector of his family, than as a co-wor-
shipper with them.* He offered to obtain for our use the

---

* An appu once told his master, apologetically, that he went on pilgrimage to the Kçlani vihára and dágoba, "to please the womans."

priests' house on the Peak, but this we would not consent
to. 'Returning therefore once more to the terrace, we
stationed ourselves near the entrance at the southern angle,
and watched the companies of pilgrims as they came up.

The ascent from the bambu shed at the Ehela-kanuwa
is usually made without a pause; the peril appearing so great
that any check, allowing a glance around or beneath, might
bring on giddiness and result in fatal falls.* Many, if not
most of the women were completely worn out with fatigue
by the time they had attained this point; they had therefore
to be assisted up the acclivity by their male companions,
who hauled them on to the terrace, and bore them, faint and
utterly exhausted, to the nearest shrine, where they bent
them down and forced them to make the requisite prostrations, and then carried them, all senseless as they were—
some in death-like swoons—to be recovered by the care and

---

* Under ordinary circumstances, weather permitting, any one with a
cool head and steady nerves, may go up and down these cliffs with perfect
safety. But accidents do sometimes occur, though happily but rarely.
Major Forbes mentions, that in 1815, "several natives were blown over
the precipice, and yet continued clinging to one of the chains during a
heavy gust of wind; but in such a situation, no assistance could be
rendered, and they all perished." And Dr. Davy was informed, that only
a fortnight before his visit to the Peak, in April 1817, two natives
looking down the precipice, "became giddy, and frightened, fell, and were
dashed to pieces." In April, 1869, three natives were said to be blown
down the precipice by the force of a fierce storm that then came on ;
and it was alleged, that at the same time several others perished from
fatigue, and the intensity of the cold to which they were exposed.

attention of their friends, wherever they could find a vacant space to go to.

The heavens above us were clear, the stars were shining bright, and the glorious full-orbed moon was scarcely past the zenith. From the Peak, ablaze with light, to the Heramiṭipína station, similarly lighted up, the whole of the pilgrims' path was filled as it were with a living chain of fire, connecting the two points together, and formed by the torches of the multitudes going to and fro. On our right, to the north, above, and beyond Heramiṭipána, towered Unudiya, the gigantic rocky Alp that crowns the Kunudiya-parvaté; to our left, and almost rivalling in height the mountain just mentioned, was the Béna Samanala. These, with the Peak on which we stood, sublimest of them all, rose sharp and distinct, from two to three thousand feet above the clouds, which like an immense plain of snow, with irregular rifts blown into fantastic shapes along the level, hid all below from view. The mother-of-pearl tint of the apparent plain, the moon-lighted tops of the fleecy rifts, the darkened shade of their caverned sides, and the shadows they threw upon the motionless mantle of cloud and mist thus suspended in mid-air, and spread westwards to an illimitable distance, was a spectacle that once seen can never be forgotten, and well illustrated the inspired assertion of the Royal Psalmist, that "the heavens declare the glory of God, and the firmament sheweth his handywork."

The wonderful beauty of this scenery of the skies did not however prevent us from noticing what was going on around.

On the Ratémahatmayá's family coming up to view the
foot-print, one of their retinue unceremoniously swept from
off the altar-table the whole of the floral offerings previously
placed there, and pitched them over the terrace wall, in
order to make room for those his party were about to
present. The chief himself seemed to take little heed of
anything but the welfare of the ladies of his family, the
younger members of which were evidently greatly interested,
and not a little amused, by the novelty of all they saw.
They were welcomed by the musicians with a special burst
of wild discords, improvised to do them honor in the presence
of the assembled crowd.

The night had considerably advanced, and the east,—
hitherto bounded by the dark mountain ranges whose out-
lines broke black against the deep blue sky,—began to shew
indications that day-break was at hand.

> The cloudless blue paled into grey,
> The grey to amber tints gave way
>   Then flushed a rosy red;
> The red grew crimson, then aflame
> With brighter brightness all became,
>   While dawn and dayspring spread.

As the advancing light became more and more diffused,
the mountain chains of the central zone grew more distinct,
and the stars above grew dimmer and yet more dim. Then,
heralding the advent of the sun from his tabernacle at the
end of the heavens, the morning star arose from behind

the (12 miles) distant Kirigallepotah* (7,871 ft. high) and
rapidly mounted upwards in the cœrulean arch

> "As if an angel-sentinel of night
> From earth to heaven had wing'd his homeward flight
> Glorious at first, but lessening by the way
> And lost insensibly in higher day."†

Behind the mountain ranges, the light grew stronger,
broader, and more and more intense, until, from north to
south, the arc of the horizon glowed like a molten looking
glass; and rising from the Nuwara Eliya plains (6,600 ft.
above the sea), the purple dome of Pedurutalágala (8,295 ft.
high, and 22 miles distant in a direct line), could be distinctly
traced behind the peak of a northern range:

> .   .   .   .   .   .   "the heavens
> Wax'd more and more resplendent, till on earth
> Her mountain peaks burn'd as with rosy flame."
>
> DANTE.

The morning star had attained an altitude of about twenty
degrees above the mountain tops, and had already paled in

---

* Or "Kiribat-gal-kanda." The Kandians in the neighbourhood of this
mountain say, that when any important personage living near it is about
to die, a great voice is heard to proceed during the night from its interior.
This they allege has happened thrice within the memory of living men;
once, a few days before the death of Doloswala Dishwa; again, at the
death of Gálle Náyaka unánse, in 1836; and a third time, a few days
before the death of the late Sumangala Náyaka unánse, in 1858, both of
whom were Chief-priests of Adam's Peak.

† "The World before the Flood."

brilliancy, when, with electric speed, a seeming stream of golden fire ran right and left through the fringe of forest trees which marged against the sky the brows of the mighty hills in the distant east, and from the core of the arc, behind the peak of Totapella(7,720 ft. in height and 21 miles distant), the light increased and radiated, until at last, with a vehement blaze, and an indescribable flush of effulgency,—all the more intense and intolerable to sight from the darkness of the mountain in its front,—the sun itself burst with a blinding flash on the eyes of the multitude who had assembled on the eastern side of the dizzy pinnacle where we stood, to gaze upon the brightness of his coming, and watch his going forth on his circuit to the ends of the earth.

> " With such ravishing light
> And mantling crimson in transparent air
> The splendors shot before us.   .   ‾.
> .   .   .   Each mount did seem
> Colossal ruby, whereon so inwrought
> The sunbeams glow'd, yet soft, it flamed intense
> In extasy of glory."
>
>   DANTE.

Old legends state, and devotees believe, that as the sun rises, he seven times salutes the Foot-print on the Samanala Peak. We noticed several yellow-robed unanses intently looking at the blazing orb that rose before us; and could well understand how easily their dazzled eyes would lead their minds to endorse the mythic tale. Well, too, could we

appreciate at that moment, the thought that prompted the
lines of the Laureate Southey, in his Sonnet on the Sun.

> " I marvel not, O Sun! that unto thee
> In adoration men should bow the knee,
> For like a god thou art, and on thy way
> Of glory sheddest with benignant ray
> Beauty and life and joyance from above."

But it was Easter Sunday morning, and we did not forget
the event then celebrating throughout the Christian world,
nor fail to breathe a prayer that the Sun of Righteousness
who then arose with healing in his wings, triumphing over
the night of Death and the darkness of the Grave, would
hasten the time when the knowledge of his glory, here and
elsewhere, should fill the land, as the waters of the sea fill
the channels of the mighty deep.

The lustre of the moon was meanwhile fading fast; and
warmer tints began to tinge the still cloud-covered west;
but we who had witnessed the wondrous glories of both
night and morn, and under their subliming influences had
but slightly felt the effects of fatigue and want of sleep, now
found our bodies yielding to nature's just requirements, and
therefore hasted to return. We thus missed two sights, the
magnificence of either of which amply repays whatever toil
a traveller may endure to behold them.   To see these was
partly the reason why the present writer again, and yet once
more again, journeyed to the Peak.   The weather was such
on the second excursion, that he did not ascend to the Sri-

Páda, but contented himself with making observations about the base of the mountain, and around Heramiṭipána. The following however is an extract from the graphic account written by one of his two companions who then went up.

"Having just returned from an excursion to Adam's Peak, I am told that it is the correct thing to write an account of my journey. Everybody does, so they say. Giving all the weight to this argument that it deserves, I don't know that I could add much of interest to the literature respecting the Peak. Like Canning's knife-grinder, I have 'no story to tell.' And yet perhaps my journey possesses some elements of novelty, from the season in which it was taken, and the weather by which it was accompanied. The season was of the wettest, the ground was saturated by the rains which were constantly falling, the jungle was in a streaming state, the mountain water-courses were swollen, and the rivers in high flood. The prospect also which we obtained from the top of the Peak, although doubtless it has often been witnessed before, has not, so far as I am aware of, been described. Many no doubt have seen it, but they have not cared to write the description. It was not the prospect which so many visitors have sketched, that wide outlook over subjected mountains and rolling hills and far stretching forest, and open plain, and meandering shining rivers, all enclosed in the remote distance by the blue rim of the all-surrounding ocean. It was not this same view, as it is seen in calm beauty, sleeping in the silver light of the meridian moon, which sheds over all a pale faint lustre; softening irregularities, imparting

to all the scene an air of repose, and harmonising all into a
picture of loveliness and peace. Not the view of daybreak,
when the wan light of morning is ascending in the east, the
shades of night hastening away before the march of the
morning light, although still lingering in places where
sheltered by the shadows of intervening hills, while the dawn
is advancing and

.   .   .   .   .   .   "jocund day
Stands tiptoe on the misty mountain tops,"

and the great red orb of the sun is bursting into view, and its
roseate beams are leaping from hill to hill and chasing far
away the last vestiges of darkness and night. These views
many have seen and many have described. That which we
saw was not like these, but what it was, its like will be
described. . . . The day broke dark and dreary. The same
thick cloud wrapped all the prospect. It was evident that
though we might go up the Peak, we should see nothing
from the top; but my younger companion and I determined
to make the ascent. At any rate we should see the road,
and should also have reached the summit, and so have
defeated the prognostications of many friends who prophesied
that we should never get there. Accordingly we set out.
The road up to nearly the top, as also for the least few miles
of our yesterday's journey, bore traces of the late presence
of an evidently large number of elephants, and the coolies,
as we went on, endeavoured by constant shoutings to scare
them from our path. The road was not difficult. It was, in

fact, a long rough, rocky staircase. We were, to speak mathematically, ascending the terms of an infinite series—of steps. . . . On nearing the top and getting on the rock-cut steps, by the sides of which the numerous chains lie intended to assist the ascent, the coolies who were accompanying us, evidently considering that our lives were only safe in their hands, made a frantic rush at us, caught hold and tried to hurry us at railway pace up the steps. We objected to this and preferred to take our own time. . . . Well! we reached the top and looked around at the prospect. The view was one of the thickest cloud, above us, below us, and all around. We were upon a little point of rock, a small air-suspended island in an ocean of mists. We knew that there were precipices around us, but we could not see them; that there was a wide stretching prospect below us, but it was all invisible. A strong westerly storm-wind blew in wild but fitful gusts, and howled and raved as it swept past us and beat on the rocky surfaces of the weather-assailed peak. . . . . When we were leaving to start on our excursion, we were informed that we should never reach the summit. It was impossible to do so in such weather, the fury of which was indicated by the fact that the iron chains at the top were so lashed by the tempest that their clanking could be heard two miles off. I believe that up to this hour one of my companions fondly clings to the belief in this statement. Indeed the idea is rather a poetic one, and creditable to the imagination that originated it. I think it is rather sublime to think of the mountain assailed by spirits of the storm;

rocking to its base when smitten by the tempest blows, and
the chains swinging and clanking in harsh horrified accompaniment. The fiction is grand, but it is a fiction. They
don't clank at all. Not a clank. They there lie and rust
in motionless idleness, and would do so if all the tenants of
the cave Æolus were to spend their utmost rage upon and
around that high summit.*

"We strolled about the little enclosed platform, climbed
up to the shrine, and examined the sacred foot-print. The
latter is what Mr. Wackford Squeers would call 'a rum
and a holy thing.' Still, I was not altogether satisfied
with it. It is, I think, some five and a half feet long, but
how is it that it is not bigger? Why do they stop at five
and a half feet? This would only give a stature to Buddha
or Sivá of some forty feet. But I like to think of Sivá as
rather a tall party. Then, the shape of the thing? Why
do they call it a foot-print at all? Certainly, by adding a
lot of cement, and bits of tile, and by other devices, they
have made it look something that may pass for being a very
lame representation of a foot on a rather large scale, but
who was the first imaginative genius who thought that
that depression in the rock resembled a foot in any way?

---

* The chains certainly did not clank when the writer of the preceding
sketch was on the Peak. But there is nothing to hinder them doing so,
when the wind is blowing strongly from particular quarters, since they
hang loosely down from their fastenings at the top of the cliff; and the
natives positively assert that at such times they clank loudly.

The same mark might as well be the impression of any other part of the body as the foot. If Buddha or Sivá had sat down on the rock, the impression made by the divine comboy might have been not unlike that. Down at Palá-baddala they show in the temple what they call a *facsimile* of the foot-print. The fact is, that it is no *facsimile* at all. It is perhaps the facsimile of what the foot-print ought to have been, if it was to preserve resemblance at all. The whole affair, with its patchwork of cement and tile, smacks of Brummagem rather too much. . .But yet we ought not to laugh at this specimen of superstition and credulity. There was a period when our own ancestors believed in the miraculous virtues of bits of the 'true cross,' at a time when there were enough pieces of wood in Europe under that name to have built a three-decker, and enough 'true nails' to have furnished the iron for engines, boilers, screw, anchors, cables, and standing rigging. We should think of these things, and not judge harshly of uneducated credulity.

"While we were upon the platform my attention was attracted by the devotions the coolies were paying to the shrine. They had brought with them some offerings, the flower shoots of some palms, and these they now laid reverentially before the foot-print. To see these poor coolies with such earnestness, and such apparent reverence and trust, make their lowly prayers, suggested to my mind many mixed reflections. It looked strange, contemplated from the stand-point of the sceptical nineteenth century. What with one side and the other, the claims of the one, the

scepticism and criticism of the other, they seem to have left
so little for an honest man to believe in now; and yet these
poor fellows seemed quite satisfied to believe that this was
the foot-print of the great Buddha."

On our third visit, we started from Hçramiṭipâna at
earliest dawn, and although we thus missed the glories of
the sunrise, we had the opportunity we hoped for of seeing
the marvellous Shadow of the Peak projected above the low-
lying mist clouds, and stretching beyond the bounds of the
Island far away into the surrounding ocean.   Faint, and
not very clearly defined at first, as the sunlight became
stronger, the outline and body of the gigantic pyramid-
shaped umbra grew sharper, darker, and more distinct; and
as the sun rose higher in the heavens, the titanic shadow
seemed actually to rise in the atmosphere; to tilt up and
gradually fall back upon the mountain, shrinking and
dwarfing in dimensions as it drew closer and yet closer to its
mighty parent, until, absorbed in the forests with which the
mountain is clad, it was wholly lost to view.   So singular a
sight,—one so strangely magnificent, and even awe-inspiring,
can be seen nowhere else in the Island, perhaps nowhere
else in the world.*

---

* The Rev. J. Nicholson, who made the ascent in 1863, thus describes this scene:—"As the sun rose in the heavens, each peak and hill
gained a share of his rays, and threw its shadow upon its fellow, or into the
valley; but the longest and the best was that thrown from 'the holy
shrine.' Right beyond, at an immense distance, the dark shadow was

As the mist and clouds dispersed, the extensive views that opened out became sublimely grand. North and east, below and beyond us, were range upon range of mountains, the valleys and slopes of which, from Maskeliya to Ramboddo, from Dimbula to Haputale, were the homes of the enterprising men whose capital and industry have, within thirty years, made Ceylon the third, if not the second, largest Coffee-producing country in the world. Sweeping round to the south were the similar ranges of Sabaragamuwa and the Morawak Kóralé, where, before similar energy and enterprise, the primæval forests have disappeared, and in their stead now grows the coffee bush. Down the sides of the mountains were seen the rushing waterfalls, the nearer ones broad bands of glistening foam, and those afar mere shining threads and filaments of silver as they shimmered in the light of day. To the south and west the circling ocean met the eye,—from Point-de Galle, soon to become the great steam-harbour of the Eastern world, to Kalutara, Colombo, Negombo and Chilaw, the sites of which, with the aid of a good glass and a map, could easily be made out;—while in between lay the vast expanse of hill and dale, watered by the Kelani-ganga,

---

spread. Photographed as it were upon the clouds, as far as vision could reach, there was the picture of the sacred summit. With one hand I could cover a mountain, while the shadow from my small body was fearful indeed. I could hardly take it as a compliment if any friend were to express his desire to me—'May your shadow never grow less!' But as that shadow shortened with the advancing light, we hastened on our homeward march."

the Kalu-gaṇga, and other streams, the chief of which sprang
from the ranges that immediately surrounded the isolated
pinnacle upon which we stood.   Standing there, and seeing
all this, we felt there was not the slightest exaggeration in
what Sir Emerson Tennent has written upon this scene, and.
which he thus sums up:—"The panorama from the summit
of Adam's Peak is, perhaps, the grandest in the world, as no
other mountain, although surpassing it in altitude, presents
the same unobstructed view over land and sea.   Around it,
to the north and east, the traveller looks down on the zone
of lofty hills that encircle the Kandian kingdom, whilst to the
westward the eye is carried far over undulating plains,
threaded by rivers like cords of silver, till in the purple
distance the glitter of the sunbeams on the sea marks the
line of the Indian Ocean."

Adam's Peak.

"Steep the descent and wearisome the way;
The twisted boughs forbade the light of day; . . .
Upright and tall the trees of ages grow,
While all is loneliness and waste below :
There as the massy foliage, far aloof
Display'd a dark impenetrable roof,
So, gnarled and rigid, claspt and interwound
An uncouth maze of roots emboss'd the ground;
Midway beneath, the sylvan wild assumed
A milder aspect, shrubs and flow'rets bloom'd;
Openings of sky, and little plots of green,
And showers of sunbeams through the leaves were seen." *

CHAPTER VIII.

DESCENT FROM THE PEAK. — HERAMITIPA'NA. — ALEXANDER'S
RIDGE.—CAVE OF KHI'ZR. — SI'TA GANGULA.—DHARMA-RA'JA-
GALA. — UDA-PAWEN-ELLA.—ACCIDENTS. — PALA'BADDALA TO
RATNAPURA.

COLD as we were, and fatigued as we felt, on our March
trip, we divested ourselves of rugs and overcoats, and staff in
hand, turned westwards on our homeward journey. Down
the cliff went two of my companions, holding on by the

---

* "The World before the Flood."

chains; and down the slanting ladder went he who had
adventured up it. Arrived at the brow of the precipice, and
seeing below me but one step for my foot, and infinite space
beyond, I stopped short. Calling to the interpreter for
assistance, for without it I could not go down, an active
Vidahn* readily came forward, and with his and the interpreter's help, I accomplished the descent. This hesitation
on my part was neither the result of fear nor of dizziness,
but of the stiffened state of my limbs, which began to fail
and flag, and shew symptoms of inability to act simultaneously with the volition that directed their movements. It
behoved me therefore to be cautious. Just as I went over
the brink, my ears were saluted by a most melancholy
whining howl. Our commissary-general's dog, answering
to the name of "Tinker," who had made the pilgrimage
with us, and scrambled up to the top of the Samanta-kúta,
where he found a solitary canine friend to keep him company,
on coming to this spot shrank back, and gave doleful vent
to his dismay at the perils before him, and his grief at being
forsaken;—for there we were obliged to leave him.

We observed in our descent that some of the links of the
chains, and irons of the ladders, had short inscriptions engraved upon them; and that on the rocks here and there
longer and more elaborate inscriptions had been cut. We
were informed that in the one case they simply recorded

---

* A petty headman, or subordinate officer.

the names of those who had fixed or repaired those useful
aids to the ascent; and in the other gave an account of
pilgrims who had visited the Peak, some of whom had died
when they had reached thus far.

We got back to Hȩramiṭipána in considerably less time
than it took us to ascend from it the previous night; but we
found the journey down the Samanala, much more painful
and trying than the clamber up. We had observed the pro-
ceding day, that from some place below the station, on the
side on which we entered it coming from Palábaddala, the
pilgrims brought up their supplies of water; and on returning
from the Peak, in going down towards the Síta-gangula, we
saw a descent to our left, which mistaking for the proper
path, one of us went partially down before he discovered
his error. About fifty or sixty feet below, he saw a clearing
in a small dell, in the centre of which was a square kind of
tank; and this dell he determined to examine on the occasion
of his third visit. The result of the examination was, that
he identified the station Hȩramiṭipána, and this place, as
that described by Ibn Batúta, as "the ridge of Alexander,
in which is a cave and a well of water," at the entrance to
the mountain Serendib. The old Moor's account is somewhat confused, his notes or recollections not always carrying
his facts exactly in their due order; but half-way down the
descent, on the left hand, is a well, excavated in the rock,
in which we found about five feet of water, and which
swarmed with tadpoles. Possibly Batúta found it in the
same condition, for he speaks of the well, at the entrance,

full of fish, of which "no one takes any." At the bottom
of the dell is a cleared space; in the centre of this is a
square tank, or well, the sides of which are formed of
blocks of stone, six or eight feet long. Beyond this,
almost facing the descent, some twenty feet up the opposite mountain's side, is a cave. To this my companion and
I forced our way through the jungle, and came to the conclusion, that this was the cave of Khízr, where, Batúta says,
" the pilgrims leave their provisions, and whatever else they ·
have, and then ascend about two miles to the top of the
mountain, to the place of ₍Adam's₎ foot." In the preceding
sentence he says, " Near this [cave] and on each side of
the path, is a cistern cut in the rock." Now, no other place
that we saw, or heard of,—and we were particularly minute
in our inquiries,—answers to such a description. There
are the two wells, and the cave; and the distance to the
foot-print is also pretty fairly estimated. Making due
allowance for a few misplacements of positions, which old
travellers,—who more often than otherwise wrote from mero
recollection,—were prone to, the account Ibn Batúta gives
of the route to the Peak,* will in its general accuracy, bear

---

* It is quite possible that the route has been slightly varied since
Ibn Batúta wrote. I am inclined to think that the path originally led
direct to the dell above described, from some point lower down the ascent
to Hẹramiṭapána, and that the ascent to the Peak was also made direct
from it. Hẹramiṭipána is however a better situated and more healthy
position for a pilgrim station.

comparison with that of any narrative of any writer of the age in which he lived.

The slopes of the mountain leading to Heramiṭipána are thickly clad with noble forest trees. The vegetation on the crest of the ridge, as well as the undergrowth amongst the trees, consists principally of several varieties of the Nilloo plant, * which we found in full bloom in the month of September, when too, it is evidently a favorite food of some of the denizens of the forest, for the shrubs bore marks of having been browsed upon in all directions. The *Datura arborea* also added its quota of magnificent white gigantic trumpet-shaped flowers to the floral beauty of the spot; and the headman and interpreter pointed out to us other flowering plants, some of which are used by the natives for medicinal purposes; such as the Adútodá, the Agal-ádára, the Páwatta, and the Wæta-hira.†

---

* The Nilloo (*Strobilanthes*) is a brittle jointed plant, well known in the mountain districts of Ceylon, where it formes a complete undergrowth in the forest. When in bloom the red and blue flowers with which it is covered are a singularly beautiful feature in the landscape, and are eagerly searched by the honey bees. Some species are said to flower only once in five, seven, or nine years; and after ripening their seed they die.

† The above are the native names. The Adútodá and the Agal-ádára, are species of the Malabar nut; the Pawatta is the *Paretta indica*, Willd., the Wæta-hira, is a kind of hedge plant, the botanical name of which I am ignorant of.

Stopping at the station on our March excursion just
sufficiently long to be able to get a cup of coffee, we started
for the Síta-gangula, where we purposed bathing and
breakfasting.   Two of my companions, younger and lighter
than L. and myself, soon shot ahead; but we found (and so
did they) that the going down was a very different matter to
the going up;—then, it was only the lifting muscles that
were brought into action, now it was the lowering ones,
with the whole weight of our bodies to be sustained, at each
descending step, upon our already strained ankles and troubled knees.   With the perspiration streaming from every
pore, and with feet swollen and inflamed, we hobbled and
stumbled on our way, objects of compassion to many who
passed us, and especially to one old sympathizing native—our
benisons on his venerable head !—who pausing to look at us
for a few seconds, drew from his wallet a fine orange, and
with a smile of encouragement handed us the refreshing
fruit,—a gift we most gratefully accepted.   By the time we
arrived at the river, I was obliged to seek the assistance
of a coolie, in addition to that of the alpenstock I grasped.
Having resolved upon a bath here, we scrambled up the
bare smooth rock in search of a convenient pool, out of sight
of the pilgrims at the ford, and in so doing, I came to grief;
for on passing one of the fissures between the boulders, my
foot slipped, and down I went, feet first, into an ugly-looking hole filled with water, dragging my attendant coolie in
with and upon me.   Instinctively throwing my arms across
the chasm, (about three feet wide), I brought myself up

when immersed to the waist, although I touched no bottom with my feet. The coolie quickly recovered himself and helped me out; but I slipped again at the first step I attempted, and this time went souse up to the arm-pits, receiving blows upon my elbows and knees which did not facilitate my after progress. Helped out again, I stripped off boots and socks, and made my way bare-foot to where my companions were disporting themselves; laughing merrily at my mishaps, which they had witnessed though a crevice between the rocks; an amusement in which I could not help joining, for the whole affair was irresistibly ludicrous. A brisk shampooing, combined with the bracing coldness of the waters, greatly revived us, and our subsequent breakfast on the rocks below was not the least relished meal of our trip. In a small stream which here joins the Sita-gangula, we observed some good-sized crabs, about four inches broad in the body, and were not a little amused at the voracity with which one seized with both claws the wing and breast bone of a fowl, and commenced tearing off with its mouth the fragment of flesh that had been left upon it.

The ascent from the river to the Dharma-rája-gala was comparatively easy work—a gentle shove behind from one of the following coolies being a most efficient upward help. When we reached the rock, an English-speaking Sinhalese who there overtook us, gravely declared that no two people could arrive at the same number in counting the steps, it being a standing miracle, ordained by Buddha, that their number should never be exactly known. Unbelievers as

we were, and one of our party having counted them on the
journey up, we agreed, for the satisfaction of our informant,
to count them again—our interpreter also counting with us.
When we came to the bottom and compared notes, each one's
count corresponded with the other's—exactly 130; a matter
of fact which evidently exceedingly puzzled our casual
acquaintance in the smart jacket and comboy.

After passing the ruined resthouse at Diyabetma, when
near the site of Getanctul-gala ambalama, a beautiful view
of the country below is obtained from an opening on the left
of the path. The whole of Gílimalé lies mapped out before
the eye, with glimpses of the Kalu-gaṇga meandering through
its plains. Further on, at a lower elevation, on the right
of the path, a similar view is obtained of the Kuruwiṭi
valley, watered by the Kuru-gaṇga. But more welcome to
our longing eyes than scenery, however beautiful or picturesque, was the rustic Nílihela ambalama, when we came
within view of it. For our progress, slow from the first,
had now become most painfully so. D. and G. had long
since distanced L. and myself,—and gradually our pace had
become reduced to that of a snail's gallop. The old man
who had made his 56th pilgrimage, decrepid from age, and
bowed and bent with infirmity, was, with the help of his staff,
and son and grandson, proceeding as fast as ourselves, and it
became a question whether he or we would reach Palábaddala first, as we passed and repassed each other on the
rocky path. He had gone on to the foot-print, while we
stayed at Heramiṭipána, and had returned and recruited

there, and started on his way back to Ratnapura before us; but we had overtaken him after leaving Diyabetma. Some extra steep places, I could only, as an emerald islander would say, face backwards, holding on by the coolie; others I literally crawled down crab-fashion. For first, an ankle gave way, and then a knee, and when we came to a somewhat level patch of the length of a yard or two, we found ourselves staggering to and fro, from positive inability to walk as was our ordinary wont.

A little beyond this, as we were toiling on, dog "Tinker" came bounding up. He had somehow contrived to overcome his difficulties, and his demonstrations of joy at having come up with us were excessive; the stump of his tail wagged with a rapidity that threatened to disjoint it altogether; and his jumps and fawnings about us had in them an odd mixture of the ludicrous with the pathetic. Soon after, L., seeing that my haltings were becoming more and more frequent, generously volunteered, although scarcely less fatigued than myself, to make a push forward and send back coolies to help me on. This he did, and the welcome help came none too soon; for though I perseveringly hobbled on, upon the principle that each step brought me nearer to my journey's end, when about three-quarters of a mile from Palábaddala, both ankles and knees had so completely given way, that even with the assistance of a coolie and my staff, I could scarcely move a step. Supported under the arm pits on either side, and gently forced forward from behind, I at last reached Palábaddala, where our former quarters had been placed at our disposal, and where my companions were already at rest.

Before the arrival of the additional coolies, when passing through Uda Pawen-ella, where there is a large open tiled ambalama, the old gentleman who had made his 51st pilgrimage, and was there halting with his family, came forward and led me to a seat. He saw at a glance the plight I was in, and probably fancied that I was worse than actually was the case, for he soon began to question me, while a crowd gathered round to hear the result of his inquiries. But as none of the natives present understood English, and my knowledge of Sinhalese was by no means extensive, we had to fall back upon the language of signs, for a proper understanding of each other. First he felt my pulse, and then pointed to and felt my ankles; at this I shook my head, and said, Naraki (bad); he then pointed to my knees and thighs, to which I responded, Bohomi. naraki (very bad); this, if I have any skill in the interpretation of looks, brought into play many expressions of sympathy and commisseration. He then pointed to my chest, whereupon I smiled, and said Hondi (good). Hondi and Bohomi-hondi were repeated in cheering tones by him and by the bye-standers; and all seemed to think that if the chest was not affected, it did not signify much what ailed the muscles. With a benevolent smile and a hearty hand-shake, he bade me good-bye, and I saw him no more; but the recollection of his kindness, and of his sympathetic conduct, will be lasting. He was without a doubt, one of the good Samaritans of a country, of whom it

is in many respects a libel to say—no matter upon what high
authority—that in it "man is only vile." My coolie now cut
up and handed me, at the instigation, I believe, of my worthy
native friend, some pieces of sugar-cane, the juice of which
I found both refreshing and reviving. After munching
these, and partaking of a draught of water, I again set out,
and in a few minutes met the help that had been sent me.

That morning's journey is one which none of us is likely
ever to forget, for none had ever experienced in so great a
degree such intensity of muscular pain or such severity of
fatigue. Our frequent halts had however enabled us to
note more closely the features of the track we traversed;
and we found that in many places it narrowed to a mere
ridge of a rock, bounded on either hand by a tremendous
precipice, the terrors of which were happily hidden by a
luxuriant growth of jungle and forest.

The mosses and ferns, some of which were gathered and
brought home by G., were singularly graceful; and one of
the latter proved to be a rare and seldom seen specimen.
Tiny flowers, with stalks so slender and delicate that they
looked like filaments of gossamer brightly shining among
the rain-drops with whose moisture they were bedewed,
clung to the faces of the rocks, encrusting them with
an exquisite gem-like efflorescence, which would baffle the
efforts of the most skilful artist to imitate. Admiring
their beauty, we gathered samples of all within reach; but
unfortunately, the coolie to whom they were entrusted,
contrived to lose them. We strongly suspected that, not

appreciating our tastes, or our love of the beautiful as manifested botanically, he simply deemed them a lot of valueless weeds, and as soon as he safely could, rid himself of the trouble of carrying them by throwing them away.

The forests were magnificent,* especially where iron-wood abounded.† Perhaps no tree is more beautiful than this, when on a trunk fifty feet in height, with a girth on the ground of four or five, and with branches symmetrically tapering to a point above, the whole mass of its leaves presents to the eye a gorgeous cone of carmined foliage, of almost every possible hue, from palest pink to deep blood red. In other seasons, when the leaves are not thus full of sap, they are more of a sober sage-green colour, which admirably contrasts with the profuse bloom of flowers with which the tree is then covered. These in appearance are not much unlike some kinds of white roses, the large petals surrounding a cluster of prominent delicate yellow stamens. They emit an agreeable, but somewhat strong perfume, and are favorite flowers for offerings at Buddhist temples.

The river scenery was varied and exceedingly picturesque. The views at the ferry before reaching Gilimalé, and at the spots where we there bathed, were charming, but both were eclipsed by the greater beauties displayed at the junction of the Hatula with the Kalu-ganga; while at Maskeliya,

---

* For a vivid description of Ceylon forest scenery, see Appendix K.; and for an account of the Botany of Adam's Peak, Appendix L.

† *Sing.* Na gaha. Mesua ferrea, L.

and at the Kalu-ganga at Palábaddala, and the Síta-gangula, and other highland streams, the aspect of the country is wholly changed; and the sylvan gives place to the wild and the grand, occasioned by the presence in and around them of rocks and boulders and frowning precipices and mountains huge, and towering Alps, and gloomy forests dense.

In the higher parts of each of the mountains we had descended, we saw numerous traces of elephants, and were at first puzzled to make out why their paths through the cane brakes on either side of our track were so frequent and so close. A little consideration however shewed, that in these places, evidently favorite feeding grounds, the sagacious brutes, who always choose for themselves the easiest possible gradients, had made a series of zigzags up the ridge; and as these crossed our path every few feet, we understood at once both the steepness and the narrowness of the ridge we were descending, and a very little divergence to the right or left gave us ocular proof of the fact. We once thought we heard their trumpetings in the distance; and all along the region of their tracks the pilgrims shouted and chanted lustily, evidently with the view of keeping them out of the way.

There was one piece of fun which the wags of a party were very fond of. Dropping behind their companions, they would send up a loud imitation trumpeting, and startle those before them into swifter movements down the mountain slope. Some however, like ourselves, were unable to quicken their

paces, and there were one or two poor women whom we
passed, lying prostrate on the rocks, who seemed as if they
would gasp out their lives ere they could reach their homes;
they were however carefully tended by their accompanying
friends.

Of butterflies, although supposed to be in the region of
their homes, we saw but few; they were principally of the
large-winged blue and purple-coloured varieties. The pest
of leeches, the dread and torment of the route in damp and
rainy seasons, we at this time luckily escaped, owing to the
dryness and the heat; not more than two or three of those
voracious bloodsuckers having assailed our persons. We
saw one or two reptiles, the green whip-snake, and a
rat-snake; and on our third journey a tic-polonga was found
in the ambalama at Nilibela. At Uda Pawen-ella we saw
an exceedingly ugly-looking centipede, at least eight inches
long, with legs spread out for half an inch on each side of
its body. Some crabs were also seen at the same place,
apparently of the same kind as the one we noticed at Sita-
gangula.

Comparing notes with, and laughing at one another's
experiences, we spent the afternoon of Easter Monday, and
before retiring to our primitive sleeping bunks, each had his
limbs shampooed, and well rubbed with an embrocation of
diluted Arnica, which one of us was provided with. The
recollection of this excellent restorative was suggested by a
visit paid us by a 'wederale,' a native medical man, who had
heard one of us was ill and came to proffer his services. Our

rascals of coolies grinned at the fun as we winced under
their hands while they operated upon us; for the muscles
of our thighs and the calves of our legs ached to agony,
and our nerves shrank and quivered with pain at the slightest touch; but we felt all the better afterwards, and slept
more soundly that night than we had done during the three
preceding.

Expert cragsmen, hardy mountaineers, and members of the
Alpine club, may smile at this account of our sufferings; and
we should doubtless have not felt anything like what we did
had we been in proper training for the work we undertook;
but as we saw numbers of lithe wiry-looking Siŋhalese
suffering in a similar manner,—pain manifest in every step
they took, with their swollen ankles, feet, and limbs,—we
have reason to think that the pilgrimage to and from the
Peak, on foot as we performed it, is a feat that would fatigue
even the hardiest and the best trained mountain-climbers
amongst our countrymen. When we woke the following
morning each movement was still the cause of considerable
pain; but another shampooing, and a cup of coffee, enabled
us to make an early start; and as the remainder of our journey was on much more level ground, as we warmed with
exercise we managed to get on more vigorously than we
at first anticipated.

On our second excursion the return to Palábaddala was
lonesome There were none on the path besides ourselves,
and we were struck by the quietude of everything around.
At Nílihela, where on our upward route we saw eight

water-falls leaping down the mountain precipices, there was
now not even a rill, but

> . . . . " deep the hush; the torrent's channel dry
> Presents a stony steep, the echo's haunt."
>
> GRAHAME.

An old woman, and a child or two, stared in wonderment as
we passed Uda Pawen-ella; and the priests and good people
at Palábaddala rejoiced at our return, for they had tried to
dissuade us from going, and prognosticated that evils would
surely befall us for not listening to their persuasions. One
accident certainly did occur, and it was irreparable. The
coolie who carried the box of glass plates and photographs
taken on the journey, slipped, stumbled, and fell, just
before reaching the bridge above the village; the box flew
off his head, struck against a rock, and in an instant the
whole of its contents were shivered to atoms. It was a
serious loss to the artist, and my readers also lose the
advantage which such illustrations would have afforded in
their perusal of these pages. Another accident also occurred, but not to our party; although the medical and surgical
knowledge which one of our number happened to possess was
thereby brought into active operation. On our way up we
had passed a poor purblind old man, who was then staying
at Uda Pawen-ella. After our return to Palábaddala, about
8½ or 9 P. M. the same man was brought into the village in
a most pitiable plight. He too, in venturing to come to the
village, had slipped, and fallen on or down the rocks; his

scalp, and temple, and cheek bone, were laid open by the accident, and his face was covered with clotted gore. He was certainly a very deplorable looking object when presented to us; but by the use and application of sponge, scissors, lint, lotion, sticking-plaster and bandages, he was in a short time made tolerably comfortable. The result however, was, that all the halt, maimed, ailing, withered, old, blind and decrepid of the village, immediately swarmed in and solicited aid, and to the best of our ability we prescribed and doctored right and left, until our drugs and medicaments were exhausted; then, but not till then, did our would-be patients leave us to ourselves.

On our third journey, we were accompanied by one of the Bandáras from Gílimalé. After we had visited the Peak, and were preparing to return from Heramiṭipána, the coolie who had been sent on from Colombo with provisions, made his appearance. He had come up to Ratnapura the day after we left, and followed our steps thus far; but had left his load on the rocks half way between Síta-gangula and Heramiṭipána, not being able to carry it further, owing to an attack of fever and ague, with which he was then shaking. We gave him a strong dose of brandy and quinine, and then hasted down to look after his load; for though there was no likelihood of any human being making free with it at that season of the year, we did not feel quite so sure about the elephants, whose spoor indicated that they were not far off. We had, besides, just finished our stock of provender, and the contents of that box were of special

interest to us at that particular juncture. Finding it where
the man had left it, and waiting to see all our party safely
over, we were detained some time in crossing the Síta-
gangula; while there, the Colombo coolie pointed out to us
a cave in the river bed, formed by three or four rocks piled
against each other, where, foodless and fireless, he had spent the
preceding night, the river roaring on either side, and the rain
pelting down on the rock above him. It was the dreariest
resting-place conceivable; but we saw several similar caves
about; and in dry weather, a party on a moonlight night might
do worse than encamp in the rocky caves there, supposing
always they were well supplied with food and fire. From
thence our journey that day was most fatiguing, and through
constant rain. We were not able to proceed as far as
Palábaddala, but halted at Uda Pawen-ella, where Bandára
made us as comfortable as circumstances would permit; and
although our lodging was on the cold ground, and our bed
but a water-proof wrapper, we had nevertheless, a roof over-
head, and a good supply of creature comforts; and conscious
that we might have fared much worse, we contrived to enjoy
ourselves, and slept soundly through the night.

· From Palábaddala to Ratnapura the return journey is
comparatively easy. My companions on the first excursion
re-crossed the Maskeliya by the unfinished bridge, while I
preferred the river's bed; on the second and third occasion
we all had to do the same. After crossing in December we
saw in the jungle on the river bank a remarkable spider, or
what we supposed to be one, which we regretted that we

could not secure. Its body was oblong, about an inch in length, and two-thirds of an inch broad; of a pale green colour, with a black stripe down the centre: as it held on to the cane on which we saw it, its legs extended an inch in front and an inch behind. We halted and bathed, and were well shampooed, and breakfasted or dined, and slept at Gílimalé, on each occasion, as circumstances permitted or rendered desirable.

> " Meantime unnumber'd glittering streamlets play'd
> And hurléd every where their waters sheen
> That as they bicker'd through the sunny glade
> Though restless still themselves, a lulling murmur made."
>
> THOMSON.

On our second journey, when nearing the Ellapita ferry across the Kalu-ganga, we were overtaken by a most violent thunder storm.

> " The woods grew dark, as though they knew no noon;
> The thunder growled about the high brown hill,
> And the thin, wasted, shining summer rills
> Grew joyful with the coming of the rain,
> And doubtfully was shifting every vane
> .   .   .   with changing gusts of wind,
> Till came the storm blast, furious and blind
> Twixt gorges of the mountains, and drove back
> The light sea-breeze; then waxed the heavens black
> Until the lightning leapt from cloud to cloud,
> With clattering thunder, and the piled-up crowd

Began to turn from steely blue to grey
And toward the sea the thunder drew away,
Leaving the north wind blowing steadily
The rain-clouds from Olympus."*

Right glad were we to take shelter in the ferry-keeper's
hut until its fury had abated; and thankful too, that we had
encountered nothing like it while in the mountains.

At Dimbulwiṭiya, about six and a half miles from Ratnapura, we met, while halting on our first journey, Wellane-
watte Anunáyaka Unánse, the second in rank of the priesthood of the Peak. He was on his way to the Srí-páda, travelling in state,—banner-bearers and musicians before him,
himself borne in a palanquin by four tall coolies, two attendant priests on foot behind, and a retinue of servants and
followers in the rear. Shrewd and intelligent in look, and
in the full prime and vigour of manhood, he eyed us keenly,
and on learning that we were returning from the pilgrimage,
became greatly interested, questioning us as to the state of
the roads, &c. When we that day regained our starting-point
at Ratnapura, we were glad enough that our march of fifteen
miles was done. D.'s bungalow, the creature comforts he
there provided, and the delicious beds we that night slept
on, are things to be remembered as those productive of a
heartfelt satisfaction, such as one meets with only on very
rare occasions in the course of a busy but withal somewhat
monotonous life. The next day we visited the gem pits and

---

* Morris's "Life and Death of Jason."

gold diggings of Ratnapura; but as there were neither gem-
mers nor gold washers at work, we had to draw upon our
imaginations for pictures of the treasures that possibly lay
hidden beneath our feet.   We saw however some fine specimens of the Talipot palm,* that

> . . . . "sultan of the stately tribe,
> Who once a century displays
> His flow'rs to man's admiring gaze;
> For none of woman born behold
> His buds a second time unfold.
> With arch on arch successive crown'd
> The folding leaves the top surround,
> Each leaf a fan-like circle forms,
> An ample screen from sun and storms,
> By Nature kindly lent to bless
> The unrejoicing wilderness!

---

* The Corypha umbraculifera, " the stem of which sometimes attains
the height of 100 feet, and each of its enormous fan-like leaves, when
laid upon the ground, will form a semicircle of 16 feet in diameter, and
cover an area of nearly 200 superficial feet.   The tree flowers but once
and dies; and the natives firmly believe that the bursting of the sheath,
which contains a magazine of seeds, is accompanied by a loud explosion.
The leaves alone are converted by the Siphalese to purposes of utility.
Of them they form coverings for their houses, and portable tents of a
rude but effective character; and on occasions of ceremony, each chief
and headman on walking abroad is attended by a follower, who holds
above his head an elaborately-ornamented fan, formed from a single leaf
of the talpat.   But the most interesting use to which they are applied is
as substitutes for paper, both for books and for ordinary purposes.   In
the preparation of *olas*, which is the term applied to them when so

As if her bounteous care had spread
A shelter for the traveller's head,
Beneath whose umbellated leaf
His languid form might find relief."*

One had only quite recently burst into bloom; the central flower spathe towered straight up from the stem, and was surrounded by others in gracefully drooping circles, the whole forming a most magnificent floral plume. Its appearance exactly corresponded with the description given of this noble palm by Mr. A. M. Ferguson in his Souvenirs of Ceylon. "The trunk rose about ninety feet in height. The grand spike with its immense mass of primrose coloured blossoms rising thirty feet high, formed a rich contrast to the dark green of the foliage from which it sprang, and presented a spectacle perhaps the most glorious which the range of the vegetable kingdom can present."

---

employed, the leaves are taken whilst still tender, and, after separating the central ribs, they are cut into strips and boiled in spring water. They are dried first in the shade, and afterwards in the sun, then made into rolls, and kept in store, or sent to the market for sale. Before, however, they are fit for writing on, they are subjected to a second process, called *madema*. A smooth log of areca-palm is tied horizontally between two trees, each ola is then damped, and a weight being attached to one end of it, it is drawn backwards and forwards by the other till the surface becomes perfectly smooth and polished; and during the process, as the moisture dries up, it is necessary to renew it till the effect is complete. The smoothing of a single ola will occupy from fifteen to twenty minutes."—Sir J. E. Tennent's Ceylon, vol. i. pp. 109, 110.

* "The Wanderer in Ceylon."

Adam's Peak.

"A gentle river wound its quiet way
  Through this sequester'd glade, meandering wide;
Smooth as a mirror here the surface lay:
  Where the pure lotus, floating in its pride,
Enjoy'd the breath of heaven, the sun's warm beam,
And the cool freshness of its native stream.

"Here o'er green meads whose tresses waved outspread,
  With silent lapse the glassy waters run,—
Here in fleet motion o'er a pebbly bed,
  Gliding, they glance and ripple to the sun:
The stirring breeze that swept them in its flight
Raised on the stream a shower of sparkling light."
  THE POET'S PILGRIMAGE.

CHAPTER IX.

THE KALU-GANGA. — KALUTARA. — PA'NADURE'. — MORATUWA.
  — RATMALA'NA. — COLLEGE, OF PRIESTS. — GALKISSA. —
MOUNT LAVINIA.— COLLUPITIYA.—GALLE FACE.—COLOMBO.

BEING pressed for time on our March excursion, we
returned to Colombo by the Ratnapura Coach; a course
adopted, for the same reason, on our Christmas and New-
Year's trip. But in September we determined upon taking
the river route to Kalutara, and from thence to return to
Colombo, by the Galle road. We accordingly engaged a

páda-boat,* and as the resthouse is very near the river, this was brought for our accommodation to a landing place close by. Sending our horse home by road, for he would not enter the boat, we dismounted our carriage from its wheels and stowing it with our boxes in the centre of the boat, took up our quarters in the fore part, while our servants and a portion of the crew occupied the hinder end. The crew consisted of a tindal or steersman, and six rowers; a complement which allowed four to be always working the sweeps on the overhanging prow, while two rested, spell and spell about. A good supply of fresh rice straw, covered with empty coffee bags, over which we spread our rugs, made excellent couches; while a clay hearth near the stern, with a few bricks and earthenware pans, served all the purposes of a kitchen. Our arrangements being quickly completed, we started from our mooring shortly after daybreak. It was a lovely morning, although the night had been rainy; it seemed indeed as if we were now about to have a return of fine weather, so auspiciously broke

> " the dewy morn
> With breath all incense, and with cheek all bloom
> Laughing the clouds away with playful scorn
> And living as if earth contained no tomb
> And glowing into day."   BYRON.

---

* A large flat-bottomed barge, about fifty feet long, with a roofing of cadjans, raised sufficiently high in the centre to allow a man to stand upright; the ends of this are separately made so as to slide backwards and forwards over the central portion.

A little delay occurred when we had advanced a couple of miles. The tindal went ashore to pray at the Saman Déwálé for a safe passage down the river, and especially to entreat the god's protection against the dangers of the rapids lower down. Heathen as the man was, he herein set an example which it would be well for more enlightened Christian folk to follow; for there can be no doubt that, as

so

> "To grease the wheel delayeth none,"

> "To church to pray doth hinder none,"

two pithy sayings, which the mother of the great Reformer, Luther, was in the habit of impressing on the minds and memories of her offspring. In about an hour we passed the junction of the Haŋgomu-gaŋga* with the Kalu-gaŋga; there was here a perceptible increase in the strength of the current, and some care was required to avoid rocks, which, as the river was pretty high from the late rains, were not visible above water. About 1 P. M. we passed the junction of the Kuru-gaŋga, and half-an-hour later shot swiftly down Peṇigala-eḷla, the first of the rapids, amongst the rocks of which our tindal, with an additional steersman, and all his men on the *qui vive*, skilfully guided his apparently unwieldy

---

* About three miles up this river is the Potgulu-vihára, or "vihára of libraries," the belief being that there was once here a large collection of all the Buddhistical writings. It is in this vihára that the mouth of one of the supposed subterranean passages exists, referred to at page 114.

craft. Here, on the right-bank of the river, is the Kiri-ęlle-déwálé, where the natives are accustomed to make offerings to Saman, as well as at the Saman-déwálé, higher up the stream. About 4, P. M., we passed the Náragala-ęlla, the second and largest of the rapids; and at 5, the Kotapata-ęlla, the third. Besides these, there are several minor rapids, which obstruct the navigation, called by the boatmen "holombuwas." Darkness coming on, and the moon not rising until after midnight, the tindal would go no further; the boat was therefore moored for the night to the stem of an overhanging cocoanut tree. Submitting to circumstances, we dined on board, and after passing a pleasant evening together, were lulled to sleep by the gentle plashing of the waters against the sides of the boat, as the river ripplingly ran by. Before the break of day, we were again astir, and ere long had passed a remarkable rock in the middle of the river, split or as it were cloven in two in a vertical direction. There is an inscription upon the face of the rock in very ancient characters; and from the position of the letters it is evident that the fracture took place subsequent to the time of their engraving. The belief amongst the natives is that the rock was split by the hard swearing of some perjured individuals. They have indeed a proverbial saying, that "perjurers can swear hard enough to split a rock."

The sun had not risen when we found ourselves alongside the Kalutara bridge, a sort of wooden-pile causeway, about three-quarters of a mile in length, the roadway of which was not much more than six feet above water-mark at the time; and here we had to wait awhile, until a drawbridge, over the principal channel of the river, was raised, to allow our páda-boat to pass; this being done, a quarter of an hour's further rowing brought us by 6 A. M. to the mouth of the river, close to the Kalutara Resthouse.

The scenery all down the Kalu-ganga, from Ratnapura to Kalutara, is most varied, picturesque, and beautiful. The Peak range is seen again and again, the Samanala and the Bena Samanala combining and grouping in different ways. Other ranges seem here to close in upon and narrow the stream, there to recede from and allow it to spread out in lake-like bays. Long, straight river vistas, bordered by dense forests, were succeeded by sweeps and reaches with shelving cultivated banks; and at every turn new beauties were revealed to our admiring gaze.

Monkeys of several species sat chattering among the trees or sprang from bough to bough, as we glided by; and an occasional charge of small shot among the leaves, that may have alarmed but certainly could not hurt them, gave us an opportunity of seeing the prodigious leaps which some of the larger quadrumana can make, when under the influence of fear.

There were places passed, to which the following lines are applicable to the very letter:

"Sweet was the scene! apart the cedars stood,
A sunny islet open'd in the wood;

With vernal tints the wild briar thicket glows,
For here the desert flourish'd as the rose;
From sapling trees with lucid foliage crown'd
Gay lights and shadows twinkled on the ground;
Up the tall stems luxuriant creepers run
To hang their silver blossoms in the sun;
Deep velvet verdure clad the turf beneath
Where trodden flowers their richest odours breathe;
O'er all the bees, with murmuring music, flew
From bell to bell, to sip the treasured dew;
While insect myriads, in the solar gleams,
Glanced to and fro, like intermingling beams;
So fresh, so pure, the woods, the sky, the air,
It seem'd a place where angels might repair,
And tune their harps beneath those tranquil shades,
To morning songs or moonlight serenades." *

Birds of bright plumage were continually glancing in the sunbeams; in their flight like " flashing rays of rainbow light;" this was particularly the case with the kingfishers, many species of which we saw dart into the stream from the overhanging branches where they watched their finny prey.

Nor were there wanting other sights and scenes. Small, frail-looking canoes were being paddled about here and there near the numerous landing places that led to adjacent villages. Sawyers and carpenters were busy on both banks felling and cutting timber, and preparing it in floats to be taken to Moraṭuwa or Kalutara. Vihâras and Déwâlés peered out

---

* " The World before the Flood."

from clustering trees on knolls and crests of hills; near each
of which a few boats or canoes were sure to be seen moored.
Rafts of timber and bambus were floating down the stream in
charge of one or two men, who were nearly as much in the
water as out, except when perched on one end of the float in a
small hut in which they could scarcely squeeze themselves.
Large páda boats similar to the one we were in, were being
poled up the river, slowly creeping alongside the banks, where
the force of the current was less than elsewhere, their crews
now helping themselves on with a haul at the canes and
creepers which fringed the water's edge, and anon availing
of a slant of wind, when they quickly stretched a wide-
spread sail on light elastic bambu masts. Altogether, to
quote the words of my companion—"I can imagine nothing
more delightful to a lover of nature than our boating trip
down this river. . .Its banks are lined with clumps of the
tall bambus, nodding to their own image in the stream
below; with lofty forest trees, many of them richly overgrown with a foliage not their own—ferns, orchids, parasites
of many kinds,—and with others, up which climbers ascended in stout twisted cables, and then fell in cascades of
green foliage from branch to branch, and hung in heavy
masses to the surface of the river. Besides these, there
were, as one descended the river, more and more of the
kitul palms, the arrow-like arekas, and the bending stems
of the cocoanuts. All these with a background of hills,
and the whole repeated again by reflection in the surface of
the smooth gliding water. And so we came slowly down

the middle of the stream, and shot hurriedly through the
rapids, till the increasing roar of the ocean surf told us
that we were nearing Kalutara."

The pleasant town of Kalutara is twenty-six miles distant
from Colombo ; the healthiness of its situation, facing the
sea-breeze from the southwest, has always recommended it
to Europeans as one of the sanataria of the Island, and not
a few deem a residence in its neighbourhood preferable to a
visit to the colder region of Nuwara Eliya.   The resthouse,
formerly the residence of the District Judge, is one of the
most commodious in Ceylon.   Views of picturesque scenery
are to be had in all directions from the surrounding emi-
nences ; the most extended being that from a vihára, about·
six miles off, on the top of the steep rocky hill, Vehera-gala-
kanda, "the mountain of the temple rock," the residence of
a Buddhist priest, celebrated amongst the Siṇhalese for his
extraordinary medical knowledge.   The old fort on the
promontory commanding the mouth of the river, has its own
peculiar historic interest.   It was originally the site of a
Buddhist Vihára, destroyed by the Portuguese for the purpose of converting the place into a fort. A mile or two from
the town, a very singular Banyan tree, in front of a Moorish
mosque, droops from an over-hanging branch its aerial roots
like a thick veil right across the road.   Coçon-nut plantations, gardens, roperies, distilleries, fisheries, busily occupy
the inhabitants; so many of whom are Moormen, that Madam
Ida Pfeiffer, led astray by the venerable bearded faces of
the numerous Israelitish-looking ancients whom she saw,

says, iu her description of the town, that its population consists principally of Jews. A District Court and Minor Courts of Justice and a Jail, provide for the litigants and the criminals of a numerous population; while schools and places of worship, well attended by children and adults, shew that the educational and spiritual wants of the people are not neglected.

The low pile bridge, already referred to, was constructed to supersede the old "tara," or ferry, across the Kalu-gaṇga, and forms a connecting link of the Galle and Colombo road, the beauty of which, as it skirts the sea-coast, and passes through groves of palms, and noble forest, or cultivated bread and jack-fruit trees, calls forth the admiration of every traveller. About a mile and a quarter from the bridge, iu a prominent position on the road side, is a Dharma Sáláwa, or preaching hall, belonging to the Waskaduwa Buddhist community, presided over by Saranápála Unánsé of the Amarapura sect, whose principal pupil is the learned Subhúti Unánsé, known in the literary world as the editor of a recent edition of the Abhidhánappadipíká, an ancient Páli dictionary, composed about A.D. 1153, by the théra Moggelána. A drive of nearly eight miles further brings one to the town of Pánaduré;* a thriving populous place,

---

* There are three derivations given for this name; one 'pánu' rock, 'dura' distance, referring to the rock Góná-gala or "elk-rock," seen at a distance from the resthouse of about two miles out at sea: the second is connected with a legend, which states that Dewol-dewiyó sailing hither

and the head quarters of a Police Magistracy. Here is the
Gal-kanda, an extensive vihára, presided over by Guna-
ratana Unánse,a priest of portly presence and much affability.
Being but sixteen miles from Colombo, Pánnduré is a very
favorite spot for an occasional visit. Folk from the capital,
whose business will not allow of long absences, can with
ease run down on the Saturday and return on the Monday
morning. The resthouse is admirably situated, facing the
mouth of a broad estuary, bounded by a sand bank, against
which the waves of the ocean fret themselves and break into
foamy surf; the resthouse keeper is proverbial for the soli-
citude with which he studies the comfort of his visitors;
excellent bathing is always attainable; fresh fish may be had
in abundance, morning, noon, and night; and a trip in a
canoe up the estuary to visit the curious cane-wicker fish-
kraals, or the rocks from whence the oysters are obtained,
is most interesting and enjoyable.

Crossing the estuary by the bridge, a further drive of
four miles leads to the town of Moratuwa. Here we enter

---

with seven ships, and being wrecked, and escaping on seven stone rafts,
saw a lamp shining at a déwálé, and endeavoured to effect a landing; but
the goddess Pattini, the presiding deity of the déwálé, objecting to Dewol-
dewiyó landing near her domains, caused the light of the lamp to recede
as the dewiyó drew near; whereupon Dewol-dewiyó desisted, remarking
" pána durayi," the lamp is too far. The third is connected with the
time of the invasion of Ceylon by Wijaya, and refers to some event connected with the breaking of lamps, respecting which I have not been able
to obtain particulars.

the region of Cinnamon; and from thence to Colombo the
road passes by or through almost continuous gardens of this
renowned laurel,—the cultivation of the cocoanut palm distinguishing the western, while that of the fragrant cinnamon
bush marks the eastern side of the road. Moraṭuwa,* for
a purely native town, is perhaps the handsomest in Ceylon.
The great bulk of its population of upwards of 12,000 souls
consists chiefly of carpenters of the fisher caste, who devote
themselves to the manufacture of furniture, and casks and
barrels for the export of coffee and cocoanut oil; but it also
numbers among its inhabitants some of the most prosperous
and wealthy of the Siṇhalese community ; and these, emu-
lous of one another, have erected mansions on either side
of the main road, in a style which shews at a glance the
opulence of their owners. Amongst the most eminent of
the inhabitants was the late Jeronis de Soyza, Mudaliyar of
the Governor's Gate, whose dwelling-house on the outskirts
of the town might be considered the model of a Siṇhalese
mansion, with its garden and oriental grounds. To his
munificence the inhabitants are mainly indebted for the
noble Anglican church which adorns the town,—a sacred
edifice that surpasses in its ecclesio-architectural beauty
all others in Ceylon. His liberality† was in like manner

---

* 'Mora,' a small but pleasant fruit; 'aṭuwa,' a granary or store.

† For an account of the procession and fête in Colombo and Moraṭuwa,
after Governor Sir George Anderson had conferred upon Mr. De Soyza
the rank of Mudaliyar, see Appendix M.

manifested, in the establishment of schools, the erection of
ambalamas, the making of roads, and in every kind of improvement that conduced to the welfare of his countrymen.
The Wesleyans and the Roman Catholics form a large
and influential section of the population here, and possess
spacious places of worship, and well attended schools.

Next to Moratuwa lies the village of Ratmalana, formerly
as its name imports, " a forest of red flowers," but now famous
for its extensive cinnamon cultivation; and for its pansala
or monastery, where a college of priests is assembled under
the presidency of Hikkaduwe Samangala, the Chief priest of
Adam's Peak, elected to that office in 1866, because, in the
opinion of his brethren—an opinion shared by all the literati
of Ceylon—"his reputation for piety and scholarship stands
super-eminent among the priesthood of the Malwatta establishments of the Island of Ceylon."* The pansala is

* There are two sects of Buddhist priests in Ceylon, the Siamese and
the Amsrapura; the former has two establishments, the Malwatte, and the
Asgiriya.   Of these, the latter establishment is the more ancient, and was
originally located in a dell on Asgiriya, "the horse rock," a hill in the outskirts of the town of Kandy.   The former was established by King Kirti Sri,
on the re-establishment, or resuscitation of Buddhism which took place in
his reign.   It was placed under the charge of the Saṅgha Raja, Weliwiṭa,
Chief-priest of Adam's Peak, at Mal-watta, "the flower garden,"—a place
bordering the Kandy lake, given by the king to be prepared as a residence
for the priests from Siam, upon their arrival in Ceylon; and the privilege
was conferred upon it of taking precedence over the Asgiriya establishment.
Its members were supposed to be more subservient to the royal will;
but the doctrines and practices of both are precisely the same.   The

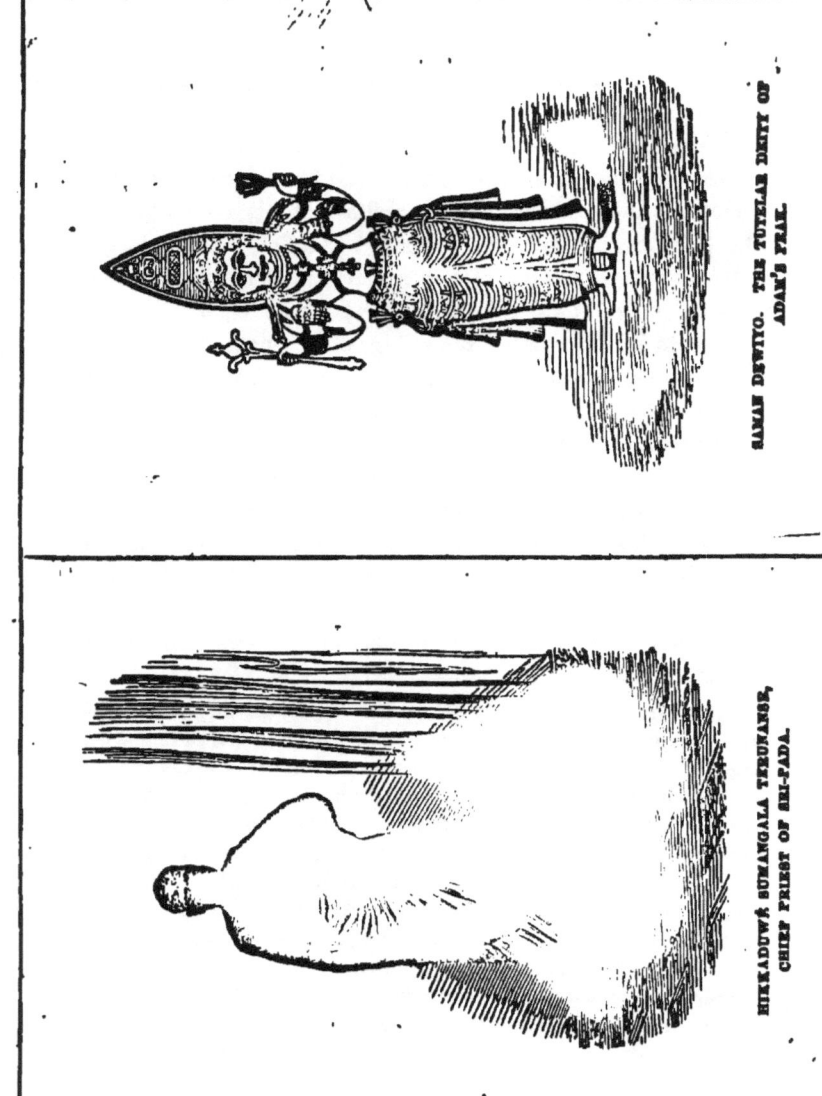

HIKKADUWÁ SUMANGALA TERUNANSE,
CHIEF PRIEST OF SRI-PADA.

SAMAN DEWIYO. THE TUTELAR DEITY OF
ADAM'S PEAK.

pleasantly situated about half a mile to the east of the road, surrounded by groves of fruit bearing and other trees. We paid our respects to the learned Chief-priest on our return from the pilgrimage. He was agreeably surprised to learn that we had succeeded in reaching the Samanala, as the reports he had received about the weather, and the state of the roads, had led him to believe that we would be forced to return without accomplishing the object of our journey.

A few miles further on, on the western side of the road, is Mount Lavinia, a rocky headland projecting into the sea, on which is situated what Sir Emerson Tennent describes as "the remains of what was once the marine palace of the Governors of Ceylon; an edifice in every way worthy of the great man by whom it was erected—Sir Edward Barnes."

Amarapura sect was established about the year 1808, by a priest named Ambagahapitiya, who, with eight others, obtained the Upasampada orders from the Sangha Raja of Amarapura at Burmah. The two sects are distinguished from each other by a slight difference in dress and personal appearance. The Siamese priests leave their right shoulders uncovered by their robes, and shave their eyebrows; those of Amarapura cover both shoulders with their robes, and leave their eyebrows in their natural state. The Amarapura sect has prospered principally in the Maritime provinces of the Island, where, since their establishment, their numbers have increased until they are about equal to those of the Siamese fraternity, which word is perhaps the better distinguishing term, since their differences are not doctrinal but merely ritual. They have a few members in Sabaragamuwa and U'va; but there, and in all the other Kandian districts, the priesthood of the Siamese ordination form a preponderating majority.

After being dismantled by orders from the home government, then undergoing a "paroxysm of economy," it underwent a variety of changes, and was bought and sold, again
and again, until a speculative purchaser ventured to repair
it throughout, for the purpose of converting it into a private
boarding-house.   It did not, however, remain long in his
hands; and being once more put up for sale, has now become
the property of a company, who let out its apartments to
invalids and others desirous of recruiting their health, or
of enjoying the sea-breezes more fully than is possible
elsewhere, for many miles along the coast.   And for both
these purposes, as well as for pic-nic parties from Colombo, it
is most admirably adapted.   A cool airy barrack, officers'
quarters, and the rifle butts of the European regiment
stationed in Ceylon, adjoin Mount Lavinia.

Mount Attidiya, a residence nearly opposite, but a little
distance inland, once as famed for the beauty of its grounds
as for the hospitality of its owner—a gentleman then high
up in the Ceylon Civil Service—is now an abandoned ruin.

At Galkissa,* the village next passed through, "the traveller has the opportunity of seeing a temple which may
serve as an example of modern Buddhist buildings of this
class in Ceylon.   It is situated on a gentle eminence close
by the high road, surrounded by groves of iron-wood,

---

* The name is derived from the words *Gal-kessa*, "stone-key";
'kessa,' being an old and obsolete term for key.   There is a legend that
an important key was hidden here in ancient times.

murutas, champacs, and other trees, offerings of whose
flowers form so remarkable a feature in the worship of the
Siηhalese. The modest pansala in which the priests and
their attendants reside is built in the hollow, and the ascent
to the Wihara above it is by steps excavated in the hill.
The latter is protected by a low wall decorated with mythological symbols, and the edifice itself is of the humblest
dimensions, with whitened walls and a projecting tiled roof.
In an inner apartment dimly lighted by lamps, where the air
is heavy with the perfume of the yellow champac flowers,
are the *pilamas* or statues of the god. One huge recumbent
figure, twenty feet in length, represents Buddha, in that
state of blissful repose which constitutes the elysium of his
devotees; a second shows him seated under the sacred bo-tree
in Uruwela; and a third erect, and with the right hand raised
and the two fore-fingers extended (as is the custom of the
popes in conferring their benediction), exhibits him in the act
of exhorting his earliest disciples. One quadrangular apartment which surrounds the enclosed adytus is lighted by
windows, so as to exhibit a series of paintings on the inner
wall, illustrative of the narratives contained in the *jatakas*,
or legends of the successive births of Buddha; the whole
executed in the barbarous and conventional style which
from time immemorial has marked this peculiar school of
ecclesiastical art.

" As usual, within the outer enclosure there is a small
Hindu *dewale* (which in this instance is dedicated to the
worship of the Katarngam deviyo), and near to it grows

one of the sacred bo-trees, that, like every other in Ceylon, is said to have been raised from a seed of the patriarchal tree planted by Mahindo, at Anarajapoora, more than two thousand years ago. The whole establishment is on the most unpretending scale; for nine months of the year the priests visit the houses of the villagers in search of alms, and during the other three, when the violence of the rain prevents their perambulations, their food is brought to them in the pansala; or else they reside with some of their wealthier parishioners, who provide them once a year with a set of yellow robes."[*]

From the populous village of Galkissa the traveller enters the suburbs of the capital, and soon begins to find himself among the residences of the European inhabitants of Colombo. Chief among these is the mansion long known as Bagatelle, where a generation ago the father of the present senior member of the Ceylon Civil Service dispensed with lavish hand most liberal hospitalities. It is now the property of Mr. Charles De Soyza, only son and inheritor of the vast wealth of the Mudaliyar to whom reference was made when treating of Moratuwa. Rebuilt and extended, it is here that its opulent owner had the distinguished honor of entertaining His Royal Highness the Duke of Edinburgh on the occasion of his visit to Ceylon in April of the present year [1870].[†] A drive of two miles along what is now called the

---

[*] Sir J. Emerson Tennent's Ceylon, vol. ii. pp. 144—146.
[†] For an account of this entertainment, see Appendix N.

Kollupitiya* road, brings one on to the Galle Face, or Faas, so called by the Dutch from its being in front of the fortifications that faced the direction of Galle. This fine open space—the general parade ground for the troops, and great lung of Colombo, is nearly a mile in length, and half a mile or more in breadth, and is traversed by three excellent roads, —one in the centre, one by the sea-side, and one past the neat Gothic church belonging to the Church Missionary Society, the bridge leading to Slave Island, the Lake, and the Garrison Burial Ground;—all converging together and uniting in one that *once* led past the frowning Dutch batteries, the deep broad moat, and the quaint old gate, that gave access to the inner defences of the Fort of Colombo.

The road that *once* led past I write,—for while this work has been in hand, the fortifications of Colombo, or that portion of them which overlooked the Galle Face, have disappeared,— have been razed and levelled with the ground; the moat from whence the earth work of the batteries was originally dug has received back into its bosom the soil rent from it a century and a half ago; the pick and the mine and the mamoty† have so far restored the site of moat and mound to its pristine state, that no one now can say with Captain Anderson:

"Upon that further point of land,
  See yonder frowning fortress stand,

---

* 'Kollu,' a kind of pulse used for feeding horses; 'pitiya,' a plain.
† A kind of short-handled hoe.

Whose mouldering but majestic walls'
Its former grandeur yet recalls
As when the conquerors of the isle
First rear'd the firm commanding pile,
To keep their slippery footing sure,
An infant empire to secure ;
To overawe a savage foe
And their superior science show.
Now like a veteran decay'd
Who once the sword of valour sway'd,
You trace upon its evening hour,
The vestige of its noontide power!"

There was a certain stern picturesqueness about the
frowning old walls and massive batteries, with their embattled
crests and grim gaping embrasures, and ancient guns, all of
which modern science has rendered useless, but which of yore
begirt the town with a cincture of impregnable strength; and
one grew so accustomed to their appearance, that now they
exist no longer, a feeling of regret at their destruction will
occasionally obtrude itself upon the mind, especially as the
work of demolition progresses, and day by day familiar objects
are for ever lost to sight.   The ancients of the place may
mourn departed glories, as did the sages among the returning Israelites when they recollected the Jerusalem of their
younger days; but the glory of the latter times, it was pre-
dicted, should exceed by far those of the former. It needs
no prophet to make known the advantages to Colombo that
must accrue from the changes which are being made.   Like
a butterfly emerging from its chrysalis, the city stript of its

warlike garniture, becomes daily more and more beautiful to view; and with the magnificent approach to it from Kollupitiya across the Galle Face, with its public and other buildings nestling as it were in the groves of Tulip trees* that adorn and shade its broad and busy streets, it appears to the eye of the traveller one of the fairest and most pleasantly situated, as it certainly also is the healthiest by far of all the cities of the East.

---

* The *Suriya*. Thespesia populnea.

Adam's Peak.

"See frowning o'er the vale below,
Yon rifted mountain's cloudy brow!
On its most elevated crest,
Perched like the soaring eagle's nest,
Half blended with the skiey blue,
And scarce within our reach of view,
There Buddha's lonely temple stands
Revered by all the neighbouring lands!
A path that skirts along the base,
Winds up the mountain to the place;
Be toil and danger then forgot,
And let us gain the hallow'd spot." *

CHAPTER X.

FACSIMILE FOOT-PRINTS. — ANURA'DHAPURA. — KURUNEGALA. —
ALU-VIHA'RA. — NA'THA-DE'WA'LE'. — GANNORUWA. — ALA-
GALLA. — KOTTIMBULWALA-VIHA'RA. — DEWANAGALA. — KHET-
TA'RA'MA-VIHA'RA. — RAMBODA. — BADDEGAMA. — SITAKANDE.
— HOT-SPRING OF MAHAPALASSE.

JUST as in Moscow the Russians have a facsimile of the
Church of the Holy Sepulchre at Jerusalem, to which the
faithful of the Russo-Greek communion make pilgrimages,

---

* "The Wanderer in Ceylon."

and honestly, if ignorantly, believe that the merit which they acquire in such pilgrimages is only but in a very slight degree less than what they would have gained had they gone direct to the hallowed fane in the sacred city itself; so in Ceylon there are numerous facsimiles of the Srí-páda, to which the old and infirm, and those Buddhists who cannot undertake the journey to the Samanala, reverently repair, and make their offerings of flowers and perfumes; and although they admit that the merit of such offerings is inferior to that of those offered on the Srí-páda itself, at the summit of the Samanala, such as it is they eagerly covet it, distinguishing the quality of their pious merit-bringing gifts by the term "uddésika pújá," or substitutionary offerings.

Fa Hian, the Chinese pilgrim of the fifth century, refers to the foot-print on the Samanala, and also to one impressed by Buddha on some place north of the city of Anurádhapura; this latter has not been identified, but was probably a facsimile, to which no great sanctity was attached.

At Kurunégala, the capital city of the island from A. D. 1319 to 1347, there is a facsimile of the Srí-páda, on the top of the enormous Etugala, or Elephant's rock, so named from its having become so rounded and worn by time, that although 600 feet in height, it has acquired the form of a couchant elephant. Here was situated an ancient temple, to which access was had by means of steep paths and steps hewn out of the solid stone. This is still the resort of Buddhists from many parts of the island, their chief object of veneration being the facsimile Srí-páda; and from this point

they can see the towering alp of Adam's Peak, although
distant about forty miles. This copy is said to have been
originally cut to gratify the pious desires of a daughter of
one of the kings, who was unable to perform the pilgrimage
to the Peak and personally make her offerings on the holy
foot-print. Lamenting her inability, the priests had compassion upon her, and resolved that a copy of the foot-print
should be cut on the summit of Etugala; this was done; the
distress of the Princess was removed, and the place soon
became recognized as a legitimate place of pilgrimage. It
was from this place that the usurping king Vasthimi Kumá-
raya, was killed by being precipitated headlong by a band of
assassins, when on his way to join an assembly of priests to
which he had been invited. Unsuspicious of danger he
accepted the invitation and was thus treacherously slain.
This usurpation, tradition says, led to the next monarch
forsaking the place and removing the capital to Gampola.

There is another facsimile at the Alu vihára in Matale; of
the rocks of which Major Forbes gives the following account:
"Amongst the recesses of these crags the doctrines of Gautama Buddha were first reduced to writing, and under their
huge masses many temples were formed at a very early
period. These temples were destroyed by the British troops
in 1803, and only two out of eight have been since restored.
On one of the highest pinnacles is a print of Buddha's footstep, similar to that on Adam's Peak, from which it is
copied; and a small hollow is formed in the rock near it,
for the purpose of receiving the offerings of the pious. On

a neighbouring crag are the remains of a dágoba, and amidst its scattered fragments a stone cut into twenty-five compartments; in the centre one of these the relic of Buddha had been placed, and the remaining cells in the stone had contained the offerings made when the relic was deposited. Through the middle of the Aluewihare rocks there is a broad natural street of unequal height; to reach this you must ascend a flight of rude steps, then pass through a crevice, and again ascend until you come upon a flat rock, which is pointed out as the spot where the King Walagambahoo assembled the priests, who here compared their texts, which were then, or soon afterwards, committed to writing, and form the Banapota or Buddhist Bible. This took place about ninety-two years B.C.; and for two hundred and fourteen years previous to that time, if not from the date of Gautama's death, his doctrines had descended by tradition only."[*]

At the Natha déwálé in Kandy, is a third copy of the foot-print. This was formerly on the Senkadagala, a hill behind the Kandy Kachcheri. The rock bearing the impress was a few years ago conveyed to the déwále where it is now seen.

A fourth facsimile exists, (some say it is an original one), on the top of a mountain on Gannoruwa, close to Peradenia; and a fifth on the summit of a mountain at Allagala. This

---

[*] "Eleven Years in Ceylon," vol. i. p. 346.

is known to have been made by the zealous restorer of Buddhism, the Sangha Rája Saranankara, who about 124 years ago brought over to Ceylon Siamese priests of the Upasampada order, and revived the religion of the country after a long period of dormant inactivity and declension.

A sixth copy was cut on the top of the Kotimbulwala vihára rock in the Atakalan Kórálé of the Sabaragamuwa district. This was the work of a pious priest who resided in the vihára about eighty years ago. It was originally a mere outline; but the late chief priest of the vihára had it cut deeper, and made more of a facsimile than it had previously been.

At Dewanagala in the Four Kórálés there are two facsimiles, the origin of which I have not ascertained. There is also one at Khettáráma vihára, about a quarter of a mile inland from the 37th mile-stone on the Galle road, made by Mahagoda Dhammadassi Terunanse, of the Malwatta establishments.

In the Southern Province, there are two copies; one at Ramboda, on a rock adjoining the high road to Galle, near the Police Court at Balapitimodare ; and another at Baddegama, about fourteen miles southeast from Galle. The Rev. James Selkirk says of this,* " I went with the interpreter this evening to a small temple, about two miles from Baddagama, where is a mark of the Srí-páda, or blessed

---

* " Recollections of Ceylon," 1844; p. 468.

foot, similar to the one which is on the top of Adam's Peak, and to which such vast crowds of worshippers are drawn every year.* It appears that a priest in this neighbourhood, some years ago, went to the Peak, and took the measure of the 'foot,' and on his return got a stonemason to cut one out similar to it. This was erected on the top of a hill in this neighbourhood, and enclosed within a small building. Great numbers of people come at certain seasons of the year to make offerings to it. I measured the length of it, and found it to be seventy-two inches; the breadth is thirty-six inches. The length of each of the toes, which are all alike, is fifteen inches, and the breadth of each seven inches and a half. When I asked the priest, who resides at a pansala near the place, what sort of a body the person must have had who had so enormous a foot, he said, with much gravity, 'Don't you know that our Buddha is eighteen cubits high? By the cubit is here meant two feet three inches."

There is also another impression of a so-called foot-print at Sítakanda in the Magam pattu; but this is alleged to be not from the foot of a Buddha, but of some other giant. Of this I have not been able to obtain any definite information. In the neighbourhood of the place where the impression is asserted to exist, there are, close together, a hot and a cold

---

* It has been computed that during the season about 100,000 Buddhists and others make the annual pilgrimage to the Srí-páda on the summit of Adam's Peak.

spring, respecting which I am indebted to the Assistant
Government Agent at Hambaṇtota for the following information.—" The Mahápélessa hot spring is found in a deserted
hamlet, four miles from Ridiyágama, and about eighteen from
Hambaṇtota. The water gushes forth in great plenty in a
small tract of open ground in the heart of the jungle. It
appeared to me to have a temperature as high as that of the
Hot Wells at Bath, considerably, if a conjecture may be
hazarded, above 100°. I had no thermometer with me at
the time of my visit. As it issues from the ground it is
perfectly clear and limpid; but in the pool, a few feet below
where it accumulates, it acquires a dark blue tinge.
When rice is boiled in it the grains are said to be dyed blue.
The pool is much frequented by elephants, elk, and wild
buffaloes. At the time of my visit three wild peacocks,
which abound in Magam Pattu, were hopping about briskly,
or, as the Siṇhalese say, dancing, in front of the spring.
The water tastes as if it had some mineral salts in solution,
which is no doubt the case. In the spring itself is a quantity
of decayed leaves and twigs, although no large trees are
near at hand. It is possible the leaves may have been
conveyed by the action of the water from some point higher
up. People acquainted with both places say, that the
water of the Mahapélessa spring much resembles in taste
and appearance, that of the Kannea hot-wells near Trinco-
malie. For persons troubled with rheumatic, and skin, and
such like ailments, all of which are but too common in
Ceylon, bathing in the Mahapélessa spring would, no doubt,

be beneficial. In any case, the spring is a natural phenomenon of a kind rare in Ceylon (where traces of volcanic agency are very scanty) and is well worth the attention of the curious. It is much to be wished that a careful analysis of the water could be made; but, so far as I am aware, this has not yet been done.

"About 400 yards from the hot spring, is another spring, of deliciously cool water. Springs of any sort are rare in Magam Pattu, which suffers much from drought at all times. I do not doubt there was at one period a populous village near these springs. The place is now however deserted; and what was once a scene of thriving industry and plenty, is a dense jungle abandoned to the elephants, the cheetah, and other wild tenants of the forest."

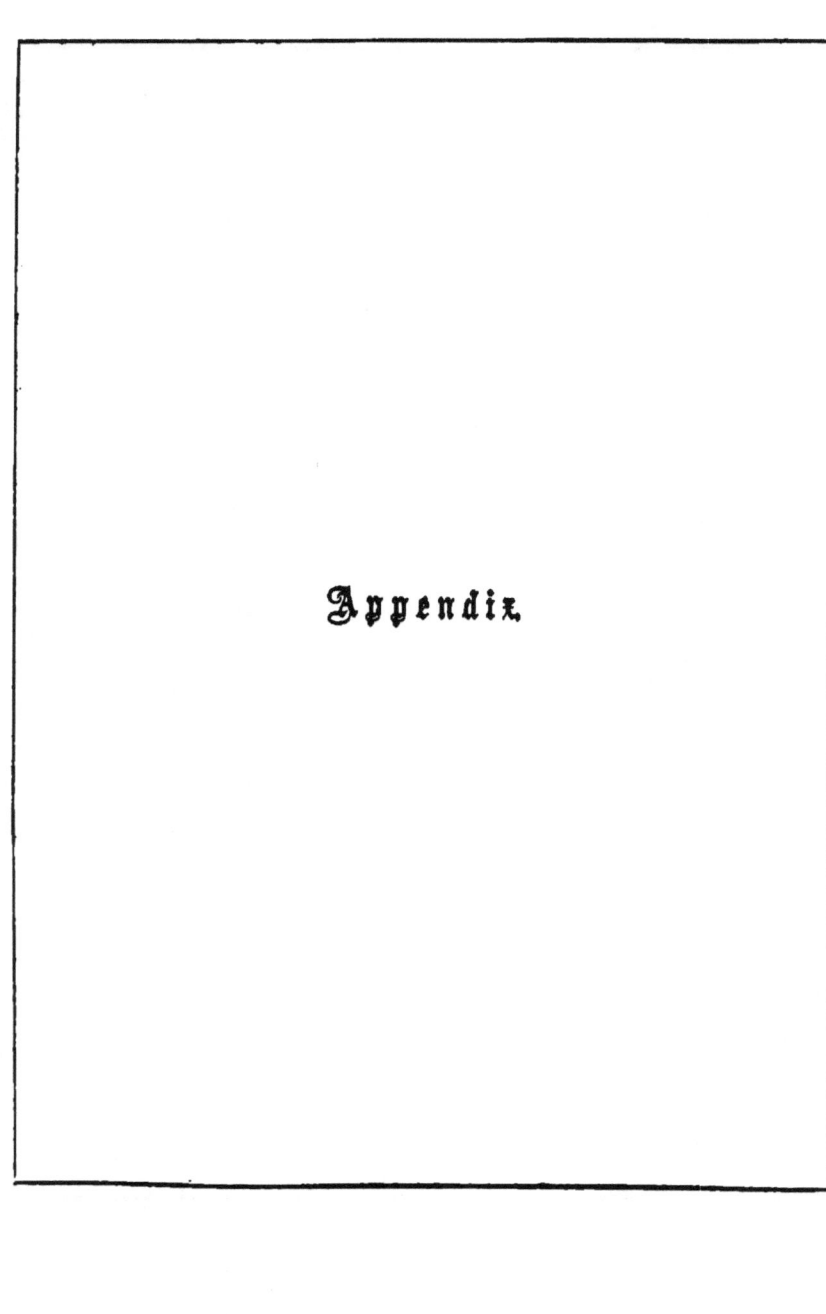

Appendix.

A.

ON THE ORIGIN OF THE SRI' PA'DA.

"THE veneration with which this majestic mountain [Adam's Peak] has been regarded for ages, took its rise in all probability amongst the aborigines of Ceylon, whom the sublimities of nature, awaking the instinct of worship, impelled to do homage to the mountains and the sun. Under the influence of such feelings the aspect of this solitary alp, towering above the loftiest ranges of the hills, and often shrouded in storms and thunder-clouds, was calculated to convert awe into adoration.

"In a later age the religious interest became concentrated on a single spot to commemorate some individual identified with the national faith, and thus the hollow in the lofty rock that crowns the summit was said by the Brahmans to be the footstep of Siva, by the Buddhists, of Buddha, by the Chinese, of Foĕ, by the Gnostics, of Icû, by the Mahometans, of Adam, whilst the Portuguese authorities were divided between the conflicting claims of St. Thomas, and the Eunuch of Candace, Queen of Ethiopia.

"The phases of this local superstition can be traced with curious accuracy through its successive transmitters. In the Buddhist annals, the sojourn of Buddha in Ceylon, and the impression of the 'sri-pada,' his sacred foot-mark, left on departing, are recorded in that portion of the *Mahawanso* which was written by Maha-naama prior to B. C. 301, and the story is repeated in the other

sacred books of the Siṇhalese. The *Raja-Tarangini* states that
in the first century of the Christian era, a king of Kashmir, about
the year 24, resorted to Ceylon to adore the relic on Adam's Peak.
The Chinese traveller, Fa Hian, who visited Ceylon A. D. 413,
says that two foot marks of Foŭ were then venerated in the Island,
one on the sacred mountain, and the second towards the north of
the island.   On the continent of India both Fa Hian and Hiouen
Thsang examined many other sri-padas; and Wang Ta-youen
adheres to the story of their Buddhist origin, although later Chinese writers, probably from intercourse with the Mahometans,
borrow the idea that it was the foot-print of Pwan-koo, "the
first man," in their system of mythology.   In the twelfth century,
the patriot King Prakrama Bahu I. "made a journey on foot to
worship the shrine on Samanhela, and caused a temple to be
erected on its summit," and the mountain was visited by the
King Kirti Nissanga, for the same devout purpose, in A. D. 1201,
and by Prakrama III. A. D. 1267.   Nor was the faith of the
Siṇhalese in its sanctity shaken even by the temporary apostasy
and persecution of the tyrant Raja Siṇha I., who, at the close of
the sixteenth century, abjured Buddhism, adopted the worship of
Brahma, and installed some Aandco fakirs in the desecrated
shrine upon the Peak.

   "Strange to say, the origin of the Mahometan tradition, as to its
being the footstep of Adam, is to be traced to a Christian source.
In framing their theological system, the Gnostics, who, even
during the lifetime of the Apostles, corrupted Christianity by an
admixture of the mysticism of Plato; assigned a position of singular pre-eminence to Adam, who, as '*Ieú, the primal man*,' next
to the '*Noos*' and '*Logos*,' was made to rank as the third
emanation from the Deity.   Amongst the details of their worship

they cultivated the veneration for monumental relics; and in the precious manuscript of the fourth century, which contains the Coptic version of the discourse on " *Faithful Wisdom*," attributed by Tertullian to the great Gnostic heresiarch Valentinus, there occurs the earliest recorded mention of the sacred footprint of Adam. The Saviour is there represented as informing the Virgin Mary that he has appointed the spirit Kalapataraoth as guardian over the footstep (skemmut) '*impressed by the foot of Ieû*, and placed him in charge of the books of Ieû, written by Enoch in paradise.'

"The Gnostics in their subsequent dispersion under the persecution of the emperors, appear to have communicated to the Arabs this mystical veneration for Adam as the great *protoplast* of the human race; and in the religious code of Mahomet, Adam, as the pure creation of the Lord's breath, takes precedence as the *Ewel' ulenbiya*, 'the greatest of all patriarchs and prophets,' and the *Kalifé-y-Ekber*, 'the first of God's vicegerents upon earth.' The Mahometans believe that on his expulsion from Paradise, Adam passed many years in expiatory exile upon a mountain in India before his re-union with Eve on Mount Arafath, which overhangs Mocca. As the Koran, in the passages in which is recorded the fall of Adam, makes no mention of the spot at which he took up his abode on earth, it may be inferred that in the age of Mahomet, his followers had not adopted Ceylon as the locality of the sacred footstep; but when the Arab seamen, returning from India, brought home accounts of the mysterious relic on the summit of *Al-rahoun*, as they termed Adam's Peak, it appears to have fixed in the minds of their countrymen the precise locality of Adam's penitence. The most ancient Arabian records of travel that have come down to us mention the scene with solemnity; but it was not till the

tenth century that Ceylon became the established resort of Mahometan pilgrims, and Ibn Batúta, about the year 1340, relates that
at Shiraz he visited the tomb of the Imam Abu-Abd-Allah, who
first taught the way to Serendib.

"At the present day, the Buddhists are the guardians of the
Srí-páda, but around the object of common adoration the devotees
of all races meet, not in furious contention like the Latins and
Greeks at the Holy Sepulchre in Jerusalem, but in pious appre-
ciation of the one solitary object on which they can unite in
peaceful worship."—SIR J. EMERSON TENNENT's Ceylon, vol. ii.
pp. 132—137.

2.

IBN BATUTA'S TRAVELS IN CEYLON.[*]

WHEN we sailed, however, (from the Maldive Islands) the wind changed upon us, and we were near being lost; but arrived at last at the island of Ceylon, a place well known, and in which is situated the mountain of Serendíb. This appeared to us like a pillar of smoke, when we were at a distance of nine days from it. When we get near the land, we saw a harbour, into which we endeavoured to put, but were threatened by the Reis, who was in the ship. The reason of this was, the harbour was in a district belonging to an infidel prince, who had no intercourse with the captains of Mohammedan vessels, as other infidel princes had. He

---

[*] Professor Lee's translation, from which this chapter is taken, is not from the original MS., but from three copies of an abridgement, or what "Mohammed Ibn Fat'h Allah El Bailúní states that he extracted from the epitomo of the Kátib Mohammed Ibn Jazzi El Kelbí, (upon whom be the mercy of God,) from the travels of the theologian Abu Abd Allah El Lawátí of Tangiers, known by the surname of Ibn Batúta." The date of his arrival at Ceylon is not stated; but it may be very nearly ascertained from several circumstances elsewhere mentioned. He resided for some time at Delhi, where he was appointed a Judge, and in 1342 was sent by the Emperor of Hindustan on an Embassy to the Emperor of China. On his way he met with many adventures and detentions, before reaching Kalicut, where he waited three months for the ship that was to convey him to China. Then, after having embarked his suite, and the presents with which he was entrusted, while

was likewise a very stupid being. He had also ships with which
he occasionally transported his troops against the Mohammedans.
Besides all this, we were in danger of drowning, unless we could
enter the port : I said to the Reis, therefore, Allow me to come on
shore, and I will ensure thy safety, and that of those about thee,
with the King. To this he consented, and myself, with some of
my followers only, were brought on shore. The infidels then came
about us and said : What are you ? I answered, I am a relation
of the King of the Maabar districts, and am on a voyage to
visit him : whatever is in the ship, is a present for the King of
Maabar. They then went to their king, and told him this. He
therefore sent for me, and I went to him. He is the king of the
city of Battála,* which is small, and surrounded by two wooden
fences. The whole of its shore abounds with cinnamon wood,
bakam, and the kalanjí aloe ; which, however, is not equal to the
Kamárí, or the Kákulí, in scent. The merchants of Maabar and
the Maabar districts transport it without any other price than a
few articles of clothing, which are given as presents to the king.

---

performing his devotions previous to embarking himself, a great storm arose, and
the ship was driven to sea without him. This caused another long detention. But
at last, ascertaining that the vessel had reached China, after a further delay he made
his way to the Maldive Islands. There he settled down, married four wives, and
was made a Judge. A child was born to him, and he became a magnate in the
land. But his prosperity became his bane ; for the Vizier, dreading his own loss
of influence, grew so hostile, that he resolved to visit the "Maabar districts of
Hindostan," whose king was married to a sister of one of his wives. Taking
all the above circumstances into account, he could scarcely have reached Ceylon
before 1347; the probability indeed is that it was later; for the capital of the
island was, at the time of his visit, Kankár, or Ganga-sri-pura, the modern
Gampola, which city was not made the capital until 1347.

    * Puttalam.

This may be attributed to the circumstance, that It is brought down by the mountain torrents, and left in great heaps upon the shore. Between this city and the Maabar districts, there is a voyage of one day and night. The king of Ceylon, Ayarí Shakarí[*] by name, has considerable forces by sea. When I was first admitted to his presence, he rose and received me honourably, and said : You are to be my guest for three days. Security shall be forwarded to the people of the ship, because your relation, the king of the Maabar, is my friend. After thanking him, I remained with him, and was treated with increasing respect.

One day, when I was admitted to his presence, he had with him a great number of pearls, which had been brought from the

---

* It is not quite clear who the individual here called the king of Ceylon was. Perhaps Ibn Batúta assigned to him the rank of king from the meaning of the name ; ' Arya,' signifying in the Sanskrit, noble ; and ' chakra-varti,' universal monarch. Major Forbes, in the Epitome of the History of Ceylon appended to vol. ii. of his work, mentions that in the reign of Bhuwanekabáhu I (A. D. 1303—1814,) Kula-sékara the king of Pándi, sent an army commanded by A'rya-Chakra-varti to invade Ceylon ; and that he took the capital Yápahu, and carried off the Dalada, which he presented to his sovereign. This relic was recovered by Prakramabáhu III. the succeeding king, who went in person to treat with the king of Pándi for its restitution. It is not stated whether the Pándian king retained possession of Puttalam or not. The Malabars or Tamils of Ceylon were settled in considerable numbers along the northwest coast, and the leading mao, or chief, may have been named Chakra-varti, which is a common enough name to this day amongst the Jaffnese ; or the Pándian General may have remained at Puttalam as the representative of the king of Pándi. In the reign of a subsequent monarch, Bhuwaneka-báhu IV. (A. D. 1347—1361,) the capital of Ceylon was removed to Gangá-sirí-pura or Gampola, which may have been the Kankár, referred to by Ibn Batúta further on ; but as the words mean only " the royal river city," they may have been applied to other cities on the banks of a river as well as Gampola.

pearl-fishery, and these his companions were sorting. He asked me, whether I had ever seen pearl-diving, in any country which I had visited. I said, yes, I had, in the island of Fínas. He said: Do not be shy; ask for what you wish. I answered: My only desire in coming to this island was, to visit the blessed foot of our forefather Adam; whom these people call Bábá, while they style Eve, Mámá. This, replied he, is easy enough. We will send some one with you, who shall conduct you thither. The ship (said I) which brought me here, shall return to the Maabar; and when I return, you shall send me there in one of your ships. He answered, It shall be so. When I told this to the commander of the ship, he refused to accede to it; and said, I will wait for you, should you be absent a whole year. This I told to the King, who said: He may stay at my charge until you return. He then gave me a palanquin, which his servants carried upon their shoulders. He also sent with me four Jogees, who were in the habit of visiting the foot-mark every year; with these went four Brahmins, and ten of the King's companions, with fifteen men carrying provisions. As to water, there is plenty of it to be found on the road. We then proceeded on our journey: and on the first day crossed a river in a boat made of reeds, and entered the city of Manár Mandulí,* which is handsome, and situated at the extremity of the territory of the infidel king, who had entertained and sent us out. We then proceeded to the port of Saláwát,† which is a small town. The roads, however, over

---

* Probably Annemadooa. Sir J. E. TENNENT says Minneri Mundal. But this lies in an opposite direction to the route to Chilaw, while Annemadooa is about midway between Puttalam and that town.   † Chilaw.

which we travelled, were rough and abounding with water. In
these there were many elephants: but they never touched either
pilgrims or strangers, in consequence of the blessing obtained by
the Sheikh Abu Abd Allah Ibn Khafíf, the first who opened this
road of pilgrimage to the foot. The infidels would not formerly
allow the Mohammedans to make this pilgrimage, but injured
them; nor would they either sell, or give them any thing to eat.
But when it happened that the elephants killed all the companions
of this Sheikh, one of them sparing and carrying him on his back
from among the mountains to an inhabited district, the infidels
ever after thought highly of the Mohammedans, admitted them
into their houses, and fed them.* And to this very day they speak
of the Sheikh in the most extravagant terms of respect, and call
him "the greatest Sheikh." After this we arrived at the city of
Kankár, which is the seat of the Emperor of Ceylon. It is built
in a valley between two hills, upon an estuary called the estuary

---

* In this statement Ibn Batúta is fully borne out by Robert Knox, who says,
speaking of the charity of the Siphalese, in his chapter "concerning their religious
doctrines, opinions and practices," part iii. ch. 5. "Nor are they charitable only
to the poor of their own nation; but as I said to others, and particularly to the
Moorish beggars, who are Mahometans by religion; these have a temple in Kandy.
A certain former king gave this temple this privilege—that every freeholder should
contribute a ponnam (fanam, 1½d.) to it; and these Moors go to every house in the
land to receive it [except in Dolosbáge]; and, if the house be shut, they have
power to break it open, and to take of goods to the value of it. They come very
confidently when they beg, and say they come to fulfil the people's charity; and
the people do liberally relieve them for charity's sake....These Moors pilgrims have
many pieces of land given to them, by well disposed persons, out of charity, where
they build houses and live; and this land becomes theirs from generation to
generation, for ever."

of rubies, and in which rubies are found.* Without the city is the
mosque of the Sheikh Othmán of Shiráz, which both the Emperor
and the people of the city visit, and for which they have great
respect.

The Emperor is an infidel, and is known by the name of Kinár.
He has a white elephant, upon which he rides on feast days,
having first placed on his head some very large rubies. This is
the only white elephant I had ever seen. The ruby and carbuncle
are found only in this country. These are not allowed to be ex-
ported, on account of the great estimation in which they are held;
nor are they elsewhere dug up. But the ruby is found all over
Ceylon. It is considered as property, and is sold by the inhabitants. When they dig for the ruby, they find a white stone abounding with fissures. Within this the ruby is placed. They cut it
out, and give it to the polishers, who polish it until the ruby is
separated from the stone. Of this there is the red, the yellow,
and the cerulean.† They call it the Maníkam. It is a custom
among them, that every ruby amounting in value to six of the
golden dinars current in those parts, shall go to the Emperor,
who gives its value and takes it. What falls short of this goes to
his attendants. All the women in the island of Ceylon have

---

* This description in some respects answers to Gampola, and in others to Ratnapura. They are both on the banks of a river, with hills on either side. Near
both is an ancient mosque. Ratnapura is certainly near "the estuary of rubies,"
or district where such gems are found; but then, on the other hand, I am not
aware that it ever was the capital, which Gampola certainly was. May not this be
the record of a not very clear recollection, in which the two places are confounded
with each other?

† The topaz and the sapphire.

traces of coloured rubies, which they put upon their hands and legs as chains, in the place of bracelets and ancle-rings. I once saw upon the head of the white elephant seven rubies, each of which was larger than a hen's egg. I also saw in the possession of the king Ayari Shakartí, a saucer made of ruby, as large as the palm of the hand, in which he kept oil of aloes. I was much surprised at it, when the King said to me, We have them much larger than this.*

---

* There seems to have been at one time, a considerable number of these large rubies, carbuncles, or amethysts, in Ceylon. Cosmas, describing the adventures of Sopater, the first traveller who gave an account of the island from personal knowledge, says, "There are two kings ruling at opposite ends of the island, one of whom possesses the hyacinth, . . . as large as a pine cone, the colour of fire, and flashing from a distance, especially when catching the beams of the sun—a matchless sight." Marco Polo says, "the king of Ceylon is reputed to have the grandest ruby that was ever seen, a span in length, the thickness of a man's arm; brilliant beyond description, and without a single flaw. It has the appearance of a glowing fire, and its worth cannot be estimated in money. The Grand Khan Kublai, sent ambassadors to offer for it the value of a city; but the king would not part with it for all the treasures of the world, as it was a jewel handed down by his ancestors from the throne." Jordan de Severac, about the year 1323, repeats the story, of the ruby being "so large that it could not be grasped in the closed hand." What became of it is not known. In the fourteenth century however, the Chinese annalists make mention of an officer who was sent to Ceylon by the emperor, to purchase a "carbuncle" of unusual lustre. "This served as the ball on the emperor's cap, and was transmitted to succeeding emperors on their accession as a precious heirloom, and worn on the birthday and at the grand courts held on the first day of the year. It was upwards of an ounce in weight, and cost 100,000 strings of cash. Each time a grand levee was held, during the darkness of the night, the red lustre filled the palace, and it was for this reason designated 'The Red Palace-Illuminator.'" Perhaps the most extraordinary statement respecting a Ceylon ruby is that given by Valentyn, the Dutch historian, who says one of the two Englishmen

We then proceeded from Kankár, and came to a cave known by the name of Istá Mahmúd, then to the estuary of Búzúta,* which in their language signifies monkeys, animals which are in great numbers in the mountains of these parts. These monkeys are black, and have long tails: the beard of the males is like that of a man. I was told by the Sheikh Othmán and his son, two pious and credible persons, that the monkeys have a leader, whom they follow as if he were their king. About his head is tied a turban composed of the leaves of trees; and he reclines upon a staff. At his right and left hand are four monkeys, with rods in their hands, all of which stand at his head whenever the leading monkey sits. His wives and children are daily brought in on these occasions, who sit down before him; then comes a number of monkeys, which sit and form a sort of assembly about him. One of the four monkeys then addresses them, and they disperse. After this each of them comes with a nut, a lemon, or some of the mountain fruit, which he throws down before the leader. He then eats, together with his wives, children, and the four principal monkeys; they then all disperse. One of the Jogees also told me, that he once saw the four monkeys standing in the presence of the leader,

---

who effected their escape from Kandy at Sítáwaka, after twenty-two years' captivity, related "that he had seen a ruby that had been found by a peasant, which was of such immense size, that for some time he had in his simplicity used it for a whetstone, without knowing what it was!" But Robert Knox, who was a captive in Kandy about the same time, makes no mention of such a gem; and it is very unlikely that had it been in existence, he would not have heard of it, or have failed to have given some account of it in his interesting account of his captivity in the country.

* Quære Batugedara.

and beating another monkey with rods; after this they plucked off all his hair.[*] I was also told by respectable persons, that if one of these monkeys happens to attack, and be too strong for a young woman, he will ravish her.

We next proceeded to the estuary of reeds, where rubies are also found. The next place we arrived at is known by "The house of the old woman,"[†] which is the farthest inhabited part of the island of Ceylon. Our next stage was the cave of Bábá Táhir who was one of the pious: the next, the cave of Síbak, an infidel king, who retired to this place for the purposes of devotion. Here we saw the fierce leech, which they call the zalaw. It remains on trees, or in the grass near water. When any one comes near to it, it springs upon him, and the part of the body attacked will bleed profusely. People generally provide themselves with a lemon for this occasion, which they squeeze over him, and then he drops off. The place upon which the leech has fastened they cut out with a wooden knife made for that purpose. It is told of a pilgrim who passed by this place, that a leech fastened upon him, so that the skin swelled; and, as he did not squeeze the lemon on him, the blood flowed out and he died.

We next came to a place called the seven caves, and after this to the ridge of Alexander, in which is a cave and a well of water. At this place is the entrance to the mountain. This mountain of Serendíb is one of the largest in the world: we saw it from the sea at the distance of nine days. When we ascended it, we saw

---

[*] This is evidently a confused account of the Veddahs and their customs. Ibn Batúta was now in their country. Sabaragamuwa, through which he was journeying, being, as its name imports, "the Veddah village."

[†] "Palábaddala," vide p. 154.

the clouds passing between us and its foot. On it is a great number of trees, the leaves of which never fall. There are also flowers of various colours, with the red rose,[*] about the size of the palm of the hand, upon the leaves of which they think they can read the name of God and of his Prophet. There are two roads on the mountain leading to the foot (of Adam); the one is known by "the way of Bábá," the other, by "the way of Mámú," by which they mean Adam and Eve. The way called that of Mámá is easy: to it the travellers come, upon their first visiting the place; but every one who has travelled only upon this, is considered as if he had not made the pilgrimage at all. The way named Bábá is rough, and difficult of ascent. At the foot of the mountain where the entrance is, there is h minaret named after Alexander, and a fountain of water. The ancients have cut something like steps, upon which one may ascend, and have fixed in iron pins, to which chains are appended; and upon those those who ascend take hold. Of these chains there are ten in number, the last of which is termed "the chain of witness," because, when one has arrived at this, and looks down, the frightful notion seizes him, that he shall fall. After the tenth chain is the cave of Khizr, in which there is a large space; and at the entrance a well of water, full of fish, which is also called after his name. Of those, however, no one takes any. Near this, and on each side of the path, is a cistern cut in the rock. In this cave of Khizr the pilgrims leave their provisions, and whatever else they have, and then ascend about two miles to the top of the mountain, to the place of (Adam's) foot. The holy foot (mark) is in a stone, so

---

[*] Rhododendrons.

that its place is depressed. The length of the impression is eleven spans. The Chinese came here at some former time, and cut out from this stone the place of the great toe, together with the stone about it, and placed it in a temple in the city of Zaitún: and pilgrimages are made to it from the most distant parts of China.* In the rock, too, in which the impression of the foot is, there are nine excavations which have been cut out: into these the infidel pilgrims put gold, rubies, and other jewels: and hence you will see the Fakeers, who have come as pilgrims to the well of Khizr, racing to get first to the excavations, in order to obtain what may be in them. We, however, found nothing but a little gold with some rubies, which we gave to our guide.

It is customary for the pilgrims to remain in the cave of Khizr for three days; and during this time to visit the foot both morning and evening. This we did; and when the three days were expired we returned by the path of Mámá,† and came down to the cave of Shisham, who is Sheth, the son of Adam.‡ After

---

* Davis in his work on China and the Chinese, says that the inhabitants of the flowery land suppose, that at the base of Adam's Peak is a temple in which the real body of Buddha reposes on its side, and that near it are his teeth and other relics.

† Sir J. Emerson Tennent somewhat vaguely speaks of Ibn Batúta's ascent "from Gampola to Adam's Peak." This would imply that he ascended by Eve's route, whereas it is plainly shewn that he made the ascent via Ratnapura; and he himself says he "returned by the path of Mámá."

‡ Vide page 43. But other Mohammedan writers hold different opinions. Thus Masudi, A D. 943, makes mention of Mount Rahwan (El Rahoun) on which Adam descended when expelled from Paradise, adding, that a race of Hindus, in the Island of Ceylon, descended from Adam, derive their origin from the children of Cain, and the analogy between the traditions of the Arabs and

this we arrived at the fish port, then at the village of Karkún, then at the village of Dildináh, then at the village of At Kalanja, where the tomb of Abú Abd Allah Ibn Khafíf is situated. All these villages and tilled lands are upon the mountain. At its foot, and near the path, is a cypress,* which is large and never drops the leaf. But as to its leaves, there is no getting to them by any means; and these people's heads are turned with some strange and false notions respecting them. I saw a number of Jogees about the tree, waiting for the falling of one; for they suppose that any person eating one of them, will grow young again, however old he may be. Beneath this mountain is the great estuary at which the rubies are obtained; its water appears wonderfully blue to the eye.†

Buddhists may probably be traced to that period of early history when both people were Samaneans ; maintaining, according to the authority of the Mefatib-el-olum, that the world had no beginning, that souls transmigrated from one body to another, and that the earth is constantly declining.—Bird's Anniversary Discourse, Journ. Bombay As. Socy. No. 5. The Rev. Spence Hardy, in his Manual of Buddhism, p. 212, commenting upon this, in connection with the Srí-páda, says, " It is probable that Rája Siŋha, A. D. 1581 would destroy the Srí-páda then in existence along with the other objects of Buddhistical veneration that fell beneath his hand." But he seems, in this instance, to have overlooked the fact, that the foot-print was venerated by the Aandiyas as that of their Supreme deity Sivá, and therefore it was not at all likely, when Rája Siŋha gave the Samanala into their custody, that he had previously desecrated or destroyed the relic which they venerated and worshipped quite as much as did the Buddhists.

* Possibly a Bo-tree, or perhaps the fancied Sansevi, the tree of life, respecting which, see p. 35.

† Probably the Kęlani-gaŋga, in whose head waters and tributary streams, rubies and sapphires and other precious stones are still found.

: From this place we proceeded, and in two days arrived at the city of Dínaur,* which is large, and inhabited by merchants. In this is an idol, known by the same name, placed in a large temple; and in which there are about a thousand Brahmins and Jogees, and five hundred young women, daughters of the nobility of India, who sing and dance all night before the image. The officers of the city revenue attend upon the image. The idol is of gold, and as large as a man. In the place of eyes it has two large rubies; which, as I was told, shine in the night-time like two lighted candles.

---

* Dondera head, or Dewandere, the Island's end, also called Dewí Newera, "the Sunium of Ceylon, and the southern extremity of the Island, is covered with the ruins of a temple, which was once one of the most celebrated in Ceylon. The headland itself has been the resort of devotees and pilgrims, from the most remote ages;— Ptolemy describes it as Dagana, ' sacred to the moon,' and the Buddhists constructed there one of their earliest dagobas, the restoration of which was the care of successive sovereigns. But the most important temple was a shrine which, in very early time, had been erected by the Hindus in honour of Vishnu. It was in the height of its splendour, when, in 1587, the place was devastated in the course of the marauding expedition by which De Souza d'Arronches sought to create a diversion, during the siege of Colombo by Raja Sipha II. The historians of the period state, that at that time Dondera was the most renowned place of pilgrimage in Ceylon; Adam's Peak scarcely excepted. The temple, they say, was so vast, that from the sea, it had the appearance of a city. The pagoda was raised on vaulted arches, richly decorated and roofed with plates of gilded copper. It was encompassed by a quadrangular cloister, opening under verandahs, upon a terrace and gardens with odoriferous shrubs and trees, whose flowers were gathered by the priests for processions. De Souza entered the gates without resistance; and his soldiers tore down the statues which were more than a thousand in number. The temple and its buildings were overthrown, its arches and its colonnades were demolished, and its gates and tower levelled with the ground. The plunder was immense, in ivory, gems, jewels, sandalwood, and ornaments of gold. As the last indignity that could be offered to the

From this place we travelled to Káli,* which is a large town; then to Kolambú (Colombo), which is the finest and largest city in Serendíb. After three days we arrived at the city of Battála, from which we had been sent by its king, with his servants, to visit (Adam's) foot. This we entered, and were received honourably by the king, who furnished us with provisions.

---

sacred place, cows were slaughtered in the courts, and the cars of the idol, with other combustible materials, being fired, the shrine was reduced to ashes. A stone doorway exquisitely carved, and a small building, whose extraordinary strength resisted the violence of the destroyers, are all that now remain standing; but the ground for a considerable distance is strewn with ruins, conspicuous among which are numbers of finely cut columns of granite. The dagoba which stood on the crown of the hill, is a mound of shapeless débris."—Sir J. EMERSON TENNENT's Ceylon, vol. ii. pp. 113—114.

. * Point-de-Galle.

Note.—While the preceding sheet was passing through the press, the writer was favoured with the following information, obligingly obtained and forwarded by H. S. O. Russell, Esq., the Government Agent of the Central Province. It will be found to throw some additional light upon the subject of the Hindu worship of the Foot-print of Siva upon the summit of Adam's Peak; the origin of which is involved in considerable obscurity. It should be read in connection with the subject discussed in chapter I., pages 27—40.

SIVANOLIPATHAM—சிவனொழிபாதம்.

In Ceylon there are places dedicated to Sivá such as Trinco-malee or Thadchanakaylaysam (தட்சணகயிலாசம்) Thirukkách-charam (திருக்கேச்சரம்) &c. There is a Puranam, (புராணம்) in Sanskrit (which is the mother language of Tamul) relating to Thadchanákaylasam or Trincomalee, called Thadchana-kaylaya-manmeium (தட்சணகயிலாசமான்மியம்.)

The following is found recorded in the 6th and 7th chapters of that book.

"In the middle of the mountain called Sivánolipatham, three rivers or kankai rise out of Siván's foot (பாதம்.)

From my (Siván's) foot, three rivers issue out, and the names are Mávillie-kankai (மாவிலிகெங்கை) Manikka-kankai (மாணிக்க கெங்கை) and Karary-kankai (காவேரிகெங்கை). Mávillie-kankai flows towards the North, reaches Siván's place at Trincomalee, and falls into the sea south of it.

Mánikka-kankai flows towards the East and passes by Kather-kamum (கதிராமம்) a place dedicated to Supermania-swamy, son of Sivá, and then falls into the Eastern sea.

Kavary-kankai flows towards the West, and passes into the place of Sivá, called Therukkachcharum (situated at Mantotte in Mannár). These three kankais are highly meritorious streams."

The names of these three rivers, the directions they take in their course, their connection with the above-named three famous places dedictated to Siván's worship; the name "Sivánolipatham" by which this peak is usually known, and the fact of these four places and the three rivers being recognised by Sivaites as places peculiarly adopted for the worship of Sivá, at the present as well as in the ancient times, shew beyond doubt that the mountain in the Central Province of the Island of Ceylon which is called Sivánolipatham in Tamul, and Adam's Peak in English, is the very mountain spoken of in the Sanskrit work Thedchana-kaylaya-manmcium written several centuries ago.

P. K. T. KANAGERATINA, MODR.

C.

SANNAS OF KING KIRTISSEL.

OUR Great and Supreme Omniscient Sovereign Buddha, the Teacher of the three worlds, who is distinguished by the beauties of thirty-two most noble marks, and eighty secondary signs, and circular beams of light, and rows of glories, who is pleasing to the eyes of all beings, and who is skilful in the distribution of the noble and glorious ambrosia of his doctrines, who is well conducted, and is of a felicitous advent, having completed all the thirty preliminary courses of *párămitás*, such as donations, observances and the like, during a period of four *asankhyas* and a hundred thousands of *kalpas*, vanquished the *mărŏyá* with all his hosts, attained into the state of omniscient Buddhaship, and who in the eighth year ascended the centre of the firmament, and came here by emitting forth clusters of his condensed beams of six colours, and carefully stamped the print of his glorious foot, endued with a hundred and eight auspicious marks, such as the noble sign of a circle and others, upon the summit of the Samantakúṭa mountain, which represents a crown of blue sapphire gems, worn upon the head of the lady of the glorious Island of Lanká, beautified with various rivers and cataracts, filled with clear water of cool springs, adorned with groves of multitudes of noble trees, loaded with flowers, and enriched with much sweet fragrance of well blossomed filaments.

When our Most High and Supreme Monarch Kírtissri Rájasiṇha,
—whose fame, glory, and majesty pervade all directions, like the
moon, the jasmin flowers, and rows of white *hansa* birds, and
are similar to the rays of the sun that dispel the darkness of the
multitudes of enemies, and who represents the central gem that
adorns the pearl necklace of many hundreds of kings from the
prime Monarch Wijaya Rája, of the solar race, that occupied the
throne of the glorious Island of Lauká, the incomparable abode
for the three kinds of relics, such as *páribhógika* like the glorious
footprint, *sártríkă* and *uddésika*,—had, like the king of the gods
alighted upon the midst of the firmament, reigning in the great
city called *Senkhanda Saila Sríwardhanapura*, which is the desire
of the eyes of multitudes, and abounds with all the glorious marks
of a city ;—engaged in the most noble pleasure of protecting the
religion of the Omniscient Buddha, by causing the decayed and
ruined temples of the glorious Island of Lauká to be cleared of the
thorns with which they were covered, and to be repaired ; and
by causing the erection of great temples, monuments, bo-trees, and
houses of images anew, by enacting rules for celebrating constant
offerings and services in the holy places, such as those in Anurádhapura, Mahiyangana, Kalyánipura, and others ; and having
presented them with gold, silver, pearls, gems, and such other
things ; and by worshipping and honoring them ; and by offering
as presents such living and non-living things as gold, silver,
pearls, gems, clothes, jewels, elephants, horses, estates, fields, men-
servants, and female-servants, in honor of the glorious tooth relic,
resembling a golden honey-making bee, which constantly dwelt
in the pink lotus mouth of the Omniscient Supreme Buddha, possessing an odoriferous sweet fragrance ; whose holy feet are enveloped in the shining clear light of the gems that embellish the

crowns of the great Brahmah, the occupant of a throne of lotuses,
and of Asuras and men; and by causing the celebration of offerings
and services in its honor; and by enhancing the prosperity of the
state and religion:—His Majesty having heard that for a long time
constant offerings and services had not been celebrated on the
peak of the Samantakúṭa mountain, where was situated the print-
mark of the holy foot of the Supreme Buddha, who is like a royal
lion that breaks open the brains of the wicked religionists, the
elephants;—it having come in the time of the divine Sovereign
Rájasiṇhu of Sítáwǎkǎ into the possession of the Aandiyas who
daub over their bodies with ashes, as protypical of their being
burnt and reduced into ashes by the most cruel and very dreadful
hell-fire;—was pleased to grant as an offering to it, the village called
Kuṭṭápitiya, the sowing extent of which is one hundred and
sixty-five amunams of paddy, situated in Nawǎdun Kóralé of the
District of Sabaragamuwa, including the houses, gardens, trees,
vegetation, dry lands, and fields in this village, in order that
offerings and services may be celebrated and well established in
this place, until the time of the extinction of the religion, unmo-
lested by the monarchs that will, hereafter, ascend the throne of
the glorious Island of Lanká; and that it may be a living for those
who supply the services in that place:—Granted with the object of
gaining the happiness of *swarga* and *nirvána* on this Wednesday,
the twelfth day of the increasing moon of the month of *Nikini*,
being the twenty-third day of the sun's entering the sign of Cancer,
(Aug. 4,) in this year named *prajápati*, which is the two thousand
two hundred and ninety-fourth of the year of the glorious Buddha,
(A. D. 1751); given in charge of the Lord Saranankará of Weliwiṭa,
resident at the Temple of Upósatháráma, who is adorned with the
magnificent qualities of *Sila* (observance) and *A'chára* (good

conduct), that the offerings may be celebrated and kept up by the succession of his pupilage. This is the enactment, and this enactment is thus recorded.

Signed, for this being a true Copy, by Saranankara Unnansé of Weliwiṭa, who had it in his charge.

(Signed.)   WELIWITA.
Translated by C. ALWIS.

D.

BUDDHA'S THREE VISITS TO CEYLON.[*]

THIS glorious Island of Lanka, was the residence of Yakshas during the non-Buddhistic periods of the world, and men dwelt there only in the Buddhistic periods. By some of the Buddhas, at the very first attainment to perfection of wisdom, the yakshas were subdued, and the Island became the abode of men. There were other Buddhas who personally visited it, subdued the yakshas, made it the abode of men, and established their religion there. And this Island of Lanka is like the Buddhas' own treasury of the three gems, as it is certain that the southern branches of the sacred trees, and the doctrines, the relics, and the religion of infinite and innumerable Buddhas, are established here.

2. The residence therefore of false religionists in this Island of Lanka is certainly as unstable as that of the former yakshas was unstable. Although, occasionally, a king of a false religion may usurp the sovereignty of the Island of Lanka, and reign over it, yet it is the authoritative mandate of the Buddhas, that the dynasty of such kings should never be permanent.

3. As this Island therefore is suitable only to the kings of the true religion, the permanence of the hereditary succession of their dynasty is sure. For such reasons as these, the kings reigning over Lanka should be assiduous in upholding the religion

---

[*] Translated by the Rev. C. ALWIS from the *Sarwajna Gund-lankdra*, ch. xxiv.

with that great love and veneration which is natural towards
Buddha, and ought to preserve the heritage of their dynasty by
keeping the influence of their jurisdiction and that of the religion.

4. Leaving aside the periods of other Buddhas of former times,
this Island was called O'jadwípa at the time of the Kakusanda
Buddha, who in this Kalpa attained to the perfection of wisdom.
Anurádhapura was then called Abhayapura; the king thereof was
named Abhaya. The present grove Maha-mewuna had the
name of Maha-tírtha-wana; the city was on the east of this grove.
The name of Piyalkulu, or the Mihintalá rock, was Déwakúta.

5. At that time a pestilential disease of fever struck such cities
as Abhayapura, over all this Island, abounding with large population and great wealth and riches; and when a great affliction of
the people prevailed, such as was in the city of Wisálá at the time
of our Buddha, people began to die. And the yakshas, being
unable, on account of the influence of Buddha, to enter the Island,
stood circumambulating round it, scattered over the sea, erecting
themselves up and observing the smell of the human carcases.

6. At that time Kakusanda Buddha, knowing the exceeding
unhappy state of the inhabitants of this Island, O'jadwípa, and
being impelled by great compassion towards them, repaired thither
in an instant through the air, accompanied by a retinue of about
40,000 holy priests, and descended upon Déwakúta (Mihintala),
and stood there like 'the moon attended by stars; he illuminated
the ten directions with his beams of six colours, and determined
with his supernatural influence, "Let all the men of this Island of
O'jadwípa see me, and as soon as they see me let all their diseases
vanish, and being sound in health, let them all come in an instant
and stand round me."

7. And at an instant, simultaneously with the thought of that

determination, all the inhabitants of the Island saw Buddha like those who see the moon in the sky. And the epidemic of fever vanished, and they all, like those who had received ambrosial water, every man from the place where he had been lying, collected themselves round the rock, as those who collect themselves into a hall in the midst of a town.

8. At this moment the kings, sub-kings and great ministers worshipped and invited him into the grove Maha-tírtha-wana (Maha-mewuna), and conducted him thither in great pomp, and completed for him a beautiful temporary court, and erected a magnificent throne for Buddha with forty thousand other seats, and presented the grove to Buddha with great ceremony.

9. In that instant the great earth gave a shock and sprang up, and all the trees throughout the grove stood embellished with supernatural flowers from their roots even to their topmost twigs. And the sentient beings, who were delighted at this miracle, with the most profound veneration, made the great priesthood, with Buddha at their head, take the repast of the alms of Chatumadhura, and presented to Buddha perfumes and flowers and other things, in proportion to the wealth which each man possessed, standing at a reverential distance.

10. At that moment Buddha preached his doctrine, and rescued forty thousand souls from transmigration; he spent the day in that place, and in the afternoon, repaired to the site of the great sacred tree, and rested there for a moment under the blissful influence of *dyána*, when he rose and thought, "I will follow the practice of the preceding Buddhas," and then stretched his right hand towards the direction of the sacred Bo-tree, and determined with his supernatural influence, "Let the sanctified priestess Ruchinanda, the chief over those priestesses of my religion who performed

miracles, appear here conveying the southern branch of the great sacred Bo-tree."

11. At that instant also the sanctified priestess perceiving the determination which Buddha had exercised, caused the king Khémáwati of the city of Khémáwati, to make a streak of yellow orpiment round the southern branch of the sacred Bo-tree, and so got it by self-cutting, and placed it in the sacred hand which the Buddha had out-stretched.

12. Then Buddha looked at the face of king Abhaya, and said, "O great monarch, follow the practices of former blessed and prosperous kings of this Island like thyself," and caused that sovereign to plant the sacred tree. Thence, on its northern direction, he sat down in the site of Lówámahápáyú, which at that time was called Sirísa-Málaka, preached his doctrine, and rescued twenty thousand souls from transmigration. He proceeded thence and sat on the site of Thúpáráms, and rose from the blissful influence of *dyána*, and preached his doctrine, and rescued in that place ten thousand persons from transmigration. And he delivered his *dharmakara* (water straining vessel), saying, "Build ye a monument here and worship the same, and make offerings to it, and be rescued from transmigration." And he left in this Island the sanctified priestess Ruchinanda, together with five hundred priestesses, and the high and holy priest Mahádéwa, with ten thousand priests. Thence he proceeded to Déwákúta (Mihintala), and standing upon the site of the Batamahasala monument advised all the inhabitants of the Island, and returned to Jambudwípa in the sight of all the living beings.

13. From that time forth during the whole of that Buddhate, every succeeding king who was born here, continued to worship the three gems, and went to the city of Nirwána.

14. Now at the time of the second Buddha, Kónágama, this Island was called Waradwípa; the name of the Maha-mewuna grove was Maha-anomá grove. The city on the south of the grove was named Waddhamanaka. It was enriched with all sorts of wealth by its king Samindha. And Déwakúta was called Sumanakuta.

15. At that time this noble Island of Lanka, which was inhabited by four noble tribes of men, and full of females like goddesses, of cows and buffaloes, and of all sorts of wealth, having had no rain for some interval of time, was overspread with a great famine like the famine called Beminitiyá Sáya at the time of our Buddha, and there was a great distress from want of food.

16. As the end of all the discourses of Buddha is aimed at (one or the other of) the three marks; he observed the time and saw the distress by famine to which men had come; and, concluding that "sentient beings could be established in faith when they had a sorrow," came here through the air attended by thirty thousand sanctified priests, and stood on the very site of the foot-marks of former Buddhas, on the summit of Sumanakuta (Mihintala), and looked at the ten directions,* and said, "Let rain fall in this Island just at this very moment, and let all the tanks and dams be filled."

17. At that instant, simultaneously with the thought of our Lord, hundreds of blue condensed clouds of rain began to present themselves to the sight, as if the reflections of mountains appeared in the mirror of the sky. Hundreds and thousands of pillars of rainy clouds began to shew themselves, resembling a pressure of pillars of blue sapphire stones spreading in the bosom of the sky, and the clouds began to roar in the sky, as if the gods had begun to play music as an offering to Buddha.

---

* The four cardinal, and the four intervening, and the zenith and nadir points.

18. Thousands of rainbows began to appear as so many divine arches, which the gods had built as an offering to Buddha. And myriads of lightnings began to shew themselves in different directions, resembling rows of banners which the gods had offered. Thousands of torrents of water proceeded, bursting the blue condensed clouds of rain like heaps of strings of pearls which gods offer to Buddha. Thousands of peacocks began to erect their tails, as if they held feather umbrellas over their heads, for the purpose of protecting themselves from the wetting of the rain.

19. At that instant throughout the whole of this Island very thick and heavy showers of rain fell, and filled the tanks, dams, rivers, and canals; and torrent-streams of fresh water floods began to run in different directions, as if they had been reddened by rage, and were moving about to find out where their enemy, the heat, was dwelling.

20. Thus Buddha having extinguished the heat by an unusual shower, caused the rain to cease, and then, in the sight of all living beings, he stood on the summit of the rock like a statue of gold, and entered the state of Samapatti of aqueous kasina, and emitting streams of water from his own body, also administered a healing to the population. And all the living inhabitants of the Island, who were delighted at the performance of this miracle, collected themselves together round Buddha, and worshipped him, immerging themselves under the beams of his toe-nails, and carried him in their arms unto the Maha-anoma grove.

21. On that very day Buddha received the grove, with a shock of the great earth, and made his repast, and at the conclusion of it, delivered his doctrines and rescued thirty thousand souls out of transmigration: and in the afternoon, as was mentioned before, he determined in his heart, and caused by his supernatural influence, the southern branch of his sacred fig-tree to be self-cut as aforesaid,

through the instrumentality of the monarch Sobhana in the city of Sobhana, and brought in an instant by five hundred priestesses, with the sanctified priestess Kanakadatta at their head, and having caused the king Samindha to plant the sacred tree, and taking seat on the site of the Lówámahúpáya, which at that time was called Núgamálaka, he delivered his doctrines, and having given to twenty thousand persons the fruits of the paths of Nirwána, proceeded thence and sat on the site of Thúpáráma, and expounded the doctrines, and liberated ten thousand souls from transmigration, and left in this Island his waist-band as a relic, together with five hundred priestesses, with the high and holy priestess Kanakadatta at their head, and one thousand priests, with the great high priest Sudharma at their head. Thence he came and stood on the site of the great stone monument called Sudassanamálaka, advised all the living beings, and returned from this Island into Jambudwípa.

22. From that time forth in that Buddhate all the princes that were born here, together with all the people, continued to worship the three gems and filled the city of Nirwána.

23. Moreover, in the time of Kásyapa, who became Buddha in the third place, this Island was designated as Mandudwípa, the grove Maha-mewuna had the name of Maha Súgara; the city on the west of it was called Wisúlápura, in which a monarch of the name of Jayanta reigned; Sumanakuta was called Subhakuta. At that time the inhabitants of this Island, with their kings, sub-kings, and great ministers, were divided into two parties, and were jealous of one another, and carried on a civil war. They engaged armies composed of four elements and arrayed in arms, and began to strike one another, saying "we will kill them and make oceans of blood."

24. Then Buddha having seen many persons perish in that civil war, impelled by great commisseration, repaired thither

through the air, accompanied by twenty thousand sanctified disciples, descended upon Subhakuta, and created a thick darkness,
and determined in his heart with his supernatural influence, "Let
no two persons see each other," and put them into a trance with
the darkness, and then dispelled the darkness.

25. And the people resumed the battle. Then he caused the
whole Island to smoke, and seeing that the rage of the people did
not subside, he entered into the state of Samápatti of the igneous
Kasina, and emitted streams of fire out of his body, which was
twenty cubits high, and terrified them by making the whole Island
like a house set in one blaze of fire.

26. Then the people seeing the mountains of fire moving about in
the air, and the sparks of fire incessantly thrown at every house, said,
"O men! what consternation is this? It is like the day of the destruction of the world; we are fighting against each other for the sake
of a kingdom, and that kingdom is now burning; our wives and
children are burning; our wealth is burning; fields and gardens are
burning; and we ourselves shall be burned presently; and what wars
shall we carry on?" And they trembling for fear of death, dropped
down the weapons which they had in their hands, and were moved
with affection towards each other, and the armies came to peace.

27. Thus Buddha, like one taking up a thorn by means of a
thorn, extinguished the fire of their rage by his miraculous fire,
and then quenched both the fires, and made himself visible to all
the living beings.*

---

* "*Similia similibus curantur.*" There is nothing new under the sun. According to this statement, Buddha was the first Homœopathist, and Hahnemann only
an imitator.

28. At that moment all men having seen Buddha, stood up with closed hands upon their heads, and enquired of him, " Lord, art thou the god of fire, or art thou the deity of the sun ? Thy face is like a full moon, thy body is like a mass of ambrosia ; but on the contrary, the fire that issued out of thy body is exceeding fierce. Can a fire spring out of water ? Lord, what sort of personage art thou ?" And when they learned that he was Buddha, the supreme over the universe, they exulted with joy.

29. Afterwards Buddha on that day caused the great earth to shake, and received the same grove, and at the conclusion of his repast he awakened the minds of the faithful by the warmth of his preaching, as heat expands the blossoms of flowers. And he gave to twenty thoussnds of souls the fruits of the paths (to Nir-wáua). And in the afternoon, he having proceeded to the site of the great and glorious sacred tree, and having, as before, determined in his heart, with his supernatural influence caused the southern branch of the sacred Nigrodha tree to be self-cut by king Brahma-datta of Benares, and brought in an instant by five hundred priestesses, at whose head was the sanctified priestess Sudharma, and planted by the monarch Jayanta; and then by the discourse which he delivered, sitting on the site of the Lówúmahúpúya, called at that Buddhate Asoka-malaka, he rescued four thousand souls from transmigration, and proceeded to the site of Thúpúráma, and preached his doctrines and gave to a thousand souls the fruits of the paths (to Nirwáua), and left in this Island his own bathing robe, and the sanctified priestess Sudharma, with five hundred priest-esses, and the great sanctified priest Sarwananda, with a thousand other priests ; and then having stood on the site of the third great stone monument Somanassa-malaka, he advised gods and men, together with all the inhabitants of the Mandadwfpa, and rose up

into the bosom of the sky and returned to Dambadiwa, like the moon attended by stars.

30. Thus also in the Buddhate of the Kásyapa Buddha, which existed for twenty thousand years, the living beings born here with passion continued to worship the three gems, and filled the city of Nirwána.

Thus should be known briefly the history of the visits of the first three Buddhas that were born in this Kalpa.

Described in Pújáwaliya.

31. Moreover our great Buddha Gautama, who became Buddha in the fourth period of this Kalpa, visited this Island of Lanka on the day of full moon of the month of *Durutu* (January), the ninth of his Buddhaship, and stood in the air over the midst of a great army of Yakshas in the full-blossomed grove of Mahánága-wana, three yoduns in length and one in breadth, situated on the bank of the river Mahawáluka (Mahaweli), where, when they had commenced a battle against one another on account of some dispute,— they were shouting with boasts like the roaring of thunders, and looking here and there with various hostile weapons in their hands, possessing hearts like flames of fire, shaking the shrunk copper coloured hair of the head, raising up the pairs of contracted cruel brows like the bow of Pluto, revolving the red eyes like inflamed balls of fire, having cheeks blistered with strokes of the extremities of tusks like crescent moons, tremulously shaking tongues thrown out of their hollow mouths, with disorderly teeth closed by the outward turned red lips, and revolving circular plates set at their ears,—he shewed himself in the air like a golden rock enveloped with many thousands of rainbows, lightnings and evening clouds, and caused a roaring of the sky and earth louder than their clamour, and created a fourfold thick darkness, and terrified the yakshas,

like Pisachas who had offended Waissrawana. Again he dispelled
the darkness, and made himself visible to them in the womb of the
sky, like the disc of the rising sun, and struck terror among the
army of yakshas by volumes of smoke emitted from his body,
and then again he stood in their sight like the face of the moon,
clear of the five obstructions, issuing ambrosial beams.

32. At this moment the army of yakshas, who had seen these
miracles, saw Buddha and prayed him, saying, "O Lord, who art
great and possessed of such influence as this, remove these calami-
ties from us, and give us safety." Then Buddha addressed himself
to the yakshas, who had supplicated him for safety, and said, "O
yakshas, if ye all wish for safety, bestow on me as much space on
the ground as will suffice for me to sit," and having obtained as
much space as would suffice him to sit, he removed the consternation among the yakshas, and sat in the midst of their army, upon
the skin carpet spread on the piece of ground given by them; the
place where Buddha sat being the site of the Mahiyangana monument; and from the four edges of the skin carpet he emitted
four streams of fire, which spreading on all the ten directions,
struck terror among the yakshas, and dispersed them in different
directions. Buddha then collected them on the sea-shore, and
shewed them as if the isle of Yakgiri had been caused to be
brought near by his supernatural influence; he then presented
that isle of Yakgiri to them, and settled the great yaksha army in
it, but he remained there on the sea-shore.

33. At that instant the chief of the gods, Sumana, resident at
the peak of Samanala, (Adam's Peak), together with all the aerial,
domiciliary, and other gods dwelling on trees, mountains and other
places, arrived there; and when they stood there making offerings of lights, incense, perfumes, flowers, and such other things;

Buddha, who was sitting in that place, declared his sound doctrines to all the gods and goddesses, presided over by the chief god Sumana, and established numerous Kelas (ten millions) of the multitude of the gods in the enjoyment of the fruits of the paths, and admitted an Asankya of gods into the initiatory *Sila*.

34.　The chief god Sumana, who on that day attained unto the holy path of Sówán, besought for a relic suitable for himself to worship and make offerings to.　Then the meritorious Supreme Buddha rubbed his head and gave a handful of hair relics to the chief god Sumana to worship and make offerings to, and circumambulated three times round the Island of Lanka, like a meteor that moved rapidly in the darkness, and gave it his protection, and returned to Jambudwípa on that very day.

35.　Then the chief god, great Sumana, placed in a golden shrine the handful of hair relic which he had obtained, and collected a heap of gems on the spot where Buddha had sat for subduing yukshas, and on the top of that heap of gems he interred the shrine with the hair relic, and built thereupon a dágoba of blue sapphire gems, and made immense offerings to it.

The first visit of Buddha to the Island of Lanka.

36.　Moreover in the fifth year of our Buddha, who is a refuge to the refugeless, and in the fifteenth day of the waning moon of the month of Bhaga (March), two Núga kings, Chulódara and Mahódara, maternal uncle and nephew, commenced a war on account of a gem throne, taking with them separate armies of eighty kelas of Nágas dwelling in water and in land, being twenty kelas of Nágas from Kelani, together with thirty kelas from Wadunnágala, against thirty kelas of Maninúga isle; and the two armies boasting violently, like two oceans stirred up by the vehemence of the wind and rushing upon the land, arranged line by line like the rows of the waves moving thereon, taking various weapons, such as swords, shields, darts, circular swords, clubs, bows, spears, lances, javelins, crowbars, maces, and arrows, and waving them like continuous flashings of lightnings, rendering the whole battle-field a universal shout, and continually running forward with bravery of heart, intoxicated with the pride of each outvieing the other, and pressing hard each upon the other.

37. Then our Buddha saw by inspiration the affliction suffered by the army of Nágas who were thus boastingly assembled in the battle field of the civil war; and impelled by compassion towards them, he started in the morning of that day from Jétawana-áráma, and came through the air under the shade of that very Kiripalu tree, which had been standing near the gate of the temple of Jétawana, and which the king of the gods, Samirdhi Sumana, who had been residing on that self-same Kiripalu tree, rooted up and held over his head, and descended at the isle of Maninága, and presented himself in the midst of the two Nága armies, who had the sharpest battle, and seated himself in the air under the shade of the blue-sapphire-banner-like Kiripalu tree. He then created a darkness for the purpose of frightening the Nágas, and afterwards threw a light upon them like that of the rising sun. The Nágas being thus frightened by the darkness, he shewed them many wonders, and preached his doctrines, and reconciled the two armies.

38. Then all the Nága people, having thrown their weapons out of their hands, brought, in company with the Nága virgins, various kinds of splendid offerings and presents, and bestowed them upon him : and they prayed Buddha to descend on the ground ; and he, sitting upon the gem throne which the Nágas had bestowed upon him, made a repast of the divine food which the Nágas gave

him, and preached his doctrines to eighty kelas of Nágas, and established them in the initiatory *sila.* And In that Nága company, the
Naga king Maniak, the maternal uncle of the Nága king Mahódara, supplicated Buddha to visit Kçlani.

39. Afterwards Buddha, having by his silence consented to the
invitation, made the Kiripalu tree, and the gem throne, páribhógika monuments,* that they might worship and make offerings
to them, in order that their advancing merits might increase; and
he sat on the gem throne, leaning against the Kiripalu tree.

40.   Thus having quelled the dissensions of the Nágas, he left as
páribhógika monuments both the gem throne which he had received,
and the Kiripalu tree, which the god had brought from Jétawana
with him, holding it as a shade over his head, in order that the eighty
kelas of Nágns, and their females inhabiting the three Nága abodes,
which have the three Nága kings, Chúlódara, Mahódara, and Maniakkha, as their chiefs, may worship and make offerings to them, in
whatever way they choose.   And he established protection to the
glorious Island of Lanka, and returned to Jétawana Vihára in the
city of Sewet in Dambadiva.

41.   Thus, the gem throne and the Kiripalu tree, which our
Buddha received when he came to Maninága isle, on his second
visit to Lanka, were placed in the oceanic Nága abode, and on
the sea shore, as páribhógika monuments.

This is the account of the second visit of our Buddha to the
Island of Lanka.

---

* Articles or relics that have been sanctified by having been used or owned by-
Buddha.

42. Moreover our great Buddha, the teacher of the three worlds, who has a glorious face like a lotus, residing in the Vihára of Jétawana, thus thought about his third visit to the Island of Lanka; namely, "when I am dead (my) tooth relic, the jaw "bone relic, the forehead relic, and about a drona* of other relics, "which the inhabitants of the city of Rambagam will receive "at my demise; the hair relics and many other relics, will be "settled in the glorious Island of Lanka; and many hundreds "and thousands of monasteries will be established there. And "as a great many people, such as Kshastrias, Brahmans, Waisyas, "Shuddras, and many others, who will delight in the three gems "will dwell there, I ought therefore to go to the Island of Lanka, "and visit the sites where the sixteen great places will have to "be situated, and indulge myself in the enjoyment of Samápatti, "and then return here."

43. So in the eighth year of his Buddhaship he, at the invitation of the great priest Sunáparanta together with five hundred sancti-fied théras, mounted upon five hundred golden palanquins which the god Sçkraia had created and presented to them, came to the territory of Sunáparant, and received the hall named Chandana-mandala-málaka, built by some merchants in the monastery of Muhulu; and there he preached his doctrines to sentient beings, and established them in the enjoyment of the fruits of the paths, and dwelt there several days, and went to the market town of Suppáraka at the invitation of the priest Purna, and preached the doctrines to the people there. While he was returning to the city of Sewet, he came to the bank of the river Nermadá, and there he, at the

---

* A measure containing about a quarter of a bushel.

request of the Nágá king Nermadá, who dwelt in the river, partook of the divine food presented by him, and gave him some
practical admonitions, and established a great multitude of Nágas
in the initiatory observance of religion.   And at the request of the
Nága king Nermadá, he made an imprint of his glorious right
foot, endowed with a hundred and eight auspicious signs, on a
beautiful strand like a heap of pearl dust, on the bank of that river,
on which the rippling waves strike and break themselves, and he
provided the Nágas with the means of acquiring merits.

44.   When the spreading waves strike over the heap of sand
on which the glorious foot was imprinted on the shore of that
river in the Yónaka country, the glorious foot-mark is covered by
the water, and when the waves retire, the imprint of the foot with
all its auspicious signs reappears, like a seal impressed upon the
surface of a lump of extremely white bees-wax, without the slightest
diminution of any of the blissful marks, satisfying the eyes of
every one who sees it.   And it imparts abundant happiness to the
world up to this day.   This is a páribhógika memorial.

45.   And from that place he proceeded to the rock of Sachchabaddha, and at the request of a certain priest called Sachchabaddha,
he imprinted on the top of the thick blue rock of that name his
glorious foot, endowed with a hundred and eight auspicious signs,
such as Siriwnsa, Swastika, and so forth, as if a foot smeared with
ointment had been pressed upon a lump of wet clay, without the
defect of a single jot of the parts of those auspicious marks, so as
to be clear to the bodily eye of every one that sees them.   This
also is a memorial of the foot of my Buddha.

46.   Thence Buddha, proceeding from the said Sachchabaddha
mountain, recollected the invitation which the Nága king Maniakkha,—who enjoys the Nága prosperity in that Nága region

which had arisen contiguous to the new stream of water named the
Kęlani river, perhaps from its resemblance to an auspicious body of
water emptying itself into the ocean, having fallen at the foot of
the rock after the entire washing and purification of the noble mountain Samantakúṭa (Adam's Peak) of the Island of Lanka, when the
water of the auspicious consecration was poured on the top of its
head for purification, previous to its sacred investment with the
mark of the glorious foot,—had made on a former occasion, when
he had gone to Mauiuága isle, for the purpose of assisting his
nephew Mahódara, the prince of the Nágas, in a war which he was
carrying on against the Nága Prince Chulódara, having seen
Buddha, who had mercifully come there,—that he should visit
Kęlani;—and on the day of full moon of the month of Wesak
(May) he began to proceed, attended by five hundred sanctified
priests, including the eighty dignitaries.

47. In the place where Buddha was residing, there was, close
to his bed chamber, a noble Nága named Sumana, enjoying great
happiness, constantly attended by sixteen thousand Nága virgins;
and he, having seen the personal gracefulness of Buddha,
greatly admired him; and he had his mother as an object of
veneration, and rendered her such services as worshipping and
honouring her, and shampooing her feet.

48. When Buddha was about to depart, he invited this noble
Nága who stood by, and said "Follow us with thy retinue." And
this noble Nága immediately obeyed these words, and said "Yea,
my Lord," and took his train of about sixty millions of Nágas, and
proceeded, holding over his head a full blossomed champack tree,
so that the rays of the sun might not strike against the glorious
person of Buddha.

49. Afterwards the meritorious Buddha, having arrived at the

Nága city of the Nága king Maniakkha at the Kelani river in the
Island of Lanka, set upon the throne completed with all sorts of
gems in the golden court, miraculously brought into existence by
Maniakkha, and remained with his attendant priests on the site of
the Kelani monument, and made refection of the divine food presented to him by the noble Nága, and delivered to him some
practical admonitions; and, at the request of that noble Nága, he
made an impression of his glorious foot under that river of Kelani,
in order that the Nága king might make offerings to him, and
he initiated many thousands of other Nágas into the threefold
refuge, and remained sitting there increasing their merits.

50. Then the great god Sumana, resident at the divine mansion on the summit of the peak Samanala (Adam's Peak), who had
heard of these circumstances, came with his numerous retinue
of gods to the site of the Kelani monument, having prepared and
brought things for offerings to him, and saw Buddha; and took
drums and other musical instruments, and offered him immense
divine fragrant flowers, lamps, incense, and other things, and
worshipped him, by applying to the ground five places of the body,
and prayed Buddha to come to the Samanala mountain, while
the Nágas remained worshipping him.

51. Then the great god Sumana, resident of the Samanala
mountain, addressed him in six such stanzas as these, standing
before Buddha, with closed hands upon his head, addressing him thus,
praying:—

52. "O great Buddha, the lord of the whole universe, it was
"with thy compassion to sentient beings that thou hadst entered
"the impassable ocean of Sansáru, and moved about during an Im-
"mense period of time, suffering pains from the moment of thy
"obtaining, at the foot of the Dipankara Buddha, the sanction to

" become Buddha, and completed the full thirty *páramitás.* I am in-
" cluded also among the number of all the sentient beings, such as
" Gods, Brahmas, Asuras, Men, Nágás, Supernas, Yaksbas, Rák-
" shas, Siddhas, Widdhyadharas, and others who enjoy the beneficial
" rewards from that compassion of thine. Have mercy there-
" fore upon me, and in that visible mountainous forest, uplifted
" and graceful in all glory, beauteous in green foliage, tender
" leaves, waterfalls, and rainbows, pressed by the striking of wind,
" delightful with clusters of lotuses and flashings of lightnings,
" resounding with the noise of gentle breezes and of the roaring
" clouds, resembling the black peak of a rainy cloud over the eastern
" horizon, sprinkled by the fall of the extremely white ambrosial
" showers of rain, situated in the midst of that visible wilderness
" like a peacock's neck, being an object eligible for the ceremonies at
" the offerings made to Buddha, being an abode for gods and
" goddesses engaged in divine sports, giving pleasure to multi-
" tudes of gods performing dances that properly correspond to the
" airs of the music variously produced by the simultaneous playing
" of the five kinds of sonorous instruments of átata, witata, witatáta,
" ghana and susira,* constantly kept up by describing various
" kinds of objects, such as trees, creepers, rivers, quadrupeds, and
" birds, and singing the airs agreeable to these on the summit of
" that peaked mountain Samantakúta, appearing like a noble
" Airáwana elephant,† whose whole body is entirely blanched with
" the white colour of the falling of dews, and who stretches forth,

---

* "A'tata," a tam-tam beaten with the hands only ; 'witata,' a tam-tam beaten
with sticks only ; ' witatáta,' one beaten with the hand on one side, and a stiuk
on the other ; 'ghana,' bells ; 'susira,' trumpets.
† The name of the elephant ridden by the god Sçkrala.

"like rows of probosces, a multitude of rivers that fall in different
"directions, graceful with rows of waves rising up at the points of
"rocks, splendid with a multitude of round and rising rocks like
"frontal globes, and of root-stems of various shapes like a mul-
"titude of tusks, dignified with cataracts, like the gently dropping
"exudation of juice; and with slabs of great stones, like temples;—
"impress there this thy tender, delicate and glorious foot, and
"improve the prosperous condition of the period of five thousand
"years."

53. The lord of the biped race, who gives commands conducive
to the happiness of the whole universe, accepted the prayer
offered by the noble god Sumana in stanzas like these, and when
he was proceeding from the city of Kelani, having ascended
the air, attended by five hundred sanctified priests, including the
eighty dignified disciples, like the great Brahmah Sahampati,
attended by the train of Brahmas, the noble god Sumana covered
himself on one shoulder with a vesture of various lustres, dressed
himself with divine ornaments of undiminished splendour, and
habited with long broad and white divine silk garments, and
himself looking like a pillar of cloud emitting torrents of rain
water, enveloped with rainbows and flashings of lightnings, stood
on the right hand side of the omniscient Buddha, bending himself
with the utmost marks of veneration, and giving him his hand,
proceeded.

54. Then in front of him proceeded in attendance many
hundreds and thousands of female deities, exhibiting various feats
of dancing, forming themselves into different concerts, shewing
their gestures comformably to the nine sentiments of dancing,
descriptive of the six acts of the foot, sixty-four of the hands, eight
of the eyes, and five of the head, and standing in the midst of a

great assembly of performers, producing airs corresponding to the various tunes,—in the same way proceeded many hundreds and thousands of divine soldiers in attendance, habited in their uniforms, overtaking one another, simultaneously raising various loud sounds of the five kinds of musical instruments, as if they were giving a violent shock upon the whole terrestrial element,—in the same way proceeded many hundreds and thousands of goddesses and companies of gods in attendance, carrying articles for offerings, such as umbrellas, fans, banners, bundles of feathers, palm-leaved fans, spreading fans, gold and silver pitchers, pots full of scented water, nosegays, garlands, and silver torches and other things.

55. In the same way proceeded Sekkras, Brahmas, great Iswaras, Nágás, Yakshas, Rákshas, Siddhas, Widdhyadharas, and others, collecting themselves together and attended by their retinues constantly spreading like canopies in the hollow of the firmament nosegays of fragrant flowers, and young branches of asóka trees, tender leaves of the honey mango trees, iron-wood trees, banyan trees, and creepers of spotted betel, and throwing, like rain, gold and silver flowers, pearls, gems, and camphor, and scattering about for offerings an immense quantity of such precious articles as godlike ornaments, divine crowns, and their upper vestures; whirling round their heads numberless divine garments like swarms of white cranes moving about the summit of a golden rock, snapping their fingers, producing sounds by the clapping of their hands, giving shouts of acclamations of joy, and filling all the points of the compass with the noise of excessive singing, intoxicated by the sports of sudhu. Thus the bands of gods proceeded through the air, together with the company of the disciples, Buddha being at their head, as if the rocks of Meru and Yugundara had landed on the shore of the great ocean, and bent their course towards the peak of Samuuala.

. 56. And in this way, while the sound adviser of all the sentient
beings, the sovereign of the world, the lord of the biped races, had
ascended the aerial path, and was proceeding, the orb of the sun
made the clusters of his beams as soft as the light of the moon,
and stood in the sky like a white umbrella held over his head for
the purpose of preventing the heat, then gentle drops of rain
began to fall slowly like a sprinkling of water upon an altar of
flowers that had been elevated to the clouded sky. And gentle
breezes mixed with perfumes began to blow from various directions,
to cool the whole universe like one orb of odour.

57. Thus Buddha suffering the pomps of the immense offerings
which the gods performed, by presenting various miracles in the
whole firmament, filled the entire universe with the clusters of
Buddha's dense beams of six colours, namely blue, yellow, scarlet,
white, red and variegated, arrived at the summit of the peak
Samantakúṭa, and stood with his face towards the west, attended
by five hundred disciples, like the orb of the rising sun enveloped
in a collection of the lustre of Buddha's beams which had come
over the top of the eastern rock, and which had looked towards the
way of the interval of the western ocean; and Buddha, at the
prayer of the great Sumana, the noble king of the gods, clearly
impressed upon the summit of the Samantakúṭa mountain, his soft
and ruddy pink coloured left foot, with all its beauties, which in
length is about three inches less than two carpenter's cubits,*
endowed with a hundred and eight auspicious signs.

58. So he properly gratified the noble god Maha Sumana,
together with innumerable sentient beings such as Brahmas and gods,

---

* Two feet three inches is said to be the measure of a Siṇhalese carpenter's
cubit; but some assert that anciently the measure was two feet nine inches.

and set his glorious foot as a seal that is impressed, purporting that the Island of Lanka was his own treasury, full of the three gems. At that moment, at the festival of the noble peaked mountain Samanala, the rocks, trees, rivers, cataracts, pools, brooks, earth, sea, and sky, like an army attendant upon it, clothed themselves with the unfolded garments of various hues of the six coloured rays of Buddha's beams, anointed with the ointment of the pouring of flowers of divine fragrance, adorned themselves with the jewelry of the showers of divine gems, decorated themselves with garlands of flowers of fully expanded and unwonted blossoms, playing on the five kinds of musical instruments like the roaring of the sea, singing agreeably to the measurement of the hum of the bees, clapping their hands as with the clash of rain clouds, shouting with applause like the roaring of the earth; and in the continual sprinkling of unusual rains they disported themselves among the waters.

59. Then the Omniscient Buddha, attended by the train of the great priests, departed from that place, and rested during the heat of the day in the cave of Bhagawá-lene on the side of that peak of Samanala, making it also a páribhógika memorial, and proceeding from that place went to the district of Ruhunu, and entered with his train into the state of samápatti, on the site where the monument of Díghanakha was to be erected, and rested there for a moment.

60. Having rested in this way for a moment's time in the state of samápatti, together with his five hundred attendant sanctified priests, at the site of Díghanakha, and having placed in that spot the deity Maháséna as guardian, and thence like a Gurulu-raja attended by a multitude of Garundas, ascended the aerial path and come to the city of Anurádhapura, he sat, by shaking the earth, on the site where the great glorious sacred bo-tree was to be placed

in the midst of the grove Maha Méghawana, and on the site where
Ratnamáll monument was to be erected, and appointed there a
deity of the name of Wísála as guardian, and he proceeded thence
and rested, by shaking the earth as before, in the state of Nirólha
samápatti, at the site where the Thupúrúma monument was to be
built ; and having appointed in that place, as guardian, a god of the
name of Prathuwimála, he proceeded thence and rested for a
moment in the state of samápatti at the site of Mirisaweti Vihára
attended by five hundred sanctified priests, including the eighty
dignified disciples ; then he rose from the state of samápatti there,
and preached his doctrines to an innumerable multitude of gods
who had collected themselves together in that place, and led them
into the four rewards of the four paths, and commanded the god
Indra to guard that place, and thus awakened the minds of the people.

61.   From that place he proceeded and rested a moment with
his retinue at the site where Lówámahápáya was to be erected, at
the site where the house of Lahabat was to be erected, at the site
where the pool Dantádhara was to be constructed, and at the site
where Ruwanwelipaya was to be built ; and he preached his doctrines
to the assembled gods in these places, and distributed the four rewards of the four supreme paths ; from that place he proceeded and
sat upon that most delightful spot of ground on the summit of the
rock of Mihintala where Mahasclasáya was to be erected ; and he
brought to his subjection those Gods, Brahmas, Nagas, Garundas,
Siddhas, Widdhyádharas, Rakshas, Gandharwas, and others who
were gathered near him, and he made them drink of the ambrosia
of his doctrines, and straightened the path of the duration of San-
sárn, and displayed to them the happy way which speedily leads
to the city of Nirwúna.

62.   He went thence, together with five hundred sanctified

priests, and entered the state of samápatti at the place where the
venerable dágoba of Kataragama was to be built, and in that place
also he caused the earth to shake, and for the future protection of
that place he located the noble god Ghósha, and departed thence and
entered the state of Niródha samápatti as before, at the site where
Tissa Maha Wihára was to be erected, and caused the earth to
shake as before, and he placed there for guarding it a god called
Manibhúraka. He left that place and coming to Nága-Maha-Vihára,
entered the state of samápatti as before, and caused the earth to
shake, and he placed there for its protection a god named Mihinda,
and proceeded thence and entered the state of Niródha samápatti
with the five hundred sanctified priests at a very delightful spot
of ground, near Séruwila on the southern bank of the river Mahaweli, and caused the great earth to shake, and rose from his seat.

63.   Then when the Nágarája Sumana had plucked some flowers
from the champac tree which he had in his hands, and had gone to
that place and offered them to Buddha and stood by him, he ordered
that Nágarája Sumana should reside there as the guardian god of
that place, and then he gave his own protecting influence to the
glorious Island of Lanka, and returned to Jambudwipa.

64.   This is the third visit of our Buddha to the Island of
Lanka. Thus all the fourteen places, at which he spent some time
in moving about, by way of standing, or sitting, and so forth, in
the three visits which the exalted sovereign of the wholesome
doctrines paid to the Island of Lanka, are páribhógika memorials.

Z.

The Legend of Sudiladewi.

"The following romantic legend, connected with Kellania, is to be found in Siphalese histories ; the period is about 200 B.C.

The beautiful Queen of Tissa, King of Kellania, having been seduced by his brother Uttiya, and their intercourse detected, he fled to Gampola ; from thence he soon after sent an emissary disguised as a priest. This person was instructed to mix in the crowd of priests, who, along with their chief, daily attended at the palace to receive their alms ; at which time it was expected the messenger might find an opportunity of safely delivering a letter with which he was entrusted to the Queen, who always assisted at the distribution of alms. The disguised messenger entered the palace along with a multitude of priests, and, having caught the eye of the Queen, dropped the letter (an ola) : the sound of its fall was heard by the King, who immediately turned round and seized it. The King, having perused the guilty communication, in the height of his fury decided that the High-priest must be cognizant of the intrigue ; for not only had the messenger come as a priest in his train, but the letter appeared to the King to have been written by the High-priest. He was forthwith thrown into a cauldron of boiling oil ; at the same time, the Queen was bound and cast into the river, and the messenger was hewn in pieces. The real writer was afterwards ascertained, and it was then remembered that Uttiya had been a pupil of the unfortunate High-priest, and had acquired exactly the same method of writing."

The above circumstances are thus referred to in the Sela-lihini Sandése:—

> Then in the mansion beautiful,—in memory built,
> By men with merit blest, of deed of tragic guilt,—
> Within the hall whose paintings the story vivid tell
> Of priest slain ruthlessly by kingly passions fell ;—
> Where Tissa in the cauldron of boiling oil had prone
> The Rahat innocent on blind suspicion thrown ;—
> There, on that sacred spot, to Buddhists ever dear,
> The Sage's ardent image, O fairest friend, revere !

"Not long after these events, the sea began to encroach rapidly on the west coast of Ceylon, and the King became persuaded that this calamity was a judgment against him for the cruel and unjust sentence he had executed on the High-priest. In hopes of preventing the onward progress of the waves, and to appease the wrath of those gods who control the waters, Tissa determined to sacrifice his virgin daughter Sudhádéwi ; and, having secured her in a covered golden canoe, on which was inscribed "a royal maiden," he caused it to be launched into the ocean. The flood continued to increase ; and the monarch, mounted on his elephant, had proceeded to view the destructive effects of the raging waters : while thus engaged, the earth opened, and the King disappeared amidst flames which burst from the sinking wreck of his richest provinces. Before the waves ceased to encroach upon the land, six hundred and forty villages (four hundred and seventy of which were principally inhabited by divers for pearls) had been overwhelmed, and the distance between Kellania and the sea-coast had been reduced from twenty-five to four miles.

The vessel in which the young Princess was immolated, having been drifted to the south-west, was discovered and brought to land by some fishermen in the Mágam district, which was at that time a separate kingdom, under the control of Kawantissa Raja. He, having heard of the mysterious appearance of the golden canoe, proceeded to the coast at Totalu Ferry; and, after reading the inscription, released the Princess, whose name he changed to Wihari Dewi, and whom he afterwards married.

Wihari Dewi became the mother of Dootoogaimoonoo, a prince who restored the Siphalese power, and expelled the Malabars, to whom both Kellania Tissa and Kawantissa had been tributaries. Many Buddhists believe that her merits and good fortune are so great, that, in a future transmigration, she will become the mother of Mytrée,* the expected Buddha."—FORBES' Eleven Years in Ceylon, vol. i. pages 154—156.

---

* In a Vihára recently built at Cotanchina, and not yet completed in its internal decorations, there is a statue of the expected Mytrée, who is represented as a white man.

F.

The Dalada-Malagawa; and the History of the Tooth.

"The principal objects in Kandy worthy of any notice, are the palace, and the different temples of Boodhoo and the gods. The palace did occupy a considerable space of ground. Its front, about 200 yards long, made rather an imposing appearance: it looked towards the principal temples, and rose above a handsome moat, the walls of which were pierced with triangular cavities for purposes of illumination. At one extremity, it was terminated by an hexagonal building, of two stories, called Pateripooa, in which the king, on great occasions, appeared to the people, assembled in the square below. At the other extremity, it was bounded by the women's apartments, on the front of which the sun, moon, and stars, (not out of gallantry, but as insignia of royalty,) were carved in stone, and in which, at the public festivals, the king and his ladies stationed themselves to witness the processions. The intermediate space was occupied chiefly by the great entrance to the palace, and by the temple (the Dalada Malegawa) a little in the rear. The entrance was by a drawbridge over the moat, through a massive archway, on one hand, up a flight of huge steps, and through another archway to the hall of audience; and, on the other hand, up another flight of steps to the temple and the hexagonal building . . . The hall of audience, where the king usually transacted business and kept his court, is a long room, in which nothing ornamental is now to be seen, excepting the carved wooden pillars by which the roof is supported . . . The principal temples in Kandy and its immediate neighbourhood, are the Dalada Malegawa, the Malwatté, and the Asgirie Wihares,—and the Nata, Maha-Vishnu,* Katragam, and Patiné Dewalés. The Dalada Malegawa, was the domestic temple of the king, and is the most venerated of any in the country, as it contains the relic, the tooth of Boodhoo, to which the whole island was dedicate, and which is considered by good Boodhists as the most precious thing in the world. The temple is small, of two stories, built in the Chinese style of archi-tecture. The sanctum is an inner room, about twelve feet square, on the upper story, without windows, and to which a ray of natural light never penetrates. You enter it by folding doors, with polished brass pannels, before and behind which is a curtain. The splendour of the place is very striking; the roof and walls are lined with gold brocade; and nothing scarcely is to be seen but gold, gems, and sweet-smelling flowers. On a platform or stage, about three feet and a half high, and which occupies about half the room, there is a profusion of flowers tastefully arranged before the objects of worship to which they are offered, viz. two or three small figures of Boodhoo,—one of crystal, and the other of silver-gilt, and four or five domes or caskets, called karanduns, containing relics, and similar in form to the common Dagobah, of which a figure has been given already. All but one of the karanduns are small, not exceeding a foot in height, and wrapped in many folds

---

* In page 103 I stated that the priests of the Maligáwa, are proprietors of the site of the Bçrçndi-kówlla at Sítáwaka; this I have since learnt is a mistake, that property belongs to the Maha Vishnu Déwálé in Kandy.

of muslin. One is of much greater size, and uncovered, and, with its decorations, makes a most brilliant appearance. It is five feet four and a half inches high, and nine feet ten inches in circumference at its base. It is of silver, from three-tenths to four-tenths of an inch thick, and gilt externally. It consists of three different pieces, capable of being separated from each other. Its workmanship is neat, but plain, and it is studded with very few gems, the finest of which is a valuable cat's-eye on its top, which is rarely seen. The ornaments attached to it are extremely rich, and consist of go'd chains, and a great variety of gems, suspended from it. The most remarkable of these is a bird hanging by a gold chain, and formed entirely of diamonds, rubies, blue sapphires, emeralds, and cat's-eyes, set in gold, which is hid by the profusion of stones. Viewed at a little distance, by candle-light, the gems about the karandua seem to be of immense value; but when closely inspected, they prove in general to be of bad quality, and some of the largest merely crystal, coloured by a foil. This great karandua is the receptacle of the Dalada, 'the Tooth,' as it is considered, of Boodhoo. Through the kindness of the Governor, I had an opportunity (enjoyed by few Europeans) of seeing this celebrated relic, when it was recovered, towards the conclusion of the rebellion, and brought back to be replaced in the Dalada Malegawa, from which it had been clandestinely taken. It was of a dirty yellow colour, excepting towards its truncated base, where it was brownish. Judging from its appearance at the distance of two or three feet, (for none but the chief priests were privileged to touch it,) it was artificial, and of ivory, discoloured by age. Never a relic was more preciously enshrined; wrapped in pure sheet-gold, it was placed in a case just large enough to receive it, of gold, covered externally with emeralds, diamonds, and rubies, tastefully arranged. This beautiful and very valuable bijou was put into a very small gold karandua, richly ornamented with rubies, diamonds, and emeralds : this was enclosed in a larger one also of gold, and very prettily decorated with rubies: this second, surrounded with tinsel, was placed in a third, which was wrapped in muslin; and this in a fourth, which was similarly wrapped ; both these were of gold, beautifully wrought, and richly studded with jewels: lastly, the fourth karandua, about a foot and a half high, was deposited in the great karandua. Here, it may be remarked, that when the relic was taken, the effect of its capture was astonishing, and almost beyond the comprehension of the enlightened :— 'Now (the people said) the English are indeed masters of the country ; for they who possess the relic have a right to govern four kingdoms ; this, for 2000 years, is the first time the relic was ever taken from us.' And the first Adikar observed, 'That whatever the English might think of the consequence of having taken Kappitipola, Pilimé Talawé, and Mudugallé,* in his opinion, and in the opinion of the people in general, the taking of the relic was of infinitely more moment.' "—DAVY's Account of the Interior of Ceylon, pp. 365—369.

---

* The three principal rebel chiefs.

The following is a brief account of the history of the Tooth, of the inestimable value of which, and of the numberless miracles wrought by it, Buddhist literature is full. Of these last, one example may be given, quoted from an antient Páli gáthá in the Attanagalu-vansa, a work written in the latter part of the thirteenth century

> Held in the lotus hand of Lanka's king,
> Like raja-hansa, bird of golden wing,
> Instinct with life, the *Danta* brightly gleam'd
> Then Buddha's form assum'd, when from it beam'd
> Effulgent flashings, which on all sides thrown
> With splendour unsurpass'd itself made known.
> Awe-struck the king the miracle beheld,
> Convinced, delighted, and by joy impell'd,—
> Such joy as fills a Chakkavatti's* breast
> When of a Chakka-ratana† possest, —
> He to th' unrivall'd relic offerings there
> Made of rich gems, and priceless jewels rare.

After the funeral rites of Gautama Buddha had been performed at Kusinara, B.C. 543, his "left canine tooth" was carried to Dantapura, the capital of Kalinga, where it was preserved for 800 years. The king of Kalinga being engaged in a doubtful conflict, directed that, in the event of defeat, the sacred relic should be conveyed to Ceylon. The event he feared occurred, and the relic was conveyed to Ceylon A.D. 311, by a princess of Kalinga, who concealed it in the folds of her hair. It was received by king Mahasen and

---

* An emperor whose dominions extend from sea to sea.

† The inestimable chariot (chakka), which is studded with (ratana) gems, and which moves on the air.

the priests with the greatest possible honors; and remained at the capital until about the year 1315, when, during an invasion of the Malabars, it was captured at Yapahoo, and carried back to Southern India. Prakramabahu III., the succeeding king, went in person to Madura to negotiate for its surrender, and returned with it to Ceylon, when it was deposited by him in Pollannaruwa. In the troublous times which followed, the tooth was carried from one place to another, and preserved or hidden at Kandy, at Delgamoa in Sabaragamuwa,* and at Cotta, where it was captured by the Portuguese in 1560, and convoyed by them to Goa. The king of Pegu, hearing of its capture, offered an immense ransom for it; which Don Constantine, the Viceroy of Goa, would have accepted, but for the determined opposition of the Archbishop, who in a solemn assembly, convened for the purpose, reduced the tooth to powder in a mortar, and then burned its remains in a brasier, the contents of which he then cast into the river. In 1564 however, Brama the king of Pegu having sent ambassadors to Ceylon for the purpose of obtaining a princess of the blood royal as a bride, these, when about to undertake a pilgrimage to Adam's Peak, were secretly informed by the chamberlain of the Singhalese monarch, that he was still in possession of the genuine tooth of Buddha, and that what had been destroyed by Don Constantine was a counterfeit. The king and his chamberlain, both of whom were in the power of the Portuguese, had, in fact, manufactured a facsimile out of stag's horn, and thought by this means to effect

---

* About half a mile on the Colombo side of the Katutlyambaráwa vihára; where there are the remains of a Portuguese fort, still known as "Delgomuwa Malua."

their purpose of palming off a daughter of the latter on the king of Pegu, the Siṇhalese king being childless, and to effect an alliance, by which his prosperity might be restored. The ambassadors, believing in the genuineness of the tooth, negotiated for its removal, with the bride, to Pegu. In this they were not at first successful, but the lady was sent to Pegu, and married to the king. When however the discovery was made that she was the daughter of the chamberlain of the king of Cotta, and not of the king, although of royal blood, the ambassadors informed Brama of the existence of the tooth, and the willingness of Don Juan to part with it. Valuing the tooth above every thing else, Brama forgave the deception as to the parentage of his wife, and eagerly made overtures to Don Juan for the possession of the relic. It was accordingly sent to him, and received with every demonstration of honor, and the most profound adoration ; the king, Don Juan, receiving in return, an immense amount of treasure. But now, another tooth turned up. For the king of Kandy, learning what had happened, and influenced by envy, despatched au envoy to Pegu, who being received with distinction by king Brama, informed him of the deceptions practised by Don Juan ; but added "that the king of Kandy, anxious to ally himself with the sovereign of Pegu, had commissioned him to offer in marriage a princess who was in reality his own offspring, and not supposititious; besides which he gave him to understand, that the Kandyan monarch was the possessor and depositary of the genuine tooth of Buddha, neither the one which Don Constantine had seized at Jayawardana, nor yet that which was held by the king of Pegu, being the true one,—a fact which he was prepared to substantiate by documents and ancient olas. Brama listened to his statement, and pondered it in his mind ; but seeing that the princess had already received the oaths of fidelity as queen, and that the tooth had been welcomed with so much solemnity, and deposited in a wihare, specially built for it, he resolved to hush up the affair; to avoid confessing himself a dupe, (for kings must no more admit themselves to be in error in their dealings with us, than we in our dealings with them). Accordingly, he gave as his reply, that he was sensible of the honour designed for him by the proffered alliance with the royal family of Kandy, and likewise by the offer of the tooth; that he returned his thanks to the king, and as a mark of consideration would send back by his ambassadors a ship laden with presents."[*]

This latter tooth is no doubt, the one now preserved in the Malí-gáwa at Kandy, which Sir J. E. Tennent describes as "a clumsy substitute manufactured by Wikrama Bahu in 1566, to replace the original *dalada*. The dimensions and form of the present dalada are fatal to any belief in its identity with the one originally worshipped, which was probably human, whereas the object now shewn is a piece of discoloured ivory, about two inches in length, and less than one in diameter, resembling the tooth of a crocodile rather than that of a man." This description shews that the fabricators were in all probability unacquainted with the appearance of the original, which had been preserved as the palladium of empire by the king and priests at Cotta; but that accepting the tradition of Buddha's stature of thirty or forty feet as a fact, they made a .tooth big enough for a being of such an enormous height.

---

[*] Diego de Couto, Decade viii., ch. xiii.

G.

ACCOUNT OF THE ASCENT OF ADAM'S PEAK, BY LIEUT. MALCOLM, OF THE 1ST CEYLON RIFLE REGIMENT.

"On the morning of 26th April, 1815, I left Batugedera with a small escort of a sergeant and four Malays, (of the First Ceylon Regiment,) for the purpose of ascending Adam's Peak; for I had been so repeatedly disappointed in expectation of guides, which the Headman of Batugedera, Dolip Nillamé, had promised, that I determined to take my chance of obtaining them at Gillemallé on my way. I merely took with me a few blankets, a quadrant, and measuring chain, and three days' provisions for my party. The route winded with the Kalu·Ganga, or Kaltura river, which, about two miles from Batugedera, receives the Mugellé-Oya, about two chains in breadth at the confluence. On the left bank, there are ruins of a Kandyan fort, erected during the late war to command the ford.

"From the Mugellé river to the rest-house of Gillemallé, the distance is about three miles and a half. At this place I procured two guides, after some delay, and leaving the Gillemallé rest-house, we immediately crossed the Malmelloo river, and about half a mile further on, the Maskellé river.

"From the banks of the latter, we entered a forest of magnificent trees, straight as pines, and from fifty to seventy feet in height; and about four P. M. we arrived at Palabadoolla, ten miles and eighteen chains from Batugedera. Here there is a considerable temple of Buddha, and a large rest-house for pilgrims on their way to the Peak.

"About two hundred pilgrims, of both sexes and of all castes and conditions, were here assembled, some on their way to, and others on their return from, the Peak. The dance was continued without intermission, to the sound of Tam-a-tams and other instruments of Singhalese music, until the pilgrims, who were about to ascend the mountain, began to prepare their lights; and at about eight P. M. they proceeded onwards in distinct parties.

"The Head Priest, from whom I received every possible attention, tried all the persuasive rhetoric he could muster, to prevent me from proceeding further towards the Peak ; assuring me, that 'no white man ever did and never could ascend the mountain.' I soon convinced the benevolent Oonansé that I was not a white man to be dissuaded from the attempt through any dread of ulterior danger ; and therefore, having been well refreshed, and our chules ready, we took leave of the priest, and left Palabadoolla about eleven at night.

"After passing three small forts that had been thrown up during the war, we began to ascend the first mountain, and reached the summit in four hours. From the next, the Kalu-Ganga descends rapidly ; and, about five A. M., we breakfasted upon the rocks bordering its stream, and then continued our route up the mountain, Adam's Peak still towering far above our heads ;

"Nil mortalium arduum est—Cœlum ipsum petimus,"

and, after surmounting two other distinct ascents, equally steep, but of less height, we came to the foot of the Peak itself. The face of the hill here appeared quite perpendicular, and the pilgrims,

in advance of my party, were seen climbing up the precipice by
the assistance of the iron chains which are fixed in the rock for
that purpose. We halted a few minutes to take breath, and after
great exertions, we reached the top between eight and nine A. M.
of the 27th April,

"The view from this great elevation far surpassed my most
sanguine expectation, it was so magnificently extensive. On one
side displaying a vast extent of mountain, champaign, and forest
scenery, the latter so variegated in foliage and so irregular in form,
that I could only compare it to an ocean of woods, whose waves
had suddenly become fixed in an unalterable position; on the
others, the tops of the hills rising above dense fogs, and resembling
innumerable islands covered with wood and scattered over the sea
that apparently filled the space below. Batugedera was seen on
one side, as if almost under our feet, and on the other, in the
distance, the Kandyan mountains, interspersed with clouds.—But,
alas! whilst in the full enjoyment of this splendid scene, a thick
fog arose from the bottom of the mountain, and drew a curtain over
its sublimity.

"The area of the summit of the peak is 72 feet long and 54 broad,
and is enclosed by a parapet wall five feet high; this has partly
fallen down on the east side, which is covered with scarlet Rhododendrons (*Rhododendron arboreum*), and the remainder is sadly
out of repair. In the middle of this area is a large rock of Kabooo
or iron-stone, upon which is a mark of Adam's left foot, called *Sri
Pada* by the Singhalese; but it requires a great deal of help from
imagination to trace it out. This sacred footstep is covered over
with a small building formed of the most durable wood, 12 feet
long, 9 broad, and 4½ to the tiles, with which it is surmounted.
Upon the inside it is enclosed by a frame of copper fitted to its

shape, and ornamented with numerous jewels set in four rows, but not of the best or *most precious gems* the island has been known to produce, for to me they looked very like glass.

"We were not, I regret to say, provided with an 'Union Jack,' but we fired three vollies, to the great astonishment of the Buddhists, as a memorial to them that a British armed party had reached the summit, spite of the prediction of the priest of Palabadoolla. The priest having warned us of approaching rain, we *had* some faith in that warning, as the result of his experience, and made the best of our way down the mountain, which we found far more laborious to descend than it had been to climb.

"The rain, which fell in torrents, increased the difficulties of the abominable roads, over rocks and fragments of iron-stone, to Palabadoolla, which we reached about 4 P. M., and returned to my quarters at Batugedera the next morning.

"Sound lungs and hard feet are indispensable to the performance of such a trip, for in many places we had to climb barefoot over the iron-stone. As to palankins, they are quite out of the question. There may be some risk in ascending Adam's Peak in heavy rains, but surely not in fine weather.

"The summit of the mountain was only clear about a quarter of an hour, which did not even allow me time to satisfy my curiosity, or to take any bearings, which latter circumstance I particularly regret."—BENNET's Ceylon and its Capabilities, pp. 380—383.

The following is from the pen of an Officer who ascended Adam's Peak shortly after Lieut. Malcolm.

"While we were in Saffregam, we resolved to put in execution a project which we had talked of at Colombo, and before our return to visit Adam's Peak. This plan we have accomplished. Leaving Baddegeddera on the morning of the 6th, we gained the summit on the next day at half past two in the afternoon. Our first march from Baddegeddera was 5½ miles of tolerable road through a fine and interesting country, along the left banks of the Caltura river, to the royal village and extensive lawns of Gillomalley. From this place, the King received his store of jaggery. There are about 250 inhabitants, who are well looking and of a creditable appearance. Their houses are numerous and comfortable. From Gillemalley, at three o'clock, we set out for Palabatula, situated on the top of the Allehentenne mountain, at the distance of 4½ miles in a northeast direction. The ascent is about 2½ miles in length. Here is a small religious establishment, where the priests live who have the care of the Holy Impression of the Foot on the Peak, and there is good shelter for travellers. We slept at this place, and soon after daylight next morning, renewed our journey, accompanied by one of the priests as a guide. The road leads for a mile and a half over a very rugged and abrupt ascent to the northeast, up the Neela Hella, at the bottom of which, about a quarter of a mile from Palabatula, we crossed the Caltura river, and all the way up to the top of the hill we heard it on our right hand running below. The next ascent is the Hourtilla Hilla, of three quarters of a mile, still more rugged and difficult than the former, the road at some places having an angle of full 50 degrees. We then ascended the Gonatilla Hilla, about half a mile, still more steep, and

the air became cooler and clearer. The next stage is to Deabetme,
rather more than a mile, and this is the summit of the mountain,
the road up which is one continual rise of four miles without any
intervening descent, although the hill has four names, and each
division is marked by a whitewashed stone on the right side of
the road. There is here a small Ambelam (a Cinhalese resthouse)
and the ruins of a building erected by Eyheylapollo (the late
Dessave of Saffregam). The Adikars, and Dessaves, were accustomed to be carried as far as this point, when they visited the Peak,
which opens to the view bearing E. by N. The road now extends
in a northeast direction four miles over the hills of Durmarajah,
Pedrotollagalla, Male Malla Kandura, and Andea Malle Hella, and is
excessively steep and difficult. From the latter the Peak itself rises
about a mile or three quarters in perpendicular height from this
place. The way is fair climbing; the direction at first N. E., then
S. E., again N. E., and lastly N. W., when the perpendicular ascent
is encountered : this is only to be surmounted by the help of
several massy iron chains, which are strongly fastened at top, let
down the precipice, and again secured below. These chains are
donations to the Temple, and the name of the donor is engraved on
one of the links made solid for that purpose. The height of the
precipice is about 200 feet, and many holes are worn in the face of
the rock by the feet of the numerous pilgrims who have ascended
it with the assistance of the chains. At half-past two in the afternoon we reached the summit. It is an area of about one fifth of
an acre, surrounded by a stone wall four feet and a half high, of
four unequal sides, with two entrances, one on the south and
another on the east, and an opening to the west in form of an
embrasure. In the middle is a rock about nine feet high, on which
is the fancied impression of the Holy Foot. It has in fact a most

shapeless appearance, bearing little resemblance to a human foot,
and what is most unfortunate for the tradition of its being the last
footstep of Buddha, when he strode from Ceylon to Ava, the toes,
if they can be discerned, are turned towards the west. The clouds
which arose as we were ascending prevented our having any view,
and we occupied ourselves till four o'clock in taking a plan of the
summit; we then found it was much too late to think of returning
to Palabatula, and resolved to remain during the night on the
Peak. I can hardly attempt to describe the extraordinary grandeur
and variety of the scene that opened upon us at sunset. Above our
heads, the air was perfectly serene and clear: below, a thick bed
of clouds enveloped the mountain on all sides, and completely in-
tercepted our view; but every now and then, the beams of the
sun broke through the mass of clouds, and threw a brilliant light
over the surrounding mountains; then suddenly the opening was
closed, and all was again hid from our sight. These beautiful
glimpses were often quite momentary, and frequently repeated,
sometimes even twice in a minute, nor did the operation entirely
cease until it was quite dark. We spent a wretched night in a
most comfortless hut about thirty feet below the summit. There
was a piercing wind, and the cold was far greater than I had ever
felt since I left England. Unluckily we had no thermometer
with us, but I think the quicksilver would not have risen above
40°. The rising of the sun presented a magnificent scene, but
quite different from that of the evening. The whole surrounding country except Ouva was covered with clouds, above
which only the tops of a few mountains were visible—Hunas-
garree, Kandy, bore northeast, and a mountain that we decided to
be Idalgasina southeast. The whole country of Ouva was exposed
to view, and lay stretched out in appearance just beneath our feet.

The sea on that side was perceptible, and bore southeast, which must have been in the neighbourhood of Paltoopane; and it was perhaps the leway or great natural saltpan that we observed. At seven in the morning we began to descend the mountain, and reached Palabatula at noon."—From the Appendix to Captain ANDERSON's "Wanderer in Ceylon."

II.

THE RUINS OF SI'TA'WAKA.

"Sitawaka, the old court of the ancient Kings and Rajas, with its great gates, walls and steps, is situated at the branch of a particular rivulet flowing from the nearest promontory, and loses itself, after half an hour's sailing, in the great river of Colombo, which comes from Ruanella; all that is brought here from Colombo is warranted good, and is therefore for the house of the Dissawa; the stones of the old ruins which are heaped up in great numbers are sufficient for building a fortification in which to store Neli and Arecanuts, which come from the adjacent Korles. The situation is by nature very strong, and well protected. For the Colombo Dissawe, a better place cannot be preferred, as he is in the centre of all the Colombo lands, as well as those of the Three and Four Korles to the north; the Saffragam lands to the south; and Colombo itself on the west: all of them lying at almost equal distances from each other; for from Sitawaka to Arandora it is six hours' journey, to Saffragam eight hours, and to Colombo ten hours by land, but may be done in six hours by water."—VALENTYN.

I.

THE PERAHARA.

"THE word Perahara means literally a procession, and though the epithet may be applied to any procession, it is used emphatically of a festival held annually in the city of Kandy, [and at Ratnapura] which commenced this year [1839] on the day of the new moon in August.

We have tried in vain to obtain an account of its origin from the natives; they say that its history is lost in the darkness of antiquity. A kapurála of Udanuwara refers it to the time of Gajábáhu, who reigned A.D. 113, and says that this king was a native of some foreign country, where these processions were in common use. This account cannot be correct, as Gajábáhu was the son of a native prince; but on referring to the history of this monarch, there are circumstances related which may assist us in our researches.

Gajábáhu resided at Anurádhapura. One night, when walking through the city in disguise, he saw a widow weeping, whose sons had been taken captive by the Solli king, in an invasion of Ceylon from the continent, during the previous reign. The king made a mark upon the door of the house, and returned to his palace. Next morning he called his nobles, and asked what injustice had been committed in the city. They replied that the whole city was as free from injustice as a house wherein a festival is celebrated, when the king, in anger, sent for the woman whose dwelling he had marked, and asked her why she was crying upon the previous evening. She said that in the reign of the king's father, the people of Solli had taken 12,000 captives from Ceylon, among whom were two of her sons, and that it was on this account she wept. Upon hearing this, the king collected an army, and proceeding to Yápápatuna, (Jaffna) he informed his people that as the Solli King had taken captive his subjects, he must go and bring them back to their own homes. With Neela, a giant, he arrived at the sea shore, where he dismissed his army, and taking an iron rod he struck the sea, which divided, and he and the giant went over to the continent. The Solli king was in great fear, and to increase his terror Neela took one of the royal elephants, and dashed it against another with such force, that both the animals died. In the same manner, the giant devastated the country. The Solli king, when he heard of these things from his nobles, asked Gajábáhu why he had come with an army to destroy his realm; to which he replied, that he had brought no army besides his giant, and proceeded, "In the days of your father, when my father reigned, he went over to Ceylon and seized 12,000 persons, and brought them hither captive, and I have come to demand them." The Solli king answered forthwith, "Though you go to dewya-lókaya, and receive the assistance of the asoors, you will not be able to overcome me." Gajábáhu was greatly enraged at this refusal to deliver up the captives, and declared that he would not only take his own subjects, but 12,000 other captives as well, and he threatened to burn the royal city to ashes in case of refusal. To shew his great strength, and that the threats were not idle words, he squeezed water out of a handful of dry sand, and afterwards out of the iron rod, which frightened the Solli king to such a degree, that he delivered up the 24,000 persons demanded, the golden halamba of Pattinee, the sacred utensils of four déwálas, and "the refection dish" of Buddha; and with these Gajábáhu returned to Ceylon. The 12,000 Sinhalese were sent to their respective homes, and tho 12,000 captives were allowed to reside in Alootkúrakórla, a district to the northward of Colombo, the inhabitants of which to this day retain many marks of their continental origin.

The sacred vessels here referred to had been taken away in the reign of Walagambáhu, B.C. 90, and there can be little doubt that it was to commemorate their return the Perahara was originally established, as the carrying of the halamba and other relics seems to be the most essential part of the procession, and to the dividing of the waters also a reference will afterwards be made. It is not clear from the narrative whether the halamba had been previously in Ceylon, though from other traditions we have heard we should suppose they had; but this will make little differerence in tho intention of the festival, as it may still be held to celebrate their arrival. It is upon these relics that the heathen natives swear in the courts of justice. The origin of the Perahara is therefore to to be dated as far back as the second century of the Christian era.

The account given of the Perahara by Knox, as it was celebrated in the reign of Raja Singha II. 1670, is as follows:—

'The greatest solemnity is performed in the city of Cande; but at the same time the like festival or Perahar is observed in divers other cities and towns of the land. The Perahar at Kandy is ordered after this manner.

'The priest bringeth forth a painted stick, about which strings of flowers are hanged, and so it is wrapped in branched silk, some part covered and some not; before which the people bow down and worship; each one presenting him with an offering according to his free will. These free-will offerings being received from the people, the priest takes his painted stick on his shoulder, having a cloth tied about his mouth to keep his breath from defiling this pure piece of wood, and gets up upon an elephant all covered with white cloth, upon which he rides with all the triumph that king and kingdom can afford, through all the streets of the city. But before him go, first some 40 or 50 elephants, with brass bells hanging on each side of them, which tinkle as they go.

'Next follow men dressed up like gyants, which go dancing along agreeable to a tradition they have, that anciently there were huge men, that could carry vast burthens, and pull up trees by the roots, &c. After them go a multitude of drummers, and trumpetters and pipers, which make such a great and loud noise, that nothing else besides them can be heard. Then followeth a company of men dancing along, and after these women of such castes or trades as are necessary for the service of the pagoda, as potters and washer-women; each caste goeth in companies by themselves, three and three in a row, holding one another by the hand; and between each company go drummers, pipers and dancers.

'After these comes an elephant with two priests on his back: one whereof is the priest before spoken of, carrying the painted stick on his shoulder, who represents Allout-neur-dio, that is, the god and maker of heaven and earth. The other sits behind him, holding a round thing like an umbrella over his head, to keep off sun or rain. Then within a yard after him, on each hand of him, follow two other elephants mounted with two other priests, with a priest sitting behind each, holding umbrellas as the former, one of them represents Cotterägan dio, and the other Potting dio. These three gods that reside here in company are accounted of all other the greatest and chiefest, each one having his residence in a separate pagoda.

'Behind go their cook-women, with things like whisks in their hands, to scare away flies from them; but very fine as they can make themselves.

'Next after the gods and their attendance, go some thousands of ladies and gentlewomen, such as are of the best sort of the inhabitants of the land, arrayed in the bravest manner that their ability can afford, and so go hand in hand three in a row: At which time all the beauties in Zelone in their bravery do go to attend upon their gods in their progress about the city. Now are the streets also all made clean, and on both sides all along the streets poles are stuck up with flags and pennons hanging at the top of them, and adorned with boughs and branches of cocoanut trees hanging like fringes, and lighted lamps all along on both sides of the streets, both day and night.

'Last of all, go the commanders sent from the king to see these ceremonies decently performed, with their soldiers after them. And in this manner they ride all round about the city once by day and once by night. This festival lasts from the new moon to the full moon.

'Formerly the king himself in person used to ride on horseback with all his train before him in this solemnity, but now he delights not in these shows.

'Always before the gods set out to take their progress they are set in the pagoda door, a good while, that the people may come to worship and bring their offerings unto them: during which time there are dancers, playing and shewing many petty tricks of activity before him. To see the which, and also to shew themselves in their bravery, occasions more people tor esort thither, than otherwise their zeal and devotion would prompt them to do.

''Two or three days before the full moon, each of these gods hath a pallenkine carried after them to add unto their honour, in the which there are several pieces of their superstitious relicts, and a silver pot, which just at the hour of full moon they ride out unto a river, and dip full of water, which is carried back with them into the temple, where it is kept till the year after and then flung away.   And so the ceremony is ended for that year.

'This festival of the gods taking their progress through the city, in the year 1664 the king would not permit to be performed; and that same year the rebellion happened, but never since hath he hindered it.

. 'At this time they have a superstition, which lasteth 6 or 7 days, too foolish to write: it consists in dancing, singing, and juggling. The reason of which is, lest the eyes of the people, or the power of the jaccos, or infernal spirits, might any ways prove prejudicial or noisome to the aforesaid gods in their progress abroad.   During the celebration of this great festival, there are no drums allowed to be beaten to any particular gods at any private sacrifice.'

Knox is right in his descriptions, but wrong, as might naturally be expected, in some of his explanatory remarks.   The attendance of the giants, commemorative of the redoubtable Neela, is another evidence that it is to the reign of Gajábáhu we are to look for the origin of the festival.

In the Ceylon Almanac for 1834 is a "Description of the four principal Kandian festivals, compiled from materials furnished by a native chief."   From this document we learn, that until the reign of king Kirtisree (A.D. 1747–1780) the Perahara was celebrated exclusively in honour of the four deities, Natha, Vishnu, Katragam, and Pattinee, and altogether unconnected with Buddhism.   The sacred Dalndá relic of Buddha was first carried in procession, together with the insignia of the four gods, in 1775.   The

circumstances which gave rise to this innovation were as follow.—
The Siamese priests who were invited here by king Kirtisree, for the
purpose of restoring the Upaósampadáwa, the highest order of
Buddhist ordination, one day hearing the noise of jingalls, &c.,
enquired the cause, and were informed that preparations were being
made for celebrating a festival in honor of the gods. They took
umbrage at this, and observed that they had been made to believe
that Buddhism was the established religion of the kingdom, and
they had never expected to see Hinduism triumphant in Kandy.
To appease them the king sent to assure them that this festival of
the Perahara was chiefly intended to glorify the memory of Buddha,
and to convince them of it, the king gave directions that the great
relic should be carried foremost in the procession, dedicating his
own howdah for its reception.

There can be little doubt that the Perahara received the counte-
nance of the native princes, rather from a political than a religious
motive, though these circumstances would vary with the disposition
of the reigning king. It was one of the few occasions upon which
the monarch presented himself to the public gaze. The most
imposing edifice connected with the place was the Pattrippo, an
octagon of two stories, the upper story having a balcony that overlooked the principal square of the royal city, on one side of which
was a lake, and on the other various religious and consecrated
places. The procession was collected in the square, that the king
might see it from the balcony; and when the curtain which
shrouded his majesty at his entrance was withdrawn, and the
assembly did lowly reverence, amidst the clamor of the drums and
pipes, the sight of the prostrate thousands, the elephants richly
caparisoned, the royal guard in proud array, the countless banners
floating in the breeze, and the adigars and other chiefs at the head

of their respective clans, all arranged in due order and degree, must have produced an effect that is not often equalled even in the festive scenes of far mightier kingdoms. On some occasions the king joined in the procession, but in this there was no uniformity of observance, his majesty being at one time on foot, and at another we are told, in a golden chariot drawn by eight horses.

The Perahara afforded an excellent opportunity to the king to examine into the state of the provinces, the conduct of the governors, and the obedience of the people. The refractory were punished, the loyal rewarded, and new regulations were now promulgated, that they might be carried to the more distant districts of the island. To the inhabitants generally it must have been a time of grateful festivity, especially during the reigns of the more popular kings, as it was a spectacle of splendor, and the various chiefs were able to exhibit their consequence in the presence of the assembled kingdom.

The Perahara begins on the day of the new moon in the month of Æsala, which this year answers to our August. The commencement is regulated by the nekata, or situation of the moon; and at the appointed moment, which must be either in the evening or morning, never at mid-day, the kapurála of the Vishnu déwála cuts down a young jack tree which has been previously chosen, and is consecrated for the purpose by mysterious rites. The day before, the kapurála must bathe in pure water, anoint his head with the juice of the lime, and clothe himself in clean garments. In ancient times flowers were used, as mentioned by Knox, and these were the flowers of the æhæla, (cathantocarpus fistulata), but either because this tree does not now bear flowers in the proper season, or because another tree is more conveniently found, the jack has been substituted in its place, which, however, for the time, receives the name of æhæla. When Knox wrote, the procession was in June; when Davy wrote, in July; it is now in August; and like all other eastern festivals, from the imperfection of the native astronomy, it traverses through all the months of the year. The painted stick of Knox, adorned with flowers, appears to be commemorative of the wonder-working rod of Gajábáhu, and the jack is undoubtedly an innovation. When the tree has been cut down, it is divided into four sections, one of which is conveyed to each of the déwálas, under a white canopy, and accompanied by music. The section is cleaned at the déwála, and put into a hole, after which offerings of cakes are presented, called ganabódana. The gana are an order of inferior deities attendant upon the gods, and bódana is the Elu form of bhójana, food.

The consecrated wood is adorned with leaves, flowers, and fruit, and during the first five days the procession simply passes round it, the kapurálas bearing the sacred vessels and implements. After this time they are brought beyond the precincts of the déwála, and paraded through the principal streets of Kandy. On the night of the full moon the procession is joined by a relic of Buddha, properly accompanied, which is afterwards carried to the Adahana Maluwa, a consecrated place near which are the tombs of the ancient kings and other individuals of the royal race. The Maluwa is encircled by stones, within which, it is said, the kings had no jurisdiction; it was a kind of sanctuary. The relic receives the adoration of the crowd until the morning, when it is returned to the temple.

Towards the end of the festival the procession approaches the river, at the ancient ferry not far from the Peradenia bridge, and whilst the multitude remains upon the bank, the kapurálas enter a boat that has been splendidly decorated for the occasion. The boat is rowed to some distance, when the kapurála takes a golden sword, and strikes the water. At the same instant a brazen vessel is dipped into the river, and whilst the water is yet disparted, a portion is taken up, which is kept until the vessel can be filled in the same manner at the next festival. The water which had been taken the previous year is at the same time poured back into the river.

There is a close analogy between this striking of the river and the striking of the sea by Gajábáhu, though what is meant by the dividing of the waters we cannot tell. It is probable that there was something extraordinary connected with the passage of the king, which tradition afterwards magnified into this miracle. Were we disposed to be fanciful, we might notice the resemblance, which the striking of the sea by a rod, the squeezing of water from the dry sand, the errand of the king to demand captives, and some other circumstances, bears to certain facts in the Israelitish exodus, but we have seen so many similar constructions levelled to the ground at a single blow, that we forbear to pursue the parallel.

The general arrangement of the Perahara is the same now as in former times, but in the grandeur of the spectacle there can be no comparison. There are still elephants richly adorned; flags, penhons, and banners; several bands of drums, tom-toms, and pipes; the palanqueens of the gods; the sacred utensils; and the chiefs of the déwálas, &c., with their separate retinues. The streets are lighted by vessels of oil, placed upon poles, and carried by men, after the manner of the meshals of the Arab tribes. There are several who have a light at each end of the pole, which they whirl round at intervals with some velocity. The din of the tom-toms cannot be better described than in the words of Knox; 'they make such a great and loud noise, that nothing else besides them can be heard.' The chiefs walk alone, the crowd being kept off by their attendants; the stiffness of their gait as they are wrapped round with manifold layers of cloth, being in perfect contrast to their usual ease, indeed we may say gracefulness, of manner. The long whips were cracked before the adigar until the present year, but no one has been appointed to this office since the death of the old man whose presence we now miss, and no other individual is entitled to the honour. The whole procession may extend about a quarter of a mile, but this is only towards its conclusion, as it gradually increases in the number of its attendant elephants, &c. from the commencement. The natives who attend as spectators are now few, even in comparison with recent years, and it would seem that in a little while its interest will vanish away, with many a better remembrance of the olden time. The procession was one day prevented from taking its accustomed round, as a man had hung himself in one of the streets through which it must have passed. The natives are very unwilling to enter into conversation respecting the detail of this ceremony, and say that there are many mysteries connected with it which they cannot reveal.

The history of the Perahara is another evidence how tenaciously the people adhere to the Braminical superstitions, and would tend to prove, that even when Buddhism was predominant upon the continent of India, it must have had very little hold upon the mass of the population; and this may account for its almost total destruction after it had once the ability to erect the splendid temples that yet remain, monuments at once of its majesty and its weakness. Buddhism is too philosophical, too cold and cheerless, to be a popular creed, and it is only its present alliance with its deadly antagonist of former times that now preserves it in the place it occupies as the national religion of Ceylon."—From the "FRIEND," vol. iii. p. 41—50. 1839.

J.

Ratnapura, 15th January, 1826.

The Board of Commissioners, Kandy.

GENTLEMEN,

I HAVE the honor to acknowledge the receipt of your letter of 16th December last, wherein I am directed to select a fit person to receive the appointment of High Priest of Adam's Peak.

Having in consequence called upon the two Dissaves, and the Basnaike Nilleme, to report on the claims of those who might be candidates for the Office, their selection fell on Gallay Madankare Unanse, who though neither a candidate residing at present in the District, they conceived should be the person to be appointed, from his having been admitted into Priesthood in the District, been the pupil of Waihaille Naike Unanse, the High Priest of the Peak, and more especially on account of his piety and great learning, which are said to have procured for him a very extended reputation.

All the Upasampada Priests of the Malwatte establishment beneficed in the District were then assembled, and the individual proposed being unanimously approved by them, I signified to Gallay Unanse, who resides in the Matura District, my intention of submitting his name for the Office, under the restrictions stated in your letter, and the additional one of constant residence in the

Dissavony. He has acceded to the proposal, and I have, in conse-quence, to recommend that the appointment may be conferred upon him.

I have also to recommend that he should at the same time be appointed Chief Priest of the Saffragam Dissavony, an office which has not for some time been conferred upon any one, though the want of it has been much felt. It was intended to have renewed it in 1822, as will be seen from the annexed copy of a letter from the late Resident, but the Priest named declined accepting the situation owing to some dissensions among the priesthood. Mr. Sawers' letter, to which Sir John Doyly refers, is not on record in this Department.

I have, &c.,

(Signed)   GEO. TURNOUR,

Agent of Govt.

Ratnapura, 27th February, 1827.

The Board of Commissioners, Kandy.

GENTLEMEN,

I HAVE the honor to return the petition of the High Priest of the Malwatte Wihāre, in which he lays claim to the village Pęl-madulle. It is accompanied by a counter-statement from the Chief Priest of Saffragam and the Peak.

From the information I am able to collect, the claim of the Malwatte High Priest does not appear to be well founded.

When Rája Singha (whose capital was Sittawakka, and who died in Sacca 1514) abjured Buddhism, and became a convert to the Brahminical faith, he bestowed the charge and the emoluments of the Peak on some Andee Fackeers. The institutions of Buddha, discountenanced and depressed, soon lost the requisites for conferring the ordination of Upasampada, and that order of priesthood in time became extinct.

Subsequent kings made some efforts to re-establish these institutions, by inviting over learned priests from the Eastern continent, but the object was never effectually and permanently attained till the reign of Kirtissry.

The Upasampada ordination was then also extinct. The priesthood chiefly consisted of the Sylout order (not now in existence) who observed most of the rules of devotion and abstinence, without being able to perform any of the functions considered the most important of a priest. The head of the Priesthood was a Samanairoo, named Welwita, known by the title of Saranankero Gunin.

To the zeal and exertions of this individual the natives now owe the footing of permanency on which their religious establisment is placed. He induced Wejai Rajah to depute Wilbaagedere Mudeyanse on an embassy to Siam for the purpose of bringing over priests capable of conferring the Upasampada ordination, and of leaving behind them the means of perpetuating it.

Wejai Rajah died before the mission reached Siam, and the Mudeyanse returned to Ceylon. He was sent back by king Kirtissry, and succeeded in bringing over the Siam priests.

On the restoration of Upasampada, Weliwita was placed at the head of the church, with the title, not of Nayaka Unanse, but of Sangha Rajah (King of Priests) and with unusual powers, to preserve the new institution from innovation.

It was at this period that the Andee Fackeers were deprived of the Peak, which at that time had no land revenue attached to it.

That office, together with Koottapitteye (till then a royal village) was conferred by the king on Sangha Raja and the grant recorded on a copper Sannas.

The Andees attempted to avert this alienation, by making presents to the King, among other articles of a pair of elephant tusks, which he received from the Andees, and made an offering of, to the Peak.

According to the enclosed Statement of the Saffragam Chief Priest, the Peak, with the village Koottapitteye, was bestowed by Sangha Rajah on Maalibodde Unanse of this Province; together with the Wihare and village of Pelmadulla, which Sangha Rajah is said to have received by the dedication of Kapugankande Syloat Namma. I am inclined to think this was some private arrangement of Sangha Rajah. For by the account Wilbsagedere Mudoyanse has left of his embassy, and of these religious proceedings, it appears that the superintendence of the Peak, together with the office of High Priest of the Low Country (Saffragam and the Maritime Districts), were confided to Waihelly Nayake Unanse by the king, at the same time that the Sannas itself was granted to Sangha Rajah. This point however, is not material to the present reference.

From that period till the succession of Rajaadi Raja Singha (in Sacca 1703) four High Priests had held the Chief-priestship of the Low Country together with the Peak, residing at Pelmadulla.

The last of these was Korrattotte Nayake Unanse, who now resides in Matura District. Morraattotte Naike Unanse was the High Priest of Malwatte, and had been the tutor of his king. On the pretence that the Saffragam Priests were leagued with the Dutch, Morraattotte induced the king to deprive Korrattotte of the Peak. The Sannas was taken to Kandy by Ratnapura Nilleme, and placed, it is said, by the king's order, by Dodangwelle Adikar, the Dissave of Saffragam, in Sanguka, in Malwatte Wihare.

From that time, until last year, the Peak, with Koottapitteye, has been held by the Malwatte High Priests. The Low Country has been without any regular Chief Priest, and Pelmadulla has been the residence of the Pupils of Waihelly.

The only advantage the Malwatte High Priests derived from Pelmadulla, consisted in having eight loads of the offerings made at the Peak, transported for them to Kandy. This exaction also is not of old standing, as the removal of the offerings at the Peak to Kandy was an irregularity which gradually attained to the extent it was ultimately carried.

I have been minute in my inquiry, as my information must chiefly be derived from interested sources. I see no ground whatever for the claim preferred. Pelmadulla is certainly not a dependency of the Peak, neither does it appear to me to appertain to the Chief-priestship of the Low Country; further than from the accidental circumstance of three succeeding High Priests inheriting Pelmadulla, as pupils of each preceding incumbent. But the Malwatte High Priests hold neither of these appointments, and can have no claim on either ground.

If the present arrangement is intended to be made permanent, it would be well to remove all ground for future litigation. With this view, I recommend that king Kirtissry's Sannas should be bestowed upon the High Priest, who now holds the Chiefship of the Peak by the appointment of the present Government. The document was, I am told, in the possession of Parakumbura Unanse of Kandy, who some time ago placed it in the charge of Deheigame Dewie Nileme. The tusks also presented by king Kirtissry (which have Sree-pada carved on them) were removed to Kandy when our troops first entered the country, by Kobaikadoowe Nayaka Unanse, they are said to be now at Goddalladeneya Wihare in Ouda

Neura. I have to suggest that they should also be sent for, and restored to the Peak shrine.

I have, &c.,

(Signed) GEO. TURNOUR,
Agent of Govt.

Extract from letter of Asst. Agent of Ratnapura, July 27th, 1858.

"It will be seen from the correspondence that about Sacca 1514, king Rajasinha, who had abjured Budhism, and became a convert to Brahaministic faith, bestowed the charge of the Peak to some Andee Fakeers ; that it was subsequently conferred by king Kirtisry to Wellwita Saranankera Ganiu, otherwise Sangaraja, together with the village of Kuttapitiya, upon a copper sannas; that however the superintendence of the Peak, together with the office of High Priest of the Low Country (Saffragam and the Maritime districts) was confided to Wehalla Naika Unnanse, and from that period to the accession of Rajady Rajasinha (Sacca 1703), four High Priests had held the Chief-priestship of the Low country and the Peak, *residing at Pelmadulla.* The last of these, Karatota, was in A. D. 1827, living at Matura, having been deprived of the Peak by the King, on the instigation of Moratota, the High Priest of Malwatta, on which occasion the Sannas was removed to Kandy, by order of the King, and kept in Sangika (or common.) From that time, up to 1826, about 40 years, the Peak was held by the Priests of Malwatta, but they appear to have derived but small advantage from its emoluments.

As early as 1825 the claim set up by the High Priest of

Malwatte to the Peak was set aside, and in the letter from the Board of Commissioners dated 16th Dec. of that year, it was conveyed that the Governor had decided, that the appointment of High Priest of the Peak should be conferred on a Priest of Saffragam, it being made a condition of that appointment that the greater part of the revenue arising from the offerings should be applied to the repair and upkeep of Rest-houses, &c.

On the 15th February 1826, Mr. Turnour communicated to Government the selection by him, according to instructions, of Galle Medankara Unnanse, to succeed the late High Priest of Malwatte as Priest of the Peak, and by the letter of the Board of the 14th April 1826, was conveyed, that as a special favour to the then Maha Naika Unnanse of Malwatte, the Government had conferred on him one-fourth of the offerings of the Peak, which reverted to the High Priest of the Peak on the death of the said Maha Naika Unnanse.

On the demise of Galle Naika Unnanse, 1836, his successor, Samangala Unnanse, who died on the 21st May 1818, was elected by the priests of this district before the then Assistant Agent, Mr. Wells, under instructions of Government (see letter No. 448 of 13th May, 1836,) which prescribed the same course as had been adopted by Mr. Turnour."

Paracumbere was the next High Priest; then Galagama Attadassi Terunansi, who was deposed on 26th May, 1866.

Hikkaduwe Sumangale Terunansi of the Vibáre called Tilakarama in Hikkaduwe, was then elected; —"a priest in every respect eligible for this high and important office, and one whose reputation for piety and scholarship stands supereminent among the priesthood of the Malwatte establishment of the Island of Ceylon."—Act of the Priests, on the 10th June, 1866.

X.

Description of the Attanagalu Forest, by James D'Alwis, Esq.

"When, some years ago, I visited this part of the country,* my eyes rested on a scene which I could not soon or easily forget, Its greatest attraction was the stately forest. Whilst I stood amazed at the prodigious height to which the trees had grown, straight from the ground, the eye lingered with delight on the 'pillared shades,' thick with their dense green foliage, and laden

'with their pendent fruits and flowers.'

The Figs and the Palms which grew up together reminded me of the Cocoanut and the Bread fruit which rose, as it were, in love's embrace, in the southwest coast of Ceylon. The Talipot, the Ná, the Sapan, the Hedawaka, the Ketakála, the Del, the Milila, the Godapora, (not to mention other timber-trees), were all here seen side-by-side with the Katu-imbul, the Goraka, the Veralu, the Kaju, the Erabadu, etc., etc. There were also climbing plants in endless variety. The Potú, the Kirindi, the Kiritilla, and the Kiri-anguna, entwined themselves round the trunks as they clambered up in search of light. The ferns and the orchids, which thrived luxuriously in the hollows of old trees, waving their brilliant foliage,

---

* Attanagalu, on the road to the Hewagam Kórálé.

seemed as if they were the cultivation of some nymph of the forest.
Nothing could exceed the beauty of the flowing tresses of the Heda-
yá, of which two species were met within the cold and mossy clefts
of trees that never saw the light of the sun. Under the shade grow
the Vana Rája. Revelling in the rich and luxurious vegetable
mould, which lay several feet thick, this dwarf 'King of the Forest'
spread out its leaves, 'the most exquisitely formed in the vegetable
kingdom, and whose colour resembles dark velvet approaching to
black, and reticulated over all the surface with veins of ruddy
gold.' It is difficult to realize the beauty of the distant landscape
along the streams and marshes of the forest. The graceful Bambu
was surrounded by the magnificent Asoka. The pale azure of
the Sal, which deeply contrasted with the burnished green of the
delicately tinted foliage of the Siambalá on the hillocks, and both
with the deep emerald brushwood below,—waved over the
Gloriosa Superba (Niagalú), whose matchless flowers festooned
the adjacent heaps of verdure; whilst the Muruta overshadowed
the Bándurá, that grow luxuriantly beneath the pink-clad branches
of the former. Nothing, again, could surpass either the splendour
of the flowers, or the beauty of the leaves. Some of the latter by
themselves exhibited the hues of the former. The scarlet shoots
of the Ná, for instance, vied in beauty with the gorgeous flowers
of the Katu-imbul, the pink clusters of the Muruta with the ripe
leaves of the Kottambá, the pale yellow Champac with the tawny
Veralu, and the snow-white blossoms of the Idda with the tender
buds and cream-coloured leaves of the Mussenda."—ATTANAGALU-
VANSA, pages 91–93.

L.

VEGETATION ABOUT ADAM'S PEAK.

By G. H. K. THWAITES, Esq., F. R. S., Director of the Royal Botanic Gardens, Perádeniya.

THE forest immediately about the Peak contains a number of interesting trees of various Natural Orders, comprising

MAGNOLIACEÆ, represented by Michelia Nilagirica (Wal Sappoo of the Siphalese.)

ANONACEÆ, represented by species of Sagersoa, Goniothalamus, Uvaria, Unona, Miliusa, &c.

MYRISTICACEÆ, by Myristica Horsfieldii, and M. laurifolia.

SAMYDACEÆ, by two or three species of Casearia, and the fragrant flowered Osmelia.

PANGIACEÆ, by Hydnocarpus and Trichadenia.

STERCULIACEÆ, by the Durian-like Cullenia excelsa, and Sterculia guttata.

BYTTNERIACEÆ, by Pterospermum suberifolium, and Julostylis angustifolia.

TILIACEÆ, by species of Elæocarpus (Weraloo of the Siphalese.)

DIPTEROCARPEÆ, by species· of Dipterocarpus, Doona, Shorea, Hopea, Vateria, Isauxis, and Stemonoporus.

TERNSTRŒMIACEÆ (the Tea tribe) by Gordonia, Eurya, Ternstrœmia, and Adinandra.

AURANTIACEÆ, by Glycosmis and Atalantia.

GUTTIFERÆ, by Garcinia Morella (the true Gamboge tree), G. ochinocarpa, G. terpnophylla, Xanthochymus ovalifolius, and species of Calophyllum (Keena of the Siṇhalese.)

CELASTRACEÆ, by Kurrimia, Kokoona, and Microtropis.

SAPINDACEÆ, by Schmidelia, Sapindus, and Nephelium.

MELIACEÆ, by Milnea, Amoora and Walsura.

TEREBINTHACEÆ, by several species of Semecarpus, by Mangifera (wild mango) and Nothopegia.

BURSERACEÆ, by Canarium, Scutinanthe, and Pteridophyllum.

HOMALINEÆ, by Homalium Ceylanicum.

LEGUMINOSÆ, by Erythrina, Pongamia, Pterocarpus, and Dalbergia.

ROSACEÆ, by Photinia and Pygeum,

COMBRETACEÆ, by Terminalia Belerica and T. parviflora.

MELASTOMACEÆ, by several species of Memecylon.

MYRTACEÆ, by Eugenia, Jambosa, and Syzygium of many species.

BARRINGTONIACEÆ, by Barringtonia, Careya, and Anisophyllea.

RHIZOPHORACEÆ, by Carallia.

LYTHRARIACEÆ, by Axinaudra and Lagerstrœmia.

RUBIACEÆ (Coffee tribe) by species of Nauclea, Canthium, Ixora, Pavetta, Discospermum, Griffithia, and Wendlandia.

MYRSINACEÆ, by Myrsine.

SAPOTACEÆ, by species of Isonandra (the Gutta percha plant belongs to this genus) Dasyaulus and Dichopsis.

EBENACEÆ (Ebony tribe), by several species of Diospyros, Macreightia, and Maba.

AQUIFOLIACEÆ, by several species of Symplocos.

PROTEACEÆ, by Helicia Ceylanica, the only representative of the family in the Island.

LAURACEÆ (Cinnamon tribe), by Cinnamomum, Machilus, Cryptocarya, Tetranthera, Actinodaphne, and Litsæa.

URTICACEÆ, by several species of Ficus, and by Celtis and Sponia.

EUPHORBIACEÆ, by Cleidion, Rottlera Macaranga, Podadenia, Gelonium, Chætocarpus, Desmostemon, Sarcoclinium, Briedelia, Cleistanthus, Prosorus, Cyclostemon, Aporosa, and Antidesma.

PALMACEÆ, by Oncosperma fasciculata, and Ptychosperma rupicola.

Amongst these forest trees grow gigantic lianes; the Anamirtus Cocculus (Cocculus Indicus), Coscinium fenestratum, Kadsura Wightiana, Toddalia aculeata, Derris sinuata, D. scandens, Guilandina Bonduc, Entada scandens, Acacia Intsia, Anodendron paniculatum, Willughbeia Ceylanica, Plecospermum spinosum, and two or three species of Calamus, being particularly conspicuous.

The beautiful Kendrickia (Pachycentria, Enum. Pl. Zeyl.) Walkeri, and its allies, Medinella fuchsiodes, and M. maculata, with some species of Piper, Pothos, &c., mantle the trunks of the trees, and handsome Ipomœas scramble over their branches.

The undergrowth consists principally of shrubby Acanthaceæ, Rubiaceæ, Urticaceœ, Labiatæ, and Zinziberaceæ. The open pattanas, or savannahs, are made gay by handsome species of Exacum, Osbeckia, Desmodium, Crotalaria, Cassia, Chirita, and Burmannia.

Numerous ORCHIDEÆ occur on the trunks of trees, or on exposed rocks, and several species of Loranthus are attached parasitically (miseltoe-like) to the trunks and branches of the trees. Lovely Balsams in great variety, and pretty Utricularias abound in damp spots.

Near the top of the Peak the gorgeous Rhododendron arboreum occurs, with the Gaultheria fragrantissima, and the Vaccinium Leschenaultii, with its arbutus-like flowers. There too, may be noticed some very beautiful species of Sonerila and Osbeckia, and some pretty species of Hedyotis. Mosses and Lichens also abound upon the trees.*

---

* Further information respecting the Botany of the Island can be obtained in the Enumeratio Plantarum Zeylaniæ, by O. H. K. THWAITES, Esq., F. R. S., &c., published by Dulau & Co., Soho Square, London; in which all the known species are described, or referred to where they had been previously described.

M.

THE PROCESSION FROM COLOMBO AND WELCOME AT MORATUWA, OF JORONIS DE SOYSA, ESQ., AFTER HIS APPOINTMENT TO THE RANK OF MUDALIYAR OF THE GOVERNOR'S GATE.*

"BELOW we give a graphic and interesting account of the reception accorded at Colombo to the man whom, on account of his public spirit, Sir George Anderson has delighted to honor. The matter is more important than would appear at first sight to our English readers. The dignity conferred on Mr. De Soysa is one that has hitherto been jealously confined to the small knot of obstructives amongst the Singhalese who call themselves first class Velules; and on this occasion the Maha Modliar, we believe, did his little best to prevent the Government from shocking the prejudices of the people—meaning by that phrase a little knot of Modliars—by conferring the highest Native rank in its gift on a man of the fisher caste. All honor to Sir George Anderson for the personal courage and decision displayed by him on this occasion. The British Government is not only too generous, but also too strong, to allow its own benevolent intentions, and the wheels of progress to be any longer impeded by foolish fears of offending antiquated caste prejudices.

The newly created Modliar is a Native Coffee Planter on a large scale, very enterprising and very wealthy. But his claims to the

* From the Colombo Observer of June 15th, 1853.

dignity conferred on him rest on the erection by him, at his own cost, of public works, such as Ambalamas and Bridges, the formation of roads, &c."

Colombo, June 10th, 1853.

Sir,—The elevation of Mr. Joronis De Soysa of Morotto to the rank of Modliar of the Governor's Gate, appearing to have caused a considerable sensation of satisfaction in the native mind, with possibly a little jealousy here and there, I have thought some account of the proceedings on his return to Morotto, would not be unacceptable to your readers, especially as you have already noticed in your columns the doings of his friends in Kandy, some of whom expressed the hope that their brethren in the Western Province would not suffer themselves to be outdone in rendering due honor to the newly appointed Modliar. Nor have they, as the proceedings of the 9th instant amply testify. I don't pretend to give you a very graphic account of every thing that happened, being altogether unused to that style of composition; but, as I was present a considerable part of the day, I will endeavour to state what fell under my own observation, and from that and such other accounts as may reach you, you will be able, I dare say, to make out for your readers a much more interesting narrative than I can, —so you are welcome to use my information, and burn my MS., or publish it in *toto*, just as you please.

Well then, at 7 A. M. according to invitation, I, together with many others, assembled at Grand Pass at the house of Mr. Soosew de Soysa, the Modliar's brother, where, in all the glory of gold and jewels, Joronis De Soysa Dharma Goonewardene Wepolle Jayasooria Dessanayake Karoonaratne, Modliar of the Governor's Gate, received the congratulations of his friends.

Europeans, Burghers, Natives of rank, wealth, and influence, Hindoos, Parsees, Moormen, &c. &c. came dropping in one after the other until the house was filled to overflowing. After partaking of a slight refreshment, hospitably provided by Soosew De Soysa, the ear-piercing fifes and deafening tom-toms of the Governor's Guard of Lascoreens, as they drew up into the Verandah, warned us that the business of the day was now about to begin. The Guard having had a dusty walk, and being moreover droughthy souls, and withal not very much accustomed to their scarlet coats and conical caps, or the wielding of their venerable halberts, and antique, lion-headed, carving-knife-looking cutlasses, of course needed a dram each, by way of nerving them to their arduous duties; and judging from the apparent relish with which they tossed off their glasses, they got the genuine stuff. While this was going on, Guard No. 2 passed by. This, I believe, is the Guard belonging to the Salpitty Korle, and glories in a uniform of blue. The poor souls looked hard and longingly at their brother lascoreens in red, but, obedient to the stern commands of duty, marched on to their appointed station on Norris's road near the Racket ground.

In a few minutes the signal was given to start. The Guard, consisting of twenty-five men, preceded by the tom-tom beaters, took the lead; then came the Modliar attired in a coat of dark broad-cloth, over which was thrown his chain of honor, formed of above 150 sovereigns linked together in couples, and terminating in an ornament formed of a cluster of forty-five of the same coins;*

---

* This was a mere temporary contrivance. The precious metal was subscribed for by about 700 of the Mudallyar's personal friends, and was afterwards worked

crossing this was the sword belt of broad gold lace, from which
hung suspended the sword encased in au elaborately chased silver
scabbard inlaid with gold; the sword hilt was a mass of gems,
principally rubies and emeralds, set in gold, the lustre of which
was however completely eclipsed by the splendid jewels in the
sword knot. Altogether the dress was a very rich and expensive
affair—(I heard it estimated as worth about £1,000, but perhaps
this included the brilliant and other rings worn by the Modliar)—
and certainly it was terribly provocative to a serious infraction
of the tenth commandment.

The Modliar's only son accompanied his father; behind them
walked two lascoreens clothed in scarlet habiliments, bearing
talipots of honour over their heads. Then followed, also on foot,
the greater part of those who had assembled at the house, the
Mohandirams in full dress, with their talipot bearers, who sported
vestments of such a nondescript character, that no verbal description can do justice to them, and I am afraid no pictorial representation would be believed ; the nearest approximation I can give
your readers will be to remind them of Pantaloon at Bartholomew
Fair, or old Shàlabalar, so inseparably connected with Punch and
London street reminiscences. *Outre* as their appearance was, they

---

up into a handsome chain of honor, to which a corresponding medal was suspended,
containing the following inscription. "Presented to Joronis De Soysa, Esq.,
Dharma Goonewardene Wepolle Jayasooriya Dessanayake Karooneratne, Modliar
of the Governor's Gate ; By his numerous friends, in token of their respect and
esteem, and of the admiration with which they regard his benevolent exertions
for the relief of the poorer classes, and his patriotic endeavours to promote the
public good, &c. &c." With this chain and medal he was invested by the
Governor, at the Levee held at Queen's House, Colombo, on the 24th May, 1854.

nevertheless added to the picturesqueness of the effect produced by the groupings and costumes of the various races and nations there assembled.

The march began; guns were fired; the fifes squealed out most horribly shrill; the tom-tom beaters plied their sheepskins so vigorously, that one had to scream into his neighbour's ear to make him understand; frantic people rushed out of houses on either side of the road, and deluged with sweet-scented waters the man whom the Governor delighted to honour; and, either in their joy or for the fun of the thing, plentifully besprinkled all and sundry near them with the same; horsekeepers gravely led their master's carriages at a funeral pace in the far distant rear; and doubtless those who overtook it imagined at first they had come upon a funeral procession, for a vile cart driver, with a villainously high-piled load of black wood, looking for all the world like a hearse, *would* take the lead of the carriages.

Passing the Queen's Advocate's house, the Honourable Gentleman himself came out and congratulated the Modliar on his elevation. From thence the procession wound up Barber street, down by Wolfendahl Church, along Main street to the Esplanade, where the scarlet Guard gave place to the Halberdiers in blue. Nothing particular occurred in this part of the route, unless a few slight passing showers be mentioned, which were more grateful than inconvenient; for walking in a crowd in the middle of a dusty road under a tropical sun is not the most pleasant thing imaginable; it was however amusing to note the shifts parties resorted to in an endeavour to escape being wetted. Imagine Coweajee Cunjee,* the

---

* This gentleman, who died not long after the proceedings above described, was of the most bulky proportions; but as genial in manner as he was great in size

portly merchant of Main street, sharing with a stout Parsee friend
a small China umbrella, scarcely big enough to cover the tops of
their turbans ; and the nondescript talipot-bearers, officiously
covering their masters' heads, but taking good care at the same
time to secure the best part of the talipot to themselves ! More
scented waters were sprinkled as Cunjee's stores were passed, and
additions began to be made to the tail of the procession, which
numerically more than compensated for the loss of those who by
the calls of business and breakfast were here compelled to take
leave of the Modliar.

. Arrived at Colpetty the Modliar paid his respects to the Government Agent, by whom he was warmly congratulated; and further
on was met and complimented by Dr. Elliott, Mr. Dalziel and
others. Outside the Gravets there was a halt for some time. Here
the Fishers' Guard met the Modliar, he being a Fisher, and the
first, I understand, of that caste, ever made Modliar of the Gate.
Groups of picturesquely attired dancing boys, grotesquely masked
mummers, and singers and tumblers, besides a numerous assemblage of friends and acquaintances were also here drawn up to pay
their respects, and accompany their countryman to his home.

From this point to Morotto every step only added to the magnitude of the procession. Ascending the open carriage in readiness
for him the Modliar again moved on. Foremost went the tumblers,
singers and dancers, delighting the concourse. who surrounded
them with their songs and antics; next the bands of tom-toms and
fifes; then the Fishers' guard, followed by the Korle lascoreens
and a body of belted peons. Then the observed of all observers,
with his son and brother in the carriage, behind which still walked
the two talipot bearers in scarlet ; and after these a train of
carriages and bandies, and a constantly increasing throng of

pedestrians. Momentary halts were continually being made, so many crowded up to the carriage to congratulate its occupants. Old men from all parts, many scarcely able to totter, and some from Caltura and Pantura (the latter village being Mr. De Soysa's birthplace,) came forward with almost infantile eagerness, some so overjoyed as to lose the power of utterance, others in such a state of excitation as to be unable to restrain their garrulity, and one declaring that now he was content to die, having seen what he never hoped to see, and what he should never see again.

When opposite the residence of the Mohandiram of the Salpitty Korle, that fine old native gentleman came out and invited all who were disposed, to partake of refreshments, which he had most liberally provided, expressing at the same time his regret that official duties prevented him from having the pleasure of proceeding to Morotto with the Modliar. Further on, every village and path contributed its quota of human beings to the mass already congregated on the road ; and the din of their rejoicing, the firing of guns and the shoutings of welcome were at times quite over-powering.

A little beyond Ratmalane is the fine Ambalama erected some years back by Mr. De Soysa. At this spot a decorated arch was thrown over the road, and here the Washerman of the District waited on the Modliar, requesting that he would allow them to do him the honor of spreading white cloths on the ground for him to walk on until he reached his house. This being done, all of course dismounted and finished the journey on foot. A light fence was thrown up on each side the road from this point to Morotto, from which an elegant festoon or fringe of strips of cocoanut leaves was suspended. All along, too, the inhabitants of the adjoining villages were drawn up ; and to acknowledge and return all the salutes he received, was no slight task for the Modliar.

From this point to Morotto, it was emphatically a triumphal procession. After walking about three quarters of a mile, the Modliar's eye was gladdened with the sight of a triumphal arch erected
opposite his house. Stretching across the road, of an octagonal
form, and about thirty-five feet in diameter, with a beautiful
ceiling of open net-work, tastefully formed of the ferns and grasses
and flowers of the neighbourhood, the arch, profusely decorated
with fruits and flowers on its exterior, was unanimously pronounced
to be the most elegant thing of the kind ever erected by natives;
and it certainly was well worth a trip to Morotto to behold.

The number of people assembled at this point was immense.
Far as the eye could range along the road, and around on the
adjacent grounds, was one dense mass of humanity; men, women
and children, all eagerly straining to catch a glimpse of their
honoured countryman and benefactor. The lowest computation
gave 5,000 as the number present ; but many were of opinion
that at least 7,000 was the most correct estimate. Whichever
be correct, it was a most gratifying sight, and such a one as it is
but seldom the lot of a European to witness in Ceylon. The crush
was very great at the front of the house, where Mr. De Soysa's
numerous relatives had assembled to meet and welcome him home
with all his honors. As the meeting was of the most affectionate and
affecting kind, and more than one drew back with moistened eyes,
I shall not dwell upon that part of the subject,—suffice it to say,
that all seemed *over-joyed.*

Looking from the Verandah down on the crowd, it was one sea
of heads and up-turned eyes. The Act of Appointment was now
produced, shewn to all assembled, read first in English and then
translated into Singhalese ; whereupon one in the crowd made a
short speech, and then uprose a loud *Hurrah!* that would have

done credit to the lungs of a London mob. Now commenced a right joyous carousal. Numerous booths and open bungalows had been erected in the compound, where tables were spread; and well did multitude after multitude do justice to the good things the Modliar had provided. Inside the house a more select company or companies were entertained, consisting of Mohandirams, friends, and acquaintances specially invited. Speeches were made, healths drank, toasts proposed; and while unbounded hilarity had free exercise within, ever and anon a loud hurrah from without gave notice of what was going on there. As soon as one company retired, another took their places, and speedily fresh courses made the laden tables groan again. After dark, fireworks illuminated the gardens, and to a late hour at night the Modliar was occupied in receiving the complimentary visits, and acknowledging the salams, of the throngs who poured into the place in an almost endless stream.

M.

Festivities at Bagatelle, Kollupitiya, in honor of His Royal Highness the Duke of Edinburgh.

THE entertainment given to His Royal Highness the Duke of Edinburgh by Messrs. Susew and Charles De Soysa was one unprecedented in the annals of Ceylon, and as successful in all its details as it was unprecedented of its kind.* As soon as His Excellency the Governor communicated to Messrs. De Soysa His Royal Highness's gracious acceptance of their invitation, they commenced their preparations, and with characteristic energy—(employing daily from 300 to 500 men for several weeks,)—completed all their arrangements in the most satisfactory manner by the morning of the 22nd April, on the evening of which day the entertainment took place.

From Galle Face to Bagatelle, a distance very little short of two miles, both sides of the Kollupitiya road were lined with decorations.

---

* "For the first time in the history of the Island—for not even in the palmiest days of the Siphalese monarchy, when a liberal and large-minded ruler like Dutugemunu or Prakkramabáhu wielded the sceptre, would Royalty so far condescend as to accept of the private hospitalities of a subject—a native has welcomed a Royal guest to his house. The circumstances under which both Ruler and Ruled now live are very much changed; but notwithstanding all the progress and the advancement which the natives of this country have made in Western civilization, 'the divinity that hedges round a throne' is not a mere

These consisted of a framework of upright bambu posts, five and ten feet each in height, alternating at distances of five feet from each other—(wider spaces being left for entrances to compounds)—and crossed just above the smaller posts by longitudinal bars eighteen inches apart. From the ground to the lower bar rose skeleton arches of a gothic form. The space between the bars was arranged in continuous panels of a diagonal pattern. From the inside of the arched work hung long ribbon-like stripes of fringed cocoanut leaves, while the whole of the framework was wreathed over and ornamented with light green olas,* festoons of which swung between the larger uprights, the tops of which were surmounted with ola-formed crowns. At the Galle Face end of the road an elegant triumphant arch with three terminal spires, the central one of which rose to a height of seventy-two feet, was erected; and two similar but perhaps more elaborately decorated arches spanned the road on either side of the gate that opened into the central carriage drive of Bagatelle grounds. Each arch bore suitable inscriptions of welcome. Wild pines and other fruits, with flowers, ferns, and mosses, were added, to give greater effect to the general appearance of the decorations, the whole of which glittered at night not only with innumerable lamps, but with flambeaux in green cocoa-nut

metaphor. It would therefore be impossible for the native mind to overrate the honor which his Royal Highness the Duke of Edinburgh has done Mr. De Soysa in accepting the invitation to his Entertainment; while on the other hand it must be matter for sincere congratulation to all classes who can claim Mr. De Soysa for their countrymen, that the Island could afford a native who by position and wealth, was pre-eminently qualified to do the hospitalities of the whole race, in his own person."—*Examiner*, April 28.

* The young and tender leaves of the cocoa and other palms.

husks; while a large body of men in uniforms of red and white, each bearing a blazing torch, lined the road and lighted up the way, the brilliance of which was added to by the illuminations with which almost every mansion on the route shone and sparkled and gave evidence of the loyalty of its occupants.

Bagatelle House * and grounds, with the numerous temporary buildings and corridors leading from one to the other, were ablaze with light, and presented to the eye a picture which realized to the mind the description given by the poet of the encampment of the Princess Lalla Rookh when on her way to Cashmere.

The invitations were issued for 9 o'clock, and by 10 most of the visitors had arrived; and although there must have been an assemblage of upwards of two thousand persons present, yet the arrangements made were so admirable, that although the throng was pretty close at the principal door where His Royal Highness, the Governor, Lady Robinson, and the Queen's House party were to alight, there was no undue squeezing or crowding. "All over the grounds, there were tents, and booths, gaily decorated and brilliantly lighted, in which the various artists who had been gathered from every part of the Island, and even beyond it, were to perform their respective *rôles*. The dancing saloon in rear of the main building was a credit to its designer; for not only was it elegantly decorated and brilliantly lighted, but every attention had been paid to ventilation. The ball-room upstairs, and the private apartments for His Royal Highness, His Excellency Sir Hercules Robinson, and Lady Robinson, were all tastefully decorated; several handsome pier glasses and mirrors reflected the light from

---

* Since named "ALFRED HOUSE," in honor of the occasion.

the chandeliers, and rendered the reflected illusion superior even to the reality. The supper room was in the shape of a St. Andrew's cross, each limb holding three rows of tables with broad passages between them The floor was carpeted with coloured coir matting, and flowers and evergreens and white olas, with some hundreds of lamps burning over head, gave to the entire place the brilliance of a strictly oriental scene. The refreshment rooms were also conveniently placed, and while the liquors, from the brandy and soda, the champagne and the ices, were all of the most unexceptionable quality, the attendance was of a kind which seldom can be secured at similar gatherings. The servants were civil and obliging, and notwithstanding the incessant and too often conflicting demands on their time and attention, they never grumbled themselves, nor gave occasion for the visitors to grumble."*

While waiting the arrival of the Royal Guest, the opportunity was seized by numbers of visiting the grounds and making themselves acquainted with the localities, where in booths and tents, and kiosks and theatres, artists, dancers and actors of all kinds and varieties were to exhibit and do their best to entertain those whom Messrs. De Soysa had honored with invitations. A long spacious corridor coiled and carpeted, led from Bagatelle to what is known as little Bagatelle. From the main corridor minor ones branched off to the temporary buildings, which were laid out in three parallel rows. The principal of these was the theatre in which the Kandian tragedy named Eyehalapola, after the Adigar of that name, its principal hero, was to be performed. Tiers of broad platforms and seats circled round the interior of a spacious building; in the

---

* Examiner.

centre of which was a pit where the musicians, (tam-tam beaters), were seated. The space between these and the audience was the stage, on which all the best native performers of Colombo were to exhibit. Above this was an elegantly designed and decorated ceiling, from which hung lamps, the whole of which rotated on the central pillar of the theatre. The tragedy is based on the occurrences which took place in the Kandian kingdom, immediately before the campaign which led to its annexation by the British. In another building was to be performed the comedy of "Sihasi-wali," which refers to the supposed origin of the Siphalese dynasty of Wijaya, the Indian invader of Ceylon in the year 543 B.C. This however was delineated by means of puppets, the wire-workers of whom sang the dialogues out of sight of the audience. Printed copies of abstracts of both these Plays were liberally provided for the benofit of those who could not understand the Siphalese of the actors. In another theatre the Hungarian wizard, Professor Ruch-waldy, was preparing his feats of art-magic and legerdemain. A troupe of Hindu Nautch girls, gorgeously dressed and adorned with solid gold head pieces, jewels, satins and silks, occupied one tent. Indian gymnasts, posture-masters and contortionists another; Grotesque dancers from Hangurankettl; Rhodiya women who twirl brass plates on their fingers while dancing; Dancers in white from Panadura, who gyrate with chatties in their hands; Boy dancers in red who strike sticks to time as they wind in and out and thread in opposing couples the mazes of their dances; bands of timbrel and tambourine players, and other native musicians, each had their separate tent or booth; a large circular swing afforded exercise and amusement to all who chose to venture within it; while last but not least Dave Carson's minstrel and musical troupe, with Signor Donatto, the wonderful one-legged dancer,

pleased, delighted, and astonished all who heard and saw them.
By half past ten all but the most important of the guests had
arrived; and a most gay and brilliant assemblage they wore.
The ladies seemed to have exhausted the resources of the milliner's
art in the elegance and beauty of their dresses; for the daughters
of Lanka were by no means behind their sisters from the West
in the richness and splendor of their jewels and attire. Military
uniforms, blue and crimson and black, with gold and silver epaulettes,
facings, and collars,—worn by the Officers of the Staff, the Royal
Engineers and Artillery, the 73d Regt. and the Ceylon Rifles; as
well as Naval ones worn by the Officers from the Galatea, the
Forte, and H. I. M. S. Armorique,—contrasted with the official
dresses of numerous Siphalese Mudaliyars, Mohandirams and
Headmen, girt with quaint golden-hilted swords suspended
from variously patterned gold sashes. Chetties, and Parsees and
Moormen, in their own peculiar and characteristic habiliments,
added a further variety to the rich display of colour and costume
that relieved the sombre black of the evening-dress in which
all the rest of the male Civilians present were clad.

Gradually the principal guests, amongst whom was Commodore
Sir Leopold Heath, began to throng around the door and line
both sides of the passage leading to the upper reception room, and
shortly before eleven, His Royal Highness, the Governor, Lady and
Miss Robinson, accompanied by Captains Haig, Tweedie and
St. John, and Mr. Cockburn Stewart, drew up and alighted. Mr.
and Mrs. De Soysa received the Duke, who led in Lady Robinson,
the Governor taking Miss Robinson. Dancing commenced immediately after, the band of the 73d supplying the music for the
ball-room occupied by the Prince and the more select of the guests,
while the general company danced in the larger ball-room below to

the music of the Ceylon Rifle band. At the conclusion of the dances in the Ducal ball-room, Mr. Carson's troupe of minstrels were introduced and were most warmly and deservedly applauded. After listening awhile to their songs, their music and their wit, the Ducal party adjourned to the supper room, " the Prince conducting Lady Robinson, and Sir Hercules Robinson taking down Miss Robinson. As with the other portions of the arrangements so with the supper, everything was arranged in first-rate style. After supper there were the toasts of the 'Queen;' and 'The Prince of Wales and the Duke of Edinburgh,' the Duke rising and bowing his acknowledgments in reply to the cordial way in which the toast was received. The Prince supped off a plate, with a knife and fork, all of pure gold, the champagne and wine goblets being of the same precious metal. Upon the spoon were delicately carved vine leaves, and around the stem was worked a row of pearls. Rows of rubies similarly encrusted the knife and fork. His Royal Highness left the supper room amid loud cheering, and after his departure Mr. Flinch mounted the table and called for cheers for Mr. and Mrs. De Soysa.

"After supper came fireworks. These were let off on the green in front of the house, and were very effectively rendered. Columns of light, through which rose rockets, soaring far above the triumphal arches adjacent, were intermingled with Chinese candles, and other improvements upon the fireworks of the olden times. Devices succeeded these, and the whole concluded with a grand burst of flame worthy of the decorations which surrounded it and of the company watching its eccentric movements.

"The Prince, the Governor and the ladies belonging to their party, did not confine themselves to the upper room, but paid visits to all the entertainments going on. They visited the theatre during the performance of the tragedy of Eheyalapola, and stayed some time. The nautch too came in for a share of their attention, and with the puppet show they were evidently much gratified."[*]

In the meantime dancing was resumed with spirit in the ball-room, and crowds thronged into the buildings where the different entertainments were going on. Dave Carson's minstrels attracted a constantly increasing audience, which was as much delighted with their performances, as it was astonished by Signor Donatto's marvellously graceful uni-pedal dances. Indeed so varied and so excellent were the numerous entertainments provided, and so admirable was every arrangement for the comfort and refreshment of the guests, that morning broke before the company separated. And they did so with the unanimous opinion, that the Messrs. De Soysa deserved the thanks of the entire community for the successful manner and princely style in which, voluntarily aided as they were by some of the leading gentry of Colombo, they had fêted His Royal Highness the Duke of Edinburgh, and in so doing afforded Her Majesty's lieges an opportunity of again testifying their loyalty to their Sovereign, and their affection for Her dynasty, as represented in the person of Her Sailor Son.

The following interesting sketch of the De Soysa family is taken from the Ceylon Observer of the 23rd April.

"THE DE SOYSAS.—The late Joronis Soysa was one of a large family. He inherited no fortune, so that the immense property left by him at his death is what he had himself acquired. From early life he showed signs of great enterprise, persevering application to his work, and indefatigable industry. He was the first young man

---

[*] Ceylon Observer, April 23.

who left Morotto to try the new field which Kandy, then recently acquired, presented. He commenced by taking a contract to supply firewood to the Government, and, by degrees, fresh contracts to supply rice and paddy. Having acquired some little money by these means, he began to farm out the Arrack rent. At first the rent was limited to small divisions, but by degrees it extended to the entire Kandyan District, the rent of which was purchased for many years successively by Mr. Soysa. His dealings with the Government brought him under the observation of the Honorable George Turnour, then Agent of the Central Province, who was struck with Mr. Soysa's scrupulous exactness and punctuality in his dealings, and gave him large facilities in his transactions with the Government. Encouraged by Mr. Turnour, Mr. Soysa purchased the Hanguranketti Coffee Estate in 1835, which proved a highly fortunate investment. It had been formerly the Royal Coffee Garden, and, when the jungle was cleared, large portions were found covered with Coffee trees left to grow wild. A little pruning brought all these trees into bearing, so that the very first season after the purchase Mr. Soysa obtained back not only his purchase money, but a large sum in excess. This was the turning point in Mr. Soysa's career. Shortly after he became the owner of the estate Mr. Soysa enlarged his trade greatly, purchased large farms, and became the owner of other valuable properties in Kandy and Colombo. In his business he was ably assisted by his brother Mr. Susew Soysa, the present head of the family. The Hanguranketti estate, which was enlarged from time to time, so that it now includes the whole of Dintalawa, and has about a thousand acres under cultivation, and the other estates which he purchased from time to time, were all managed by young men selected by Mr. Soysa from his native village, many of them his relatives, and he has never had a European in his employ.

As his fortune increased so did his usefulness. He gave largely in charity, and constructed many useful public works, such as tanks and dams for irrigation purposes, besides bridges and roads. The road from Harragam to Hangurankotti was constructed at his expense, and so were also canals, roads and bridges at Moraṭuwa.

In 1853 Sir George Anderson offered him, on the recommendation of Mr. Charles Buller, the Agent at Kandy, the Mudaliyarship of the Governor's Gate, which he accepted. This excited the opposition of the so-called first-class Mudaliyars, who theretofore looked upon these high ranks as exclusively theirs. What particularly called forth their ire was, that this was the first instance of a native getting such a rank *per saltem;*—in every former instance the recipient had to go through the different grades of Mohandiram, Mudaliyar, and then Gate Mudaliyar. The then Maha Mudaliyar, Ernest de Saram, had great influence with Sir George Anderson, and prevailed upon him to alter the title from Gate Mudaliyar to Mudaliyar of Moraṭuwa. This was made known to De Soysa on the morning of the day of the Levee, when the rank was to be conferred. He informed the Governor that he had not solicited any rank, and that the only one he would accept was the Gate Mudaliyarship. Sir Charles Mac-Carthy the Colonial Secretary, and Mr. Buller, took up the matter warmly, and, at the last moment, Sir George Anderson with his own pen altered the warrant, and made Mr. Soysa the Mudaliyar of the Governor's Gate, and the Maha Mudaliyar was subjected to the mortification of interpreting a complimentary speech which the Governor made in delivering to him his sword. All classes of the community, save and except the so-called first-class, joined in applauding the act of the Governor, and in congratulating Mr. De Soysa on his well deserved reward. After obtaining this rank he retired from trade, and confined himself to the cultivation of his extensive fields, and Coffee, Cinnamon and Cocoanut Estates. The principal work constructed by him after his elevation was the Moraṭuwa Church, which has cost more than £8,000, and is a monument of the deep piety for which he was always distinguished. He also established several schools, which are still maintained by the family. Sir Charles MacCarthy (then Governor) and Lady MacCarthy, the Bishop, and all the principal residents of the Town were present on the consecration, and went afterwards to the Mudaliyar's house to offer their congratulations. He died in 1862, deeply regretted, not only by his family, but by the community generally, and particularly by the residents of Moraṭuwa, by whom he was beloved for his charities. When it was known that he was ill, large numbers of the villagers flocked to see him for the last time. On taking leave of them he earnestly besought them to 'avoid the Sureya tree.' There were large Sureya trees in the compound of the old District Court, under which natives resorting to the Court used to sit. The Mudaliyar felt that the love of litigation was the bane of the natives, and always did his best to wean them from it."

The sequel to the Entertainment, given below, is extracted from the Examiner of the 27th April.

"On Sunday afternoon, the Messrs. De Soysa waited by appointment on his Royal Highness the Duke of Edinburgh and his Excellency the Governor, at Queen's House. They were very graciously received by His Royal Highness, who conveyed to them, through the Maha Mudaliyar, who was in attendance as interpreter, his acknowledgments for the entertainment given by them in his honour on Friday evening. He also thanked them for the handsome presents which they had given him, and while intimating his acceptance of the various specimens of Ceylon products and Ceylon workmanship, His Royal Highness said, he could not think of depriving them of so costly a memento of the entertainment as the service of gold plate which they were good enough to ask him to receive. He would therefore beg of them to retain it as an heir-loom in the family, in remembrance of the pleasant evening he had passed at their house. To return a present made by a native is with them considered an insult, but the handsome terms in which the Duke excused himself from accepting the gold service, took away any pain which the refusal might have otherwise given.

His Excellency the Governor next thanked Messrs. De Soysa for the munificent offer which they had made to commemorate the visit of His Royal Highness to Ceylon, by the endowment of £10,000 for establishing a Model Farm and School of Agriculture. His Excellency said, that he gladly accepted the offer on behalf of the Government, and informed the Messrs. De Soysa, that His Royal Highness had signified his approval of the institution being called the "Alfred Model Farm." His Excellency then referred to the liberality of the De Soysa family, and as this was not the first time they had employed their wealth in benefiting their fellow men, it gave His Excellency great pleasure to mark his high sense of their liberality by conferring on them the highest honours in his gift. He would therefore appoint the elder Mr. De Soysa, a Mudaliyar of the Governor's Gate, and his nephew a Justice of the Peace for the Island. His Excellency added, that as Mr. Charles De Soysa was more English in his views and aspirations, he would probably attach less weight to native rank than his uncle. His Royal Highness intimated his intention to present Mr. De Soysa with the sword and belt, and stated that, when received in Ceylon, it would give His Excellency great pleasure to invest him with that insignia of a Mudaliyar of the Governor's Gate.

His Royal Highness then asked the Messrs. De Soysa to accept
a little souvenir of his visit, and handed each of them a breast pin.
The elder Mr. De Soysa, who was the spokesman, in thanking
His Royal Highness, said, "any thing in the estimation of your
Royal Highness must be a trifle, but the moment it leaves your Royal
Highness's hands and comes to ours, it assumes the value of untold
wealth; to us the gift which your Royal Highness has given is as if
we had come into the possession of a world (Laukawak.)" The
elder Mr. De Soysa then begged to be excused for presuming to
trouble His Royal Highness again, but he could not allow the
present opportunity to pass without asking His Royal Highness
for another gift ; and on His Royal Highness's enquiry for its nature,
Mr. De Soysa begged to be favoured with a portrait of His Royal
Highness to be placed on the wall of the ball-room, in which the
Duke had done them the honor of being present on Friday last.
His Royal Highness seemed very much pleased with the request,
and promised that he would order the picture at once. The visitors
then withdrew, highly gratified with the result of their interview.

The articles which His Royal Highness accepted from the
Messrs. De Soysa were a very elegantly carved calamander-wood
gun-case, with ebony figures of Veddhas armed for the hunt at the
base; a sandal wood easy chair, very elaborately carved; a casket
containing specimens of Ceylon gems ; and a collection of the
numerous essential oils of Ceylon."

ADDENDUM.

"PHILALETHES."

THE work published under the above name having been frequently quoted in the preceding pages, the following remarks upon the identification of the author, may not be deemed out of place.

The authorship of the History of Ceylon by "PHILALETHES," published in London in 1817, has been attributed to a variety of individuals. Sir James Emerson Tennent, in the introduction to his work on Ceylon, says that "the author is believed to have been the Rev. C. Bisset;"[*] and in a note at page 90 of the second volume, on the subject of the Kandian Campaign of 1815, he remarks, "from the identity of the materials of 'A Narrative of events which have recently occurred in Ceylon, written by a gentleman on the spot,' (published in London in 1815,) with the 25th chapter of the History of Ceylon by PHILALETHES, the two statements appear to have been written by one and the same person, and evidently by one who was present whilst the occurrences he describes were in progress." This is however by no means conclusive, for the work of Philalethes consists, to a very great

---

[*] Private Secretary and Son-in-law to General Sir Robert Brownrigg, the then Governor of the Colony.

extent, of quotations, and translations, and the "narrative of events"
is only freely made use of by the author who so chose to designate
himself. There is reason to believe, as I shall afterwards shew,
that the two works were not from the same pen. The Rev. R.
SPENCE HARDY, in the "Jubilee Memorials of the Wesleyan
Mission, South Ceylon, 1864," says in a note, "It appears strange
that authors, (as in Barrow's Ceylon, past and present, 1851,) will
persist in attributing to Mr. Bisset, the work on Ceylon by PHI-
LALETHES, whose initials are H. W. B., and it is evident that he
never was in the island. It has been supposed by others that
Mr. Bennet is the author of this work, but his initials are J. W. B."

Now, on looking at the end of the preface to the work by
PHILALETHES, that name will be seen to occur at the right hand
corner of the page,—the usual, if not the invariable position in
which a writer places his name, in print as well as in manuscript.
The initials "H. W. B." stand at the left hand corner, immediately
above the date "November 13, 1816." They therefore seem to
indicate the initial letters of a place of residence, rather than the
name of an author. In Clark's Summary of Colonial Law (1834,)
p. 439, it is stated, that "the History of Ceylon, published under
the assumed name of PHILALETHES, is, in the copy deposited in
the British Museum, attributed to Mr. R. Fellowes."

My attention was originally drawn to Mr. Clark's work by
Mudaliyar Louis De Soyza; and Mr. W. N. De Abrew Rajapakse
hinted to me that Mr. R. Fellowes was probably an officer serving
in the Ceylon Rifles at the time the work by PHILALETHES was
written. Following up the clue thus given, I examined the Ceylon
Government Almanacs and the General Orders of the Ceylon
Command, for the year 1815 and onwards. The result was, that
I found Lieut. Robert Fisher Fellows, (also spelt Fellowes) served

in the 4th and 2nd Regiments of the Ceylon Rifles from March 16, 1810, to April 10, 1826, when he died in the Seven Kóralós, to which place, after serving on the Staff at several outstations, he had been appointed Commandant. In the course of his service he went to England on leave, on the 6th September, 1814, and remained in England until the 24th March, 1817. In the General Orders of April 29, 1817, notifying an extension of leave, his name occurs as Fellowes. He was therefore in England during the whole of the years 1815, 1816, and part of 1817; and the work by PHILALETHES was completed by the 13th November, 1816, and published at the commencement of the following year. But, notwithstanding this coincidence, it seemed scarcely credible, that if he was really the writer, he could have avoided intimating so much at least as would have sufficed to shew that he had written from personal recollections of the events described, or have refrained from dropping hints here and there of having been an actual participator in them. Nothing of the sort is however to be found in the book. I therefore wrote to England upon the subject, requesting information upon certain points, and in particular, that the copy of the work in the British Museum should be examined, and an exact transcript sent me of any manuscript that might be found to warrant the statement made by Mr. Clark.

In reply to my inquiries, I received the following particulars, kindly furnished under the hand of GEORGE BULLEN, Esq., the Superintendent of the Reading-room in the British Museum; who also produced the book for the satisfaction of the friend who was good enough to make the inquiry for me. "In the Museum copy the name R. Fellowes, written in pencil, follows the words, 'by Philalethes, A. M., Oxon.'" Mr. BULLEN further informed my friend, that Mr. R. Fellowes was one of the superior officers in the

British Museum at the time the work was written; that it was written by him at the British Museum; and that he himself wrote his own name in the Museum copy. There can therefore be now no more uncertainty upon the subject. The initials 'H. W. B.,' unquestionably refer to the name of a residence, possibly Holly Wood, Blackheath.

From subsequent inquiries I have learnt the following further particulars concerning PHILALETHES. The Rev. ROBERT FEL-LOWES, L.L.D., was born in Norfolk in the year 1770, perhaps at Haverham Hall, near Norwich, which is a seat of a family of that name. He went to St. Mary's Hall, Oxford, was ordained a Clergyman of the Church of England in the year 1795, and obtained the degree of M.A. in 1801. From 1799 to 1807 he published several theological works—"Religion of the Universe," "Christian Philosophy," "Guide to Immortality," "Religion without Cant," &c., which received high praise from the celebrated Dr. Parr, with whom he was on very friendly terms, as well as with Baron Maseres, who is said to have left him £200,000. He also published, in 1806, a volume of poems. The History of Ceylon, by PHILA-LETHES, in 1817, is apparently his last work. He was a stanch partizan of Queen Caroline during her prosecution, and he also took a prominent part in the establishment of the London University, where he founded two annual gold medals—called the "Fellowes' Medals." He was Editor for many years of the London Critical Review, at least up to the year 1820. In his later years he seceded from the Church of England, and joined, it is said, the Unitarian body. He died in 1847.

The fact that Dr. Robert Fellowes was the writer who assumed the *nom-de-plume* of PHILALETHES, accounts for the hitherto puzzling difficulty evidenced throughout the work, that that writer had never himself been in Ceylon. From whom then, beyond the authors he quotes, did he derive his information, which as evidently came from some one who was intimately acquainted with the country and the contemporaneous events described? I cannot but think, from the similarity of name, and the coincidence already noticed, that Lieutenant R. Fisher Fellowes, of the Coylon Rifles, must have been a relative or connection, who, during his stay in England, communicated to him the information which a service of four years in the island could not fail to have furnished him with; and that the actual writer of the work chose to attach the name "Philalethes" to his book, rather than appear before the world as the author of a volume, the substance of which had been placed in his hands by another, and that other a relative of his own. And that Lieutenant Fellowes was neither the author of, nor the furnisher of the facts contained in the "Narrative of events which occurred in Ceylon in 1815," is clear, inasmuch as he was in England at the time, having left Ceylon the previous year.

INDEX.

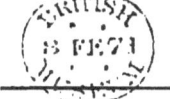

www.ingramcontent.com/pod-product-compliance
Lightning Source LLC
Chambersburg PA
CBHW021328110726
47900CB00005B/1401